Glendale College Library

The Mexican American

The Mexican American

THE
CALIFORNIA OUTLAW
TIBURCIO VASQUEZ

COMPILED BY
ROBERT GREENWOOD

ARNO PRESS
A New York Times Company
New York — 1974

Reprint Edition 1974 by Arno Press Inc.

Copyright, 1960, by The Talisman Press
Reprinted by permission of The Talisman Press

THE MEXICAN AMERICAN
ISBN for complete set: 0-405-05670-2
See last pages of this volume for titles.

Manufactured in the United States of America

364.1
Bee
1974

c~∞~ɔ

Library of Congress Cataloging in Publication Data

Beers, George A
    The California outlaw.

    (The Mexican American)
    First published in 1875 under title: Vasquez.
    Reprint of the ed. published by Talisman Press,
Los Gatos, Calif.
    Bibliography: p.
    1. Vasquez, Tiburcio, 1835-1875. I. Greenwood,
Robert, comp. II. Title. III. Series.
HV6452.C3V3 1974   364.1'092'4 [B]   73-14203
ISBN 0-405-05677-X

The California Outlaw:
Tiburcio Vasquez

Tiburcio Vasquez

THE
CALIFORNIA OUTLAW

TIBURCIO VASQUEZ

COMPILED BY
ROBERT GREENWOOD

INCLUDING THE RARE CONTEMPORARY ACCOUNT
By **GEORGE BEERS**

WITH NUMEROUS PHOTOGRAPHS AND
EXCERPTS FROM CONTEMPORARY NEWSPAPERS

———— ❧ ————

THE TALISMAN PRESS
Los Gatos, California   1960

ACKNOWLEDGMENTS

The publisher would like to acknowledge the valuable assistance of the follow-
ing individuals and institutions in the compilation of this book: Mr. Clyde
Arbuckle, director, San Jose Landmarks Commission; The Bancroft Library,
University of California; Irene Simpson, Director, Wells Fargo Bank History
Room; Dr. W. N. Davis, Jr., Historian, The California State Archives; San
Jose State College Library; Covert Martin, Stockton, California; The Cali-
fornia State Library; The California Historical Society; The New Almaden
Museum, Almaden, California; Dr. Benjamin Gilbert, Professor of History,
San Jose State College, and Ruth I. Mahood, Curator, Los Angeles County
Museum.

Contents

It is a good deal like hunting a needle in a hay stack, this hunting for a man in the mountains.

—SHERIFF HARRY MORSE

The California Outlaw: Tiburcio Vasquez

1

IN THE HISTORY of the American West, legend and folklore often overcome fact so that reality becomes romanticized. This is particularly true in the case of the Western outlaw. There are a number of reasons for this, the most important being that too few accurate records have survived from that day to the present. Another is the fact that the outlaw, by his very nature and character, led a secretive life, with the result that little is known about the lesser events in his life. Finally, many of the contemporary writers of the period, eager to write a salable and exciting book about the outlaw, disregarded what little fact was known, and like the dime novelists of the day, relied instead upon their imagination and ability to spin a good yarn.

In later years many of these "biographies" came to be regarded as factual. Perhaps the best example of this type of outlaw book is John Rollin Ridge's (or Yellow Bird's) *Life and Adventures of Joaquin Murieta.* Murieta is probably the most familiar outlaw in American history, next to Billy the Kid. But there is serious question and doubt today about the exploits attributed to this person; indeed, even as to his identity and fate. There could have been a Joaquin Murieta (a minor cattle thief in the Mother Lode country of California) but certainly not a Joaquin Murieta such as Ridge described. It is more likely that there were five bandits named Joaquin, each operating independently in various parts of California, and that their joint crimes were attributed to Joaquin Murieta. Likewise it seems safe to say that the method Ridge used to develop the character of Joaquin Murieta for his book was to represent the five as one, thereby creating the character of Murieta, and the Murieta folklore as it exists today. In this connection, it is interesting to note that there never was a consistent or accurate description of a Joaquin Murieta. The name Murieta was hardly mentioned in the newspapers of the day; there were numerous references to "Joaquin" or to "Joaquins," but rarely with a surname. There are no known photographs of Joaquin Murieta, no specimens of handwriting, no tangible proof of any kind, only the legend.

As to the famous story of Joaquin's death at the hands of Captain Harry Love and his Rangers, and their subsequent return to Stockton with Joaquin's head (later placed on public exhibition), it seems clear that when the Love expedition started out in search of the outlaw they had no clear idea of which Joaquin to look for. In sponsoring the expedition, the California legislature had named five separate Joaquins and it would appear no more was known about one than any other. As it happened, Captain Love and his Rangers came upon a group of Mexicans in the Panoche Pass in July, 1853, and when one of the Rangers said that he recognized Joaquin they promptly opened fire on the Mexicans. Several of the band were killed including the leader, said to be Joaquin, and another later identified as Manuel Garcia, or "Three-Fingered Jack." Two days later, Captain Love and his Rangers rode into Stockton with the head of Joaquin and the hand of "Three-Fingered Jack." The head was subsequently "identified" in Stockton as that of Joaquin Murieta. It seems clear that this identification was based on nothing more than rank speculation and hearsay. Even the newspapers of the day were skeptical of the whole affair. The following article appeared in *The San Francisco Alta* in August, 1853, about three weeks after the head was exhibited in Stockton:

It affords amusement to our citizens to read the various accounts of the capture and decapitation of the "notorious Joaquin Murieta." The humbug is so transparent that it is surprising any sensible person can be imposed upon by statements of the affair which have appeared in the prints. A few weeks ago a party of native Californians and Sonorians started for the Tulare Valley for the express and avowed purpose of running mustangs. Three of the party have returned and report that they were attacked by a party of Americans, and that the balance of their party, four in number, had been killed. That Joaquin Valenzuela, one of them, was killed as he was endeavoring to escape, and that his head was cut off by his captors and held as a trophy. It is too well known that Joaquin Murieta was not the person killed by Captain Harry Love's party at the Panoche Pass. The head recently exhibited in Stockton bears no resemblance to that individual, and this is positively asserted by those who have seen the real Murieta and the spurious head.

Certainly, then, the Love expedition and the decapitated head shed little light on Joaquin Murieta the outlaw. If anything, they only confuse matters further, while contributing greatly to the Murieta folklore.

If Murieta, then, is to us legendary and unreal, Tiburcio Vasquez is by contrast very real indeed. Vasquez appears upon the California scene in 1857, some five years after the demise of the Joaquins, his first recorded crime being horse-stealing in Los Angeles County. Earlier in 1853, he had been involved in the murder of a Constable in Monterey during a Mexican fandango, though he was never officially charged with that crime. With Tiburcio Vasquez, we have a rather clear and factual record of the man and his exploits. In this sense, when the record of his crimes is examined, and the degree of truth which attaches to them, Vasquez emerges as perhaps the major figure in California outlawry, overshadowing the unreal Murieta. And because the record of fact exists there is less tendency to invent a fiction. This is not to say, however, that Vasquez has not been fictionized. To some extent much that has been written about him is an attempt to romanticize. But it generally shows up as just that, for it will not jibe with the record and what we know of him. Vasquez and the legendary Murieta, however, do have a good deal in common. In some ways it would appear that Vasquez is a latter-day counterpart of Murieta. Both outlaws engaged in a similar variety of crimes: cattle and horse-stealing, stagecoach robberies, murder, pillaging, etc. Like the legendary Murieta, Vasquez was the chief of a banditti, roaming throughout California and striking in widely scattered areas. Both were regarded with admiration and fear by the native Mexican population, and with outrage by the Yankees. Both were elusive, clever, and highly skilled in horsemanship. Like Murieta, Vasquez made his principal hideout and headquarters in the wild and remote La Cantua Canyon in what was then Fresno County, and now San Benito County. Finally, both had ambitions toward effecting an uprising or revolution against the "Yankee invaders" of California. It has been said that Captain Harry Love's killing of Joaquin came just in time as Murieta was on the verge of executing a grand plan for a revolution against the Yankees. After Vasquez was captured, and while in jail at Los Angeles, he remarked in an interview with the editor of *The Los Angeles Express*:[1] "Given $60,000 I would be able to recruit enough arms and men to revolutionize Southern California." Similarity between the two is further developed when both are viewed as native Californians up-rooted from a pastoral heritage and discriminated against by the Yankees. The story of Joaquin's public whipping and beating at the hands of the Yankee miners and the ravishing of his wife by them (after which he swore to take his revenge) is an important part of the Murieta folktale. While Vasquez never suffered such fictional indignities, he shared in a feeling of genuine dislike for the Yankees and felt his rights abused by them. Vasquez spoke of this in an interview with Ben Truman, editor of *The Los Angeles Star:*

> My career grew out of the circumstances by which I was surrounded. As I grew to manhood I was in the habit of attending balls and parties given by the native Californians, into which the Americans, then beginning to become numerous, would force themselves and shove the native-born men aside, monopolizing the dance and the women. This was about 1852. A spirit of hatred and revenge took possession of me. I had numerous fights in defense of what I believe to be my rights and those of my countrymen. The officers were continually in pursuit of me. I believed we were unjustly and wrongfully deprived of the social rights that belonged to us.[2]

We would be misled, however, if we were to conclude from these statements that his life as an outlaw stemmed from these considerations alone. For while it is a matter of record that native Californians did suffer much abuse from the Yankees, these things alone do not force a person into becoming an outlaw. In making these remarks, Vasquez was trying to rationalize a life of violence and to picture himself as a social underdog. It was a notion he knew would bring him sympathy—especially from the Mexican population—and in this he was not mistaken.

The similarity between Vasquez and Murieta is indeed striking. Moreso when we consider Murieta as legend and Vasquez as fact. We might even remark that Vasquez in several ways is the Murieta legend come true, cast in that role but in a different time by some twenty years.

2

TIBURCIO VASQUEZ was born in Monterey, California, on August 11, 1835. Vasquez himself is the authority for this date, although various sources place his birthdate anywhere from 1835 to 1840. His parents were respectable citizens of the community. The Vasquez home, directly in back of Colton Hall in Monterey, is a handsome white adobe building still standing. Tiburcio had three brothers and two sisters.

He said: "I have three brothers and two sisters. Two of my brothers reside in Monterey County; one unmarried and one married; the other resides in Los Angeles County; he is married. My sisters are both married. One of them lives at San Juan Bautista, Monterey County, the other at the New Idria quicksilver mines." Vasquez further remarked that he himself had never married but had one child living in Monterey County.[3]

It is possible that the Vasquez family descended from a man also named Tiburcio Vasquez, who, in 1840, was a major-domo at the Mission Dolores in San Francisco, and colonizer of a Spanish land grant near what is now Half Moon Bay. The record is not clear on this point and must wait further proof.

The young Tiburcio attended school in Monterey and learned to read and write, an accomplishment of which he was very proud. Even when he was in San Jose awaiting trial and execution (1874-1875) he was given to while away the hours practicing his penmanship. A few samples of his handwriting have survived and the hand itself is bold, the letters carefully formed, large and graceful. Two of these samples happen to be poems, one in English and one in Spanish. This led the newspaper reporters of the day (who seemed always at his side from the day of his capture to the moment of execution) to speculate that Vasquez possessed talent as a poet. This must have amused Vasquez and no doubt flattered his vanity. No one knows for certain that he did not compose the poems but the chances are certainly against it. It is the kind of story that makes good folklore.

At the time of his trial and hanging in San Jose, Vasquez was thirty-nine years old. He presented a figure of sartorial elegance, wearing a neatly trimmed full beard and mustache and often clothed in a suit, tie, and polished boots. An interesting description appears in the records of Captain Adams, then Sheriff of Santa Clara County:

> Vasquez. He deserves credit for the manner in which he faced death. Description. Height 5′ 5¾″. Hair, dark. Eyes, dark brown. Age, 39. Complexion light for a Spaniard. He was a native Californian born in Monterey, California.[4]

Ben Truman in his book *Occidental Sketches* gives a further description, written the day after Vasquez was captured near Los Angeles:

> Not more than five feet seven inches in height, and of very spare build, he looked little like a man who could create a reign of terror. His forehead was low and slightly retreating to where it was joined by a thick mass of raven black and very coarse hair; his mustache was by no means

luxuriant, his chin whiskers passably full; and his sunken cheeks were only lightly sprinkled with beard. His lips thin and pale. His teeth white, even and firm; his left eye slightly sunken. He had small and elegantly shaped feet. Perhaps 130 pounds was as much as he weighed. His light build made it easy for the horse that bore him to perform forced marches.[5]

This description no doubt reflects the appearance of a hunted and wounded man, Vasquez having been shot during his capture the day before. The "sunken left eye" is often mentioned in descriptions of Vasquez, also his slight and unassuming build. As Truman remarks, Vasquez looked little like the man who owned a reputation for being the terror of California and the chief of a fearful banditti. But one must remember that an image of Vasquez the outlaw had long been growing in the public mind, shaped through his outrageous exploits, and enlarged upon in the sensational newspaper reports of the day, so that it was not unusual the public should have come to picture him as fierce in both appearance and deed.

Sometime in 1852, when Vasquez was but seventeen he fell into company with a group of persons in Monterey known to be of unsavory character. Chief among this group was an outlaw named Anastacia Garcia, long known to authorities in Monterey County as a horse-thief and robber. One source states that Garcia was a member of Joaquin's banditti and one of his most "desperate adherents"[6] but there is no evidence to establish this. One night Vasquez and Garcia, in company with one Jose Heiguerra, attended a fandango in Monterey. During the evening, Garcia became involved in a violent argument and fistfight. Constable William Hardmount entered the hall and attempted to establish order. What happened then is not altogether clear, but the trio resisted arrest and the Constable was slain. One report says the Constable was "shot through the heart"[7] and another says he was stabbed. Most versions agree, however, that Hardmount was murdered by Garcia (though one attributes the deed to Vasquez). Vasquez, though, was never officially charged with the crime though he was sought for questioning. That night Garcia and Vasquez fled into the hills where they remained for some time. Jose Heiguerra was seized by the Vigilantes and hanged the next morning.

The young Tiburcio is said to have served his apprenticeship in outlawry under Garcia. There is probably much truth in this. Garcia and Vasquez were definitely associated for a time and it is logical to assume that the young Vasquez, then seventeen, fell under Garcia's influence. After the murder of Constable Hardmount and du⁻ concealment in the mountains of Monterey County, there were edly numerous occasions for Garcia to instruct his pupil. One wr₁. says Garcia taught Vasquez the art of robbing stagecoaches and ambushing lone travelers. In any case, Vasquez' life as an outlaw properly begins at this point though it was not to reach its climax until some eighteen years later, in the 1870's, when his crimes would become consummate in character.

Some months after the Monterey affair, Garcia was apprehended in Los Angeles and returned to Monterey for trial. Arriving there, news of his capture swept through the town and the outraged Vigilantes broke into the jail and seized him. He was summarily hanged without trial. Whether Vasquez had been in Los Angeles at the time of Garcia's capture is not definitely known. One writer says he was. Vasquez himself said at that time he was in Mendocino County, near Ukiah, and while there was sought out by the authorities for questioning in the murder of Constable Hardmount.[8]

At about this time—the date will vary anywhere from 1863 to 1865—there is a story told by those who have written about Vasquez that he abducted a beautiful young girl, Anita, and rode off with her into the mountains. Versions of this story differ sharply in setting, circumstances, and time. In the account by Eugene Sawyer, *The Life and Career of Tiburcio Vasquez* we are told the incident occurred near Mt. Diablo, and that Vasquez, having fallen from his horse and injured himself, was taken in and cared for by a wealthy Mexican ranchero. The daughter, Anita, took an immediate fancy for Tiburcio and nursed him back to health. On recovering, Vasquez and Anita elope—as this account has it—and the father, thinking the worst, pursues and overtakes them near Livermore. The ranchero recovers his daughter after a gunfight in which Vasquez is shot in the arm. In another version of this story the father shoots both Vasquez and Anita, but both are only slightly wounded.

In George Beers' book, *Vasquez; or, the Hunted Bandits of the San Joaquin* we have an entirely different story. Here, Anita is Vasquez' childhood sweetheart who struggles unsuccessfully to win his soul from the evil influence of Anastacio Garcia. It should be pointed out that Garcia is clearly made the villain of the piece, and that Vasquez by contrast is still in a position to be saved. After Constable Hardmount is murdered, Vasquez abducts Anita with

Garcia's assistance and all three take to the mountains. There follows
a long and fanciful tale of Anita's hardship in the mountains and her
efforts to escape. She is befriended by another woman in the party,
Margarita, a companion of Garcia's, who looks after her and promises
to aid in her escape. After much traveling the party encounters a group
of Americans, a Major Baldwin, Joe Pettingill, and Grizzly Jim, all
of whom are pictured as wise, kind, and anxious to assist Anita. A
plan is devised which brings about the capture of Vasquez and Garcia.
Enroute to Monterey, Anita suddenly has a change of heart and
implores Major Baldwin to set Vasquez free, "as he has done me no
harm." Vasquez is then released and leaves for Los Angeles. For good
measure, Garcia is set free too. Anita and Margarita return to Monterey
with the Americans. Suspecting that either Vasquez or Garcia may
return and seek revenge, the Americans take up residence at Anita's
rancho. As it turns out Garcia is the one who seeks revenge (and who
now wishes to abduct Anita for himself). Garcia enlists the assistance
of Juan Soto and makes a wild attack on the rancho. In the attack
the Americans are again victorious, driving Garcia and Soto off in a
blaze of gunfire. The story ends on that note.

It is an incredible story and must be considered as fiction. There
is no evidence that such events ever occurred, nor that Major Baldwin,
Joe Pettingill, and Grizzly Jim are anything more than fictional
characters invented by the author. One must conclude that author
Beers (whose book is otherwise the most accurate and detailed contemporary work on Vasquez) wrote the story into the book for two
reasons. He was first interested in giving his readers a "love story"—
as it were—and secondly to write at some length about Vasquez' early
life, of which little is known in any detail. It is the most fanciful
version of the Anita incident and leads one to wonder whether there
is any truth in it at all.

3

ON JULY 15, 1857, Vasquez and a *compadre* descended upon a
ranch on the Santa Clara River in Los Angeles County and drove off
a herd of horses. As one account says,[9] his *compadre* in this raid was
no less a person than Juan Soto, but this cannot be verified and must
remain in question. The pair were captured while trying to sell the
horses. Indicted in Los Angeles on August 11, 1857, Vasquez pleaded
guilty as charged and was sentenced to five years in San Quentin. He
later remarked that while in San Quentin he was "roughly handled as

TOMAS REDONDO, alias Procopio, member of the Vasquez banditti. Procopio was arrested by Sheriff Harry Morse in San Francisco in 1871.

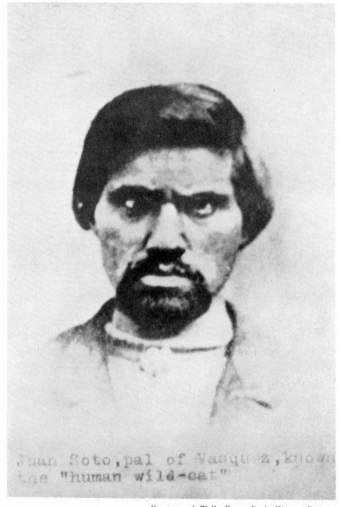

Juan Soto, pal of Vasquez, known the "human wild-cat"

JUAN SOTO, confederate of Tiburcio Vasquez, and one of the fiercest California outlaws. Soto was slain in a gunfight by Sheriff Harry Morse.

the discipline at that time was undergoing a reform."[10] He had not yet served two years of his sentence when he escaped in the general prison break of June 25, 1859. He made his way to Amador County, in the Mother Lode, where he again tried his hand at horse-stealing. He was no more successful this time than before and was returned to San Quentin on August 17, 1859. After serving out his full sentence this time he was released on August 13, 1863.

Tiburcio then turned to the bustling quicksilver mines at New Almaden in Santa Clara County where he allegedly took up professional gambling. The mines were working at full production and there was considerable prosperity in the area. But Vasquez was either a failure in gambling or else impatient and uncertain of the financial return. In Enriquita one morning an Italian butcher was found stabbed and some $400 in cash, known to have been in his possession, was missing. Captain Adams, Sheriff of Santa Clara County, investigated the murder and, ironically, employed Vasquez as interpreter at the inquest. The resulting statement rendered into English by Vasquez could hardly have proved enlightening: "The deceased came to his death from a pistol bullet, fired by some person or persons unknown."[11] Immediately after the inquest Vasquez vanished. Several days later Captain Adams received information that his interpreter, Vasquez, and one Faustino Lorenzano had committed the murder and robbery. But the evidence was not deemed sufficient to make an arrest and Vasquez was not pursued.

During the years 1864-1866, Vasquez is reported to have associated with Tomas Redondo, *alias* Procopio, *alias* Dick of the Red Hand, a familiar and notorious outlaw in Alameda County who was later arrested in San Francisco by Sheriff Harry Morse, the great California lawman. Vasquez is also said to have operated with Juan Soto, a fierce and ruthless outlaw who was killed in a famous gunfight with Sheriff Morse. Vasquez denied he was ever affiliated with either Procopio or Soto, but their names are so often linked together that we must conclude some confederation existed among them. One writer has said that Procopio was a first cousin to Joaquin but fails to specify which "Joaquin."[12] Eugene Sawyer says that Vasquez first met Procopio in San Juan.[13] Procopio is mentioned as having taken a part with Vasquez in the holdup of the Visalia stage near Soap Lake in the fall of 1871.[14] And still another report states that Procopio and Vasquez were partners in crime for over two years, and that Vasquez had only just parted company with Procopio when the latter was arrested by Sheriff Morse in San Francisco. As for Juan Soto, his most singular crime was the robbery of a store near Sunol in which the clerk, Otto Ludovici, was shot and killed by Soto. Prior to that time Soto was known primarily as a bad-tempered cattle thief. In physical appearance—unlike Procopio who was tall and handsome—Soto appeared particularly rough and ugly. In the one surviving photograph of him, he has piercing eyes, coarse black hair, and a general expression of toughness. Soto was mentioned earlier as the possible *compadre* of Vasquez in the horse-stealing episode in Los Angeles County. Soto met his death in a gunfight with Sheriff Morse, an incident in itself as rousing as anything in the literature of Western outlawry, and which for sheer courage is Morse's greatest single exploit.

In 1867, Vasquez left Monterey County and for a time operated in Sonoma County where he tried to run off a herd of cattle. This went no better than his attempts at horse-stealing. Captured by a posse, he was sentenced to San Quentin a third time. He entered prison on January 18, 1867 and was discharged on June 4, 1870, after serving a sentence of three years and six months. If he did associate with either Procopio or Soto this association could have occurred only during the years 1864-1866, or the latter part of 1870, after he was released from San Quentin. Soto was killed by Sheriff Morse in January, 1871, and Procopio was arrested by Morse in 1871. After 1870, Vasquez' confederates are rather well known and a matter of record; no mention of either Procopio or Soto occurs in connection with Vasquez after that date.

After his release from San Quentin in 1870, Vasquez returned to Monterey County. There follows a story of his relationship with a family named Salazar in San Juan. Vasquez was a frequent visitor in the Salazar home—either socially or to seek refuge—and it was not long before he became smitten with the charms of Salazar's handsome young wife. The story goes that Vasquez abducted the willing Mrs. Salazar one night and took her to Natividad. Tiring of her in a few days, he abandoned her to her own devices. In the meantime, Salazar had been told of Vasquez' treachery and threatened to shoot him on sight. The opportunity was not long in coming. Several nights later Vasquez and two companions were walking down a back street in San Juan when they came face to face with Salazar. Hot words were exchanged and Vasquez drew his Navy revolver, but the gun misfired. Salazar got his shot off, the bullet striking Vasquez in the neck and coming out below the shoulder. More shots were exchanged. Salazar retreated and Vasquez was taken away by his companions. Later Salazar swore out a warrant of attempted murder against Vasquez and the grand jury found a true bill, but Vasquez had vanished into the Panoche mountains. There is probably truth in this story. At least one writer has mentioned Vasquez bore a deep scar on his neck.

In the fall of 1871, Vasquez held up the Visalia stage at Soap Lake, near Hollister, assisted by Francisco Barcenas and Narcisso Rodriguez. As the stage approached it was surrounded and forced to a stop. The passengers were ordered out. Each was robbed and tied and laid upon the ground. The stagecoach was driven to the side of the road and concealed in a thicket. The outlaws were last seen riding in the direction of San Juan Mountain. Later that same day, on the San Juan grade, Vasquez chanced to meet on the trail Thomas McMahon of Hollister. McMahon knew Vasquez by sight and Vasquez knew McMahon. Only recently Vasquez had received word that Sheriff Morse had requested McMahon's assistance in capturing him, and that McMahon was to keep Morse informed of any information on Vasquez. Determined to "teach Tom a lesson" for his conspiracy with Sheriff Morse, Vasquez stopped him and robbed him. Here is the story in Vasquez' own words as told in an interview with Reporter George Beers:[15]

> Sheriff Henry Morse, of Alameda County, whose heroic adventures in my pursuit the newspapers of late have been full, desirous of capturing me, wrote to Tom McMahon, of San Juan Bautista, in Monterey County, who, through his relations with the creole (native Californian) population of that region could best serve him, to inform himself without delay in regard to my movements and whereabouts, and to notify him (Morse) with all possible dispatch. This coming to my ears, I determined to teach Tom a lesson . . . I took occasion to stop him at a convenient point.
>
> "How are you, Tom?" said I.
>
> "Very well, friend Tiburcio," he replied.
>
> I then inquired if I had ever done him any harm. He replied that I had not. I then told him that I had learned of his underhanded dealings with Morse, and that I proposed to repay him in his own way.
>
> Upon being called to deliver, he handed over his coin and a fine improved Colt's revolver. I then informed him that I wanted a fine ring that ornamented his handsome hand. To this he rather objected, but on being informed that I would stand no nonsense, he made a virtue of necessity, and he and the ring parted company. Then I told him I was

no assassin, I would make him a present of his cowardly life, which he was by no means loathe to accept, with permission to jog on with his fine buggy and horses.

In writing this account Reporter Beers (of *The San Francisco Chronicle*) no doubt embellished it by adding a few words here and there. But it is essentially what happened. Although McMahon was robbed of $750 in cash, he had another $500 in a shot sack hidden under the seat of the buggy which Vasquez overlooked. Thereafter when traveling, McMahon carried with him a double-barrel shotgun.[16]

Sheriff Tom Wasson of Monterey County had meanwhile organized a posse to search for the outlaws. In the hills outside San Juan, Wasson came upon the outlaw camp, surprising Vasquez, Barcenas, and Rodriguez. In the gunfight that followed Vasquez and Barcenas escaped but Rodriguez was taken prisoner. For his complicity in the robbery of the Visalia stage, Rodriguez was sentenced to ten years in San Quentin, where he died in 1873 from drinking an overdose of alcohol. The posse recovered several stolen horses and a large cache of arms and ammunition.

Traveling by night, Vasquez and Barcenas made their way to Santa Cruz. No sooner had they arrived when Marshal L. T. Roberts learned of their presence in the area. A few miles above Santa Cruz in the mountains, Marshal Roberts discovered the pair and ordered them to surrender. There was a rapid exchange of gunfire and Barcenas was killed outright. Vasquez was shot through the body, the bullet striking below the right breast nipple and ranging diagonally out under his right shoulder. Seriously wounded, Vasquez stood his ground and returned Roberts' fire, and succeeded in wounding him. With a remarkable determination, Vasquez then mounted his horse and rode a distance of some sixty miles to La Cantua Canyon where he remained until his wound healed.

It was about this time that Procopio was arrested in San Francisco by Sheriff Morse. Morse had been told that Procopio might be found at a certain fandango in company with a group of friends. Acting on the tip, Morse entered the hall and walked straight to Procopio. Taking him by the throat and pressing a gun to his head, Morse said, "Procopio, you're my man!"[17] No resistance was made and Morse marched him out. Procopio was tried and convicted of grand larceny and sentenced to fourteen years in San Quentin.

While recovering from his wound in the La Cantua, Vasquez was joined by Cleovaro Chavez, who was to become his lieutenant and most efficient *compadre*. No photograph of Chavez has been located and none may exist. The following description of Chavez is taken from Reporter Beers and will have to suffice:

> Vasquez now associated himself with a young Mexican, in whom he had full confidence, and was as desperate as the former chief, Soto, but who exercised better judgment in emergencies, and who was faithful in carrying out the plans laid down and carefully agreed upon. This was Cleovaro Chavez. Chavez is about five feet eleven inches in height, and is very muscular, weighing over two hundred pounds. His complexion is rather light for a Mexican, and he had gray eyes, short whiskers on the side of the lower jaw, small goatee, rather thin, bloodless lips, teeth regular and well preserved, a scar on one cheek, caused by a fall from a horse—a small angular cicatrix—black hair, worn rather long; short thick neck.[18]

Like Vasquez, Chavez possessed considerable talent and daring. With his arrival, Vasquez began to plan a series of crimes more ambitious than any previously undertaken. Cleovaro Chavez was to ride with Vasquez in every major raid and robbery for the next three years.

About this same time Vasquez recruited Abdon Leiva, a Chilean, into the banditti. Leiva and his wife, Rosaria, lived on a small ranch in the La Cantua with their two children. Tiburcio was quick to establish an amorous liason with Rosaria, but was cautious so that he might remain in the good graces of her husband, insofar as that was possible. In any case, the unsuspecting Leiva joined in planning the next raid. Vasquez had been told that Henry Miller, the famous cattle baron, had deposited $30,000 at Firebaugh's Ferry to pay his employees.

Plans were carefully drawn up for a raid on the San Joaquin River town. Vasquez recruited a force of six men, consisting of a Frenchman, August de Bert, Romulo Gonzales, Theodoro Moreno (said to be first cousin to Vasquez), Chavez, Leiva, and himself. Arriving at the Ferry, Vasquez learned from a storekeeper that Miller had failed to deposit the money. To compensate for their disappointment and trouble it was decided to rob the store. Twelve persons in the store were tied and laid upon the floor. Each was robbed of money and jewelry. After plundering the merchandise, the safe was opened and robbed. There is a story about this robbery which is worth noting, the type of story often told of outlaws intended to picture them as romantic and generous. The story here is all the more interesting when we consider that it is reputed to have been told by Vasquez himself, and which, if true, gives us some insight into his conceit.[19]

I took a watch away from a man named the Captain. His wife saw me, and coming up, threw her arms around my neck and begged me to return the watch; that her husband had given it to her during their courtship, and she couldn't bear to part with it. I gave it to her, and then she said, "Come with me." I followed her into another room, and from behind the chimney she took out another watch and gave it to me. The Captain said, "You haven't got a bad heart, after all!"

The story is a familiar one, an anecdote repeated of gallant outlaws wherever such stories are told. It is mentioned in all the accounts on Vasquez, usually with some variation, and we can only speculate whether Vasquez is really the proper source of the story. In such matters it is best to let the reader judge for himself.

4

AFTER THE RAID at Firebaugh's Ferry the outlaws returned to Leiva's ranch in the La Cantua, near the New Idria quicksilver mine. Vasquez was a frequent visitor to New Idria in those days and some writers have suggested that an agreement of mutual protection existed between the mine superintendent and Vasquez. The superintendent's part of the bargain was not to give information of Vasquez' movements and in exchange for this consideration Vasquez was to commit no depredation against the mine or its employees. On one occasion Vasquez and Chavez had stopped the New Idria stage to rob it. Upon ordering all the passengers out it was discovered the superintendent was among them. Vasquez ordered everyone back into the coach and on their way; no one was robbed. Another time, two officers succeeded in tracing Vasquez to New Idria but upon arriving there could learn nothing concerning his hideout. Both the miners and the officials said they had never heard of anyone named Tiburcio Vasquez. That night Vasquez left his hideout (having been informed the officers were looking for him) and trailed the officers on the road to Gilroy. When the officers broke camp the next morning they discovered their horses were gone. Vasquez, of course, had taken them. It was a capricious act and a bold one, too. But then the officers had no proof that Vasquez was the thief.

Much has been written about the protection given to Vasquez by the native Mexicans. There is much truth in this. We must remember that considerable friction existed between the native Californians and the *gringos* in that day.

TIBURCIO VASQUEZ. From a photograph taken while Vasquez was in jail awaiting trial at San Jose.

ABDON LEIVA, member of the Vasquez banditti, who later turned State's evidence against Vasquez.

To some, Vasquez must have seemed a hero dealing out his own particular brand of justice. Certainly his reputation was building fast. His exploits were now reported by the press in great detail. In some instances, the complicity of the Mexicans was probably inspired through fear rather than sympathy. Then there is the matter of Vasquez' sources of information or his intelligence regarding efforts to capture him. One writer has gone so far to say that Vasquez had a highly organized spy system with agents close to official sources. This is an obvious exaggeration. What information he got must have come to him through a sort of grapevine. In certain instances where a posse would be out searching for him it seems clear enough, however, that he knew about it.

In the summer of 1873, Vasquez worked out his most daring scheme. It was no less than a plan to derail and rob the Southern Pacific payroll train between San Jose and Gilroy. Knowing the payroll train left San Francisco the end of each month to pay employees along the line, Vasquez and his company rode to a point on the railroad known as the Twenty-One Mile House, halfway between San Jose and Gilroy. However carefully Vasquez may have planned the robbery, it never came to pass. One of two things happened. Either the bandits had not given sufficient time to removing the rails to derail the train, or the railroad had been told about the robbery plan and had re-scheduled the train. In any case, they were not able to stop the train, much less board and rob the payroll car. To compensate their disappointment, it was decided to raid the Twenty-One Mile House, a hotel and restaurant on the railroad line. An account of that exploit appeared in *The Gilroy Advocate* on August 2, 1873:

BOLD ROBBERY

Last Wednesday night, about 8 o'clock, Mr. Finley, who has charge of the Twenty-One Mile House during the owner's absence in Europe, two farm hands and a traveling agent for a sewing machine, who were stopping there for the night, were seated in the bar-room of the above wayside inn, when six Mexicans rode up, watered their horses, dismounted and entered as though for a drink. Such was not their purpose, however, for after a little maneuvering they drew their pistols, covered the unsuspecting inmates with them, and with the admonition to be quiet and make no resistance, they proceeded to bind them. The two farm hands and the machine agent were laid on the floor, bound and covered with a blanket. Finley was bound, and the leader of the gang holding a knife in most uncomfortable proximity to him, demanded to know where the money was, remarking that unless the information was forthcoming he would be dispatched to Davey Jones' locker. A second demand was not necessary, and the desired information was imparted instantly. About $155 in money was taken, together with four watches. One was taken from Finley, a fine silver watch, which he had purchased from H. C. Warner, of this city, a short time ago, and one from the sewing machine agent, together with what loose change he had upon him. Luckily the other two men had nothing valuable on them. After securing this booty one of the ruffians helped himself to something to drink, and the whole party mounted their horses and rode off in the direction of this city. Next to that at Firebaugh's Ferry, a few months since, this is the boldest robbery which has occurred in this vicinity for a long time. It is generally believed that these robbers are a portion of the band that committed the depredation of the above mentioned, and that at San Benito, a short time after, and which has become a terror to that portion of the country. They undoubtedly have their rendezvous in the mountains, from which they prowl forth to prey on sparsely settled and unprotected districts. Some effectual measures should immediately be taken to hunt out this band of lawless marauders and bring them to speedy justice.

It is interesting to note that Vasquez is not mentioned by name. But as the item appeared only three days after the raid it may have been too soon to establish any identity. It was generally known at the time, however, that Vasquez had led the raid at Firebaugh's Ferry and one can only conclude that this fact was unknown to the editor of the *Gilroy Advocate.* Another matter worth noting is the manner in which the victims were tied and laid upon the floor: this occurs in nearly all the robberies and is the Vasquez label where the victims offer no resistance.

The bandits remained in hiding at Leiva's ranch in the La Cantua for several days after the raid on the Twenty-One Mile House. It was then that Vasquez began planning the robbery of Snyder's Store at Tres Pinos, a crime which as it later developed was to become his most notorious. He expected to shift his activities to Southern California after the robbery of Snyder's Store, and in keeping with this plan he urged Leiva to dispose of his ranch and move his wife, Rosaria, and two children to Jim Heffner's ranch in Los Angeles County. Having got into some trouble with the authorities at New Idria, Leiva was agreeable to the suggestion. The ranch was sold. Rosaria and her children were sent to Heffner's where she would be joined by the outlaws after the Tres Pinos robbery. One might guess that Vasquez was continuing his romantic liason with Rosaria all this time, thus his interest in planning arrangements for her.

Plans for the robbery of Snyder's Store took shape. Vasquez described them in an interview with Reporter George Beers:[20]

> I made it a special condition that Abdon Leiva should take command for the occasion, because it became necessary that he should go into the place in the daytime, reconnoiter, and make the necessary dispositions, and that I would make my appearance at night. At five o'clock of the evening of the 26th, I sent Leiva and Romulo Gonzales ahead, with orders that they should enter the town, take a few drinks and smoke a few cigars, and ascertain the inmates of Snyder's store, and they were not to do anything until my arrival . . . They started, and in a short time I sent Moreno, and about dark I followed with Chavez.

On August 26, 1873, Leiva and Gonzales entered the store according to plan. The New Idria stage had just arrived and the clerk, John Utzerath, was sorting the mail. The pair ordered drinks and cigars and "reconnoitered" as Vasquez had put it. Then Theodoro Moreno entered the store. Drawing his pistol, Moreno ordered the occupants of the store to line up against the bar. Leiva and Gonzales tied up Andrew Snyder, John Utzerath, a small boy, and several customers, laying them upon the floor. At that point Vasquez and Chavez arrived and Moreno was stationed outside the store to guard the horses. Just then a Portugese sheepherder named Bernal Berhuri appeared in the street and started toward the store. Moreno ordered him to halt. But the Portugese, not understanding or not hearing, continued and was shot in the head by Moreno. It is not altogether clear who shot the Portugese; one account says Vasquez shot him.[21] But it is probable Moreno did; it was Moreno who was ultimately tried and sentenced for his death.

In the meantime a small boy, brother to the one who had been tied inside the store, broke out the back door and ran toward the stable. Chavez, who had been inside, gave chase and caught him, knocking him unconscious with his pistol butt. Then a teamster, George Redford, drove up in front of the store with a load of pickets. Vasquez was outside now and covered him with his Henry rifle, ordering him down from the wagon. Redford, who was deaf, did not hear the order and sensing danger, panicked, running toward the rear of the store. Vasquez shot him as he reached the stable door. One account says: "When found afterwards he lay face downward, his hands clutching tightly a wisp of hay, and his face horribly distorted from the agonies of the death struggle." [22]

Next door in the hotel, Leander Davidson, the proprietor, had heard the gunfire and was standing in the doorway attempting to close and bolt the door.   Someone shouted for him to shut the door and get inside and that he would not be harmed.   One report says Leiva shouted the warning to him;[23] another says Lewis Scherrer, a blacksmith, shouted the words.[24]   In any case, Vasquez saw Davidson and shot through the door, the bullet hitting Davidson in the chest, who fell backward against his wife.   He died instantly.

Chavez and Leiva had been robbing the hostages inside the store. Vasquez entered and sent for Snyder, who was untied.   Snyder was told to produce all the cash and valuables on the premises.   He took them into a back room and directed them to a bureau drawer containing some $200, after which he was again tied and laid upon the floor. The robbers then plundered the merchandise, taking clothing, tobacco, whiskey, and food.   Eight horses were taken from Snyder's stable and loaded with stolen merchandise.   Some $1200 in cash and valuables were obtained in the robbery.   Then, under cover of darkness, the outlaws mounted and made good their escape up Tres Pinos Creek, leaving behind three persons dead.

News of the "Tres Pinos Tragedy"—as it was called—outraged and shocked the public and many local communities feared an imminent attack from the Vasquez banditti.   Some newspaper accounts suggested that Tiburcio had as many as fifty men under arms, divided into bands, all working under his evil genius.   In Hollister an attack was expected at any moment.   Vigilantes were hastily organized and men were posted at various approaches to the town to stand watch. The Tres Pinos murders were reported at great length in newspapers throughout the state, a fact which no doubt contributed greatly to the public anxiety.   The following account appeared in *The Salinas Index* on September 4, 1873:

THE TRES PINOS CARNAGE AND ROBBERY

The brief notice of the telegraphic report of the Tres Pinos murder and robbery which came to hand as we were going to press last week, has been too truly verified, and the public have been fully acquainted with the particulars of the outrage by a party of eight desperados, the leaders of whom are well known in this country, where they have been committing their depredations for a number of years, avoiding capture by resorting to the many inaccessible canyons and hiding places which abound in the various mountain ranges. The tragedy occurred Tuesday last night, and although Sheriff Wasson was at the time in Monterey City, he reached the scene of the murder Wednesday afternoon, in company with Sheriff Adams, of Santa Clara County, who was in Gilroy at the time, and from him and Sheriff Wasson we learn the following particulars concerning the affair and subsequent events.

The robbery was commenced in Snyder's store, about dark, and the operations inside were conducted by the notorious Tiburcio Vasquez, who with his assistants, were unmasked, which fact corroborates the theory that robbery and not murder was the original intention. During the whole affair, while the shooting was going on outside, it is said that Vasquez paid no attention to it, busying himself with search for money and plunder. The shooting was all done by one man, Jose Chabo, who first shot a Portugese teamster, who was engaged in greasing his wagon wheels, and who, it is supposed, did not hear and immediately obey an order to lie down; George Redford, another teamster, who was standing on Davidson's hotel porch, started to run and was shot in the back, he gained the stable where he laid down in a manger and died. Another man, who heard the shooting, entered the hotel by the rear entrance and advised Davidson to shut up the house as soon as possible, and as the latter was in the act of closing the front door Chabo fired through it, the ball killing Davidson almost instantly. For an hour or more the robbers were engaged in going through the store, hotel, and persons of their captives, the terrified inhabitants offering no resistance, seeming paralyzed with fear. Eight of the best horses in the stables and on the premises, together with saddles, were then taken by the robbers, who decamped toward the south. If the citizens in that locality had acted with sufficient energy and promptness, and had followed the band at once, forcing every man they came across to arm and join the pursuit, a force of at least fifty men would have been on the trail in a few hours, the band would have been killed or taken, together with the stock and plunder; but the inhabitants were terror-stricken and entertained fears of a subsequent visit and revenge by the terrible Vasquez if they even attempted their own protection.

There are several statements in this article which do not jibe with other accounts of the Tres Pinos robbery. The report says eight men took part in the raid; most accounts say five or six participated. Vasquez said there were five, including himself. The Salinas article states that while Vasquez was inside the store "busying himself with search for plunder and money" one Jose Chabo did all the shooting outside the store. It seems clear Vasquez did not spend all his time inside the store. Most versions are clear on the point that Vasquez shot Davidson, and probably Redford. One wonders where the *Salinas Index* got hold of the name "Jose Chabo." There is no proof of such a person in association with Vasquez at any time. (Perhaps it is a mis-spelling of Chavez?) In any case the article is certainly in error in saying that "Chabo" did all the shooting. The Portugese sheepherder is described as a "teamster" and is not named (Bernal Berhuri). And finally, the article says that Davidson's hotel was robbed. This is not mentioned elsewhere but it may be true. It would seem logical for the outlaws to rob the hotel after shooting Davidson.

On the day of the robbery Captain Adams was in Gilroy on election business. Informed of the crime the next morning, he immediately left for Hollister to recruit a posse and pursue Vasquez. The townspeople, however, had other ideas about joining the posse, either fearful of reprisal from Vasquez or more immediately concerned with the defense of Hollister against an expected raid. Captain Adams was joined by Sheriff Wasson of Monterey; eventually four other men were deputized, making six altogether. The party set out in pursuit of Vasquez one whole day after the robbery at Snyder's Store.

Traveling up Tres Pinos Creek, the posse made their way to La Cantua Canyon where they conducted a thorough search for the outlaws. A sheepherder told them that Vasquez and his party had passed through the canyon but had not stopped. Adams thought Vasquez had headed for Tulare Lake and later found tracks in that area, but opposite the northwest corner of the lake the track scattered and was lost. Adams decided to skirt the lake and travel inland where he might catch a stagecoach or train, and by thus traveling, move ahead and cut off the bandits. So the posse started in the direction of Fresno but missed the trail in the dark and got lost in a marsh at the lower end of the lake. At daylight they found the trail to Fresno and arrived there late in the afternoon. Sheriff Wasson, not knowing the country, decided to return to Monterey and organize a further search for Vasquez in the La Cantua. Adams telegraphed to Bakersfield, in Kern County, and asked the Sheriff there to organize a posse and wait his arrival.

In the meantime, the outlaws had made good their escape into Southern California. Theodoro Moreno had parted from the group in the La Cantua to hire out on a nearby sheep ranch at Bitterwater Valley. South of Bakersfield, Gonzales' horse had given out and he remained behind while the balance of the party continued to Heffner's Ranch to join Rosaria Leiva. Later a camp was set up in Little Rock Creek Canyon, consisting of Vasquez, Chavez, Leiva and his wife.

In Bakersfield, Captain Adams was joined by two deputies and the trio immediately rode southward to Tejon Pass. At Buena Vista Lake they met a Mexican on the trail whom Adams stopped to question. Having no description of Romulo Gonzales, Adams had no way of knowing the man he questioned was actually Gonzales. In any case, had Adams known whom he was it would have been difficult to arrest him. There was no jail at the time in Bakersfield and to have taken Gonzales along would no doubt have impeded the posse in its pursuit of Vasquez. Gonzales was allowed to go his way. They found the tracks again a few miles to the south and followed the trail to San Emedio, and from there to Heffner's. At Tejon Pass, Adams telegraphed Sheriff Rowland in Los Angeles saying that he believed Vasquez to be in the vicinity and to join him with a posse. Returning to Heffner's ranch, Adams made plans for a thorough search of the entire surrounding area. Two days later Sheriff Rowland arrived with six men and an Indian guide. Having received a tip that Vasquez was in Little Rock Creek Canyon, Rowland led the posse to the mouth of the canyon where they found fresh wagon tracks in the creek bed. Riding up the canyon, one of the men found ashes of a recent campfire and a cache of food supplies. Captain Adams suggested they move further up the canyon in hope of surprising the outlaws. Rowland agreed and the posse continued to a point three miles up the canyon. Suddenly, ahead of them, Chavez rode into view from behind a clump of manzanita. One of the posse shouted: "Look! There's a man!" Chavez heard the alarm and spurred his horse up a ravine and over a rise. Having the fresher horse, Chavez rapidly outdistanced the posse. Adams and Rowland gave chase and followed to a small fork in the canyon. As they debated which fork to take, Vasquez and Chavez appeared above them atop a large boulder and commenced firing. The posse scattered as Vasquez and Chavez kept up a heavy fire with Henry rifles. Adams wanted to make an immediate charge to dislodge the outlaws from their position but Rowland disagreed, insisting they wait for the rest of the posse to re-group. The firing ceased. Fearing the outlaws were making good their escape, Adams promptly mounted and charged up the canyon unassisted. As he reached the top he caught a glimpse of Vasquez and Chavez riding into the chaparral. Adams was then joined by Rowland but as their horses were tired it was not possible to give chase. The outlaws had escaped into the wild canyon below. After a brief search nine horses were found, some of them matching description of those stolen from Snyder's stable at Tres Pinos. Recovering what they could take with them, the posse returned to Tejon Pass.

5

WE CAN ONLY SPECULATE whether Abdon Leiva was a willing recruit for Tiburcio Vasquez. But it is probable that he was, regardless of what influence Rosaria might have had in the matter. Some writers have said that Leiva was reluctant and that it was only through Rosaria's insistence he joined Vasquez. But then Leiva made no very strenuous objections to taking part in the raids on Firebaugh's Ferry, Twenty-One Mile House, or in the robbery of Snyder's Store. Reporter George Beers would have us think that Leiva began to develop a conscience about these crimes and wished to reform.[25] But there is little evidence to prove this view. The most important single factor which led to Leiva's falling out with Vasquez, and his decision to give himself up and turn State's evidence, stems from his discovery of the affair between his wife, Rosaria, and Vasquez. He began to suspect something was amiss about the time of the Tres Pinos robbery. But his suspicions were not proved until later during an incident which occurred at Little Rock Creek Canyon. Vasquez had asked Leiva to take a wagon and go for supplies. As the story goes, Leiva departed and left his wife behind with Vasquez and Chavez. Thinking the worst, Leiva obtained the supplies at a nearby ranch in order to make a hasty return to camp. Upon arriving (some two hours before he was expected) he surprised the romantic couple in what Vasquez later referred to as *fragrante delicto*. Leiva drew his pistol to shoot Vasquez when Chavez interceded and threatened to kill Leiva if he harmed Vasquez. One writer says Chavez told Leiva, "Drop that gun or I'll blow your brains out!"[26] Leiva offered to fight a duel but Vasquez declined, saying there was no point in adding to the wrong already done. An understanding was reached by the two that no gunplay would take place until they had separated. Then it would be each man for himself. The next morning, Leiva and Rosaria drove away in the wagon to Heffner's ranch at Elizabeth Lake. But Leiva's mind had been working hard at getting revenge and he decided to take it by turning himself in to the authorities and turning State's evidence against Vasquez. He left Rosaria at Heffner's and drove to Lyon's station, where he surrendered himself to Under-Sheriff W. W. Jenkins of Los Angeles.

Receiving news of Leiva's surrender, Captain Adams rode to Lyon's Station where he interviewed him at length. Leiva, then, could have been the source of information telling that Vasquez was hiding in Little Rock Creek Canyon. Leiva further told Adams that Theodoro Moreno had parted from Vasquez after the robbery at Tres Pinos and could be found at a sheep ranch in the Bitterwater Valley.

Not to be outdone in all this, Vasquez rode to Heffner's that night and abducted Rosaria. No doubt Rosaria was willing to be "abducted" —even though she later insisted she was taken at gunpoint. They then rode into the mountains and joined Chavez. On this occasion Vasquez is supposed to have ridden within one-half mile of Captain Adams, who was riding on the other side of the same hill. Adams was enroute to Heffner's to call for Rosaria, while Vasquez, having already called for her, was riding away with her on the opposite trail. Rosaria remained with Vasquez for several months, during which time she became pregnant. When her presence became an impediment to Vasquez' plans to move north again, he abandoned her in the mountains. Eventually she made her way to San Jose. An interesting account of this incident appears in George Beers' book and is reputed to be Rosaria's own version of it.[27] In brief, she says that Vasquez abducted her at gunpoint and that they hid out in the mountains. She complained of having nothing to eat but meat. Her health failed due to bad food and exposure. She mentions her pregnancy and miscarriage and says Vasquez left her "sick, helpless, and alone" in the wilderness. The remainder of her story tells of her convalescence on a ranch and her journey to San Jose.

Vasquez commented briefly on the whole business in an interview with the editor of *The Los Angeles Express*.

Reporter: Tell me about the affair with Leiva's wife.
Vasquez: A criminal intimacy had existed between myself and Leiva's wife long before I left the ranch in Monterey County. But Leiva never suspicioned us. At Rock Creek he caught us in *fragrante delicto*. He turned against me then, and sought to have me captured. Leiva had been with me a long time prior to the Tres Pinos murders.[28]

6

MORENO WAS ARRESTED at Judge Tully's ranch in the Bitterwater Valley by Sheriff Wasson of Monterey. On November 23, 1873, he was formally indicted in Salinas for the murder of Bernal Berhuri who was shot and killed during the robbery of Snyder's Store at Tres Pinos. Moreno was found guilty and sentenced by Judge Belden to life impris-

onment in San Quentin. Principal witness for the prosecution was
Abdon Leiva. One reporter said Moreno expressed himself as perfectly satisfied with the verdict, having cheated the hangman.[29]

Vasquez had returned north to his old hideout in La Cantua Canyon.
Along the way, he and Chavez had recruited four new men, Isadore
Padillo, G. Gomez, T. Monteres, and Blas Bicuna. Gomez was regarded as a noteworthy addition, having distinguished himself by
shooting the Constable in Bakersfield. Through friends at New Idria,
Vasquez learned that Leiva had testified against Moreno in Salinas
and had been returned to San Jose in custody of Captain Adams.
Matters would be considerably eased with Leiva out of the way. With
this in mind, Vasquez tried to induce Bicuna to travel to San Jose,
and by conniving with friends there, who might gain access to Leiva's
cell, administer poison to the informant, through a bottle of wine presented to him as a gift. But Bicuna had no stomach for the assign-
ment and the matter was dropped.

On December 26, 1873, Vasquez and his banditti were to further
distinguish themselves by sacking the town of Kingston.[30] Leaving
their horses just outside town in a thicket, the bandits crossed a wooden
footbridge and, dividing into groups, took possession of the town. In
less than ten minutes over thirty-five men had been tied up and robbed
by the outlaws. At Reichart's Hotel, Jacob & Epstein's General
Store, and Sweet's Store, the customers were tied and robbed and
laid upon the floor. At each store the safe was opened and robbed.
At Jacob & Epstein's General Store, the clerk refused to open the safe
and was knocked unconscious by Chavez. Vasquez entered the store
and told Epstein he would be shot unless the safe was opened immediately. All the stores were being robbed at the same moment. Across
the street at Reichart's hotel, the guests were assembled in the lobby
and robbed. Several persons were knocked unconscious when they
resisted; miraculously no one was killed. While Epstein was opening
the safe, a volley of shots rang out up the street, fired by J. W. Sutherland who had responded to an alarm at Sweet's Store. There was
general chaos as shots were exchanged in the street. Sutherland was
forced back but continued firing. Fearing the situation had got out
of hand, Vasquez rendezvoused his company at the footbridge and prepared to ride. In the scramble, Chavez had been wounded in the knee
by a shot from Sutherland's rifle. Monteres was somehow unable to
escape over the footbridge and was captured. The raid had been
interrupted but not before the bandits had obtained some $2500 in

cash and jewelry. The banditti rode to a rancho so
distant where Chavez was treated and his wound dr(
detailed Gomez to accompany Chavez to a hideout
Chane. The rest of the band rode south in the dir
Lake.

News of the "Sacking of Kingston" swept over the state. In
Bakersfield, interest in the raid was at fever pitch and the principal
topic of conversation for days. The following article appeared in
The Bakersfield Southern Californian on January 1, 1874:

Vasquez seems determined to excel
even the dare-devil exploits of the
famous brigand chief Joaquin Murieta.
After having been hunted for months
like a wild beast from lair to lair—
the banditti under his command either
killed, captured, or dispersed— and
successfully eluding the most vigilant
and indefatigable pursuit to which an
outlaw was ever subjected in this
state, has suddenly placed himself
again at the head of a band of Mexican cut-throats and ex-prison convicts,
and has entered upon another campaign of pillage and murder. On Friday evening last, between twenty and
thirty Mexicans and white men entered
Kingston, Tulare County, tied all the
storekeepers, from whom they took
safe keys and robbed all the safes.
They robbed everybody in town they
could lay their hands on, and left the
place about 9 o'clock p.m. Vasquez
was recognized as their leader. Early
next morning a teamster on the Tulare road was robbed of $100. Armed
posses from Visalia and Kingston are
in pursuit. Tuesday evening a dispatch was received here stating that
Vasquez and his people were crossing
the White River, forty miles from
this place. This created somewhat of
a sensation, and our citizens immediately placed themselves on a war-
footing, and evinced a determination,
if the foe should put in an appearance, to "welcome them with bloody
hands to hospitable graves." At present writing, however, there are no
indications of Vasquez. The natural
avenue of escape for these marauders
is through the west side of this valley
into the mountain fastnesses south
of here, or out into the Mojave desert and on to Arizona or Mexico. And
if they are hotly pursued they will
probably scatter the best they can.
We do not think, however, they will
honor us with a visit.

This article exaggerates in saying that twenty or thirty men participated in the Kingston raid. Most accounts place the number at nine
or eleven. The last section of the article expresses the very real con-
cern of the day over Vasquez' depredations and where he might strike
next. As the report says, there were many posses in the field—almost
too many—and one might wonder how many were imprudently organized on the basis of false information.

Having divided his banditti at Tulare Lake, Vasquez proceeded alone to Panama, near Bakersfield, where he says he spent several days drinking, dancing, and carousing with the charming young *senoritas*.[31] Later he rode to Posa de Chane to join Chavez, who had sufficiently recovered from his wound to ride south with Vasquez to Inyo County. About this time, on January 24, 1874, Governor Newton Booth issued a proclamation putting a price on Vasquez. Up to that time the only rewards for his capture had been posted in Monterey and Santa Clara Counties. Governor Booth offered a reward of $3,000 for Vasquez if taken alive, and $2,000 if captured but delivered dead.

On February 25, 1874, Vasquez and Chavez made a bold appearance at the Coyote Holes stage station, between Los Angeles and the Owens River. Planning to seize the station and hold its occupants as hostages until the stagecoach arrived, Chavez fired several shots into the roof of the station while Vasquez rode up to the door and shouted for everyone to come out with hands up. Everyone who came out was made to line up and sit down. While Chavez stood guard over them with his Henry rifle, Vasquez went from person to person, robbing them in turn. After that they were marched off behind a hill and tied up. Vasquez returned to the station and while searching the livery stable found W. P. Shore, otherwise known as "Old Tex," whom he ordered to lie down. Old Tex was perhaps drunk; in any case he was disposed to fight with Vasquez and was shot in the leg for his trouble. At sundown the stage rumbled to a stop in front of the station, some three hours overdue on its run from Los Angeles. Vasquez trained his rifle on the driver and ordered him to dismount and unhitch the team. The passengers were lined up against the stage and robbed. The Wells Fargo box contained no money, only stock certificates and drafts which Vasquez scattered to the wind. Six horses were taken from the livery stable and the team driven off, no horses being left behind to form a posse. Driving the stolen horses before them, Vasquez and Chavez rode south in the direction of Soledad Canyon.

Here was another daring robbery, in full daylight and on a well-traveled road. Vasquez and Chavez had succeeded in robbing some twenty men and making good their escape. We might wonder how two men could rob a group of that size. No doubt one reason was Vasquez' way with a Henry rifle and his reputation as one who would use it. The Tres Pinos murders were still fresh in the public mind. Little doubt could have existed in the minds of the passengers at Coyote

Holes that Vasquez would shoot if resisted. The stagecoach robbery was big news in newspapers all over California. The following article appeared in *The Los Angeles Weekly Express* on March 5, 1875.

Deputy Sheriff Prater, of Kernville, who arrived yesterday, says that Vasquez and one companion have just collected a heavy contribution at the stage station near Walkers pass, on the road to Inyo, known as Coyote Holes. He arrived at 1 p.m. Wednesday and remained until 6 p.m. of the same day, being compelled to make this long delay because of the non-arrival of the stage from here on time, from which he expected to collect a considerable sum of money. The first move was to secure all the horses from the stable, eight in number, six of which belonged to the stage company, and rob the four or five men who were stopping at the place, one of whom, manifesting some opposition, was shot in the leg by Vasquez himself, as a gentle reminder, he said, that such conduct was dangerous. The station is on a road that is much travelled, and while waiting for the stage, everybody that came along was detained, requested to sit down and hand out his money, until by the time it arrived the victims numbered somewhere in the neighborhood of sixteen. There were four passengers in the stage, one of whom, Mr. Belshaw, owner of the Cerro Gordo mine, they did not search him accepting his statement as true that he had no money. They broke open the express box, but it contained very little in cash. As soon as they were through with the stage they left, going in a southerly direction. Vasquez was very friendly and communicative with his victims and appeared in good spirits. As far as it is known he only secured about $250, and one watch belonging to the stage driver.

7

IN JANUARY, 1874, Governor Newton Booth and Sheriff Harry Morse of Alameda held a discussion in Sacramento to plan the organization of an expedition that would take to the field in an effort to capture Vasquez. Sheriff Morse's reputation as a superlative lawman was well known and it was deemed proper that he should head the expedition. Morse had brought a score of desperadoes to justice and no lawman might conduct so thorough and painstaking a search in tracking down an outlaw. The sum of $5,000 was appropriated by the California legislature to finance the expedition. Given a free hand in choosing his company, Morse chose the following men: Thomas Cunningham, Sheriff of San Joaquin County; Harry Thomas, Deputy-Sheriff of Fresno County; Ambrose Calderwood, formerly Sheriff of Santa Cruz County; Ralph Faville, Deputy-Sheriff of Alameda County; A. J. McDonald, of Sunol; Ramon Romero, of San Leandro, and A. B. Henderson, news-editor of *The San Francisco Chronicle*.

One method Morse had used in tracking down his quarry is worth mentioning. In order to remain unknown to both the outlaw and his friends, he would sometimes wear an elaborate disguise, comprising a beard, wig, or whatever he thought appropriate. Morse writes of one instance: "I wore an old pair of ragged pants, a gray woolen shirt, a great broad-brimmed hat that flopped about my ears like a dilapidated umbrella in a rainstorm. A pair of dark green goggles covered my eyes, and the lower part of my face was hidden by a long red beard."[32]

On March 12, 1874, the expedition took to the field and headed south in what was eventually to become a sixty-one day, 2,720 mile search for Tiburcio Vasquez. It was to take them into some of the wildest country in California but was to end without success. It would, however, provide the clue that would eventually lead to the capture of Vasquez. The following report to Governor Booth was written by Sheriff Morse following his return to Oakland. In the first paragraph, Morse is commenting upon a statement of expenditures submitted by him and equipment used in the expedition having been sold at auction:

Oakland, May 30, 1874
Hon. Newton Booth

Sir:

Herewith please find statement of account between the State of California and myself, which if you find correct, you will please forward the balance due me. I disposed of all the things that were left, and salable to the highest bidder. The matting was worn out and not salable, as were the picket ropes. Some of the pickets were lost, also the hatchet, of which I have made no accounting. It was impossible at times to obtain vouchers, being in the mountains, away from pen, ink, and paper, and most of the time dealing with the natives who could neither read or write.

It is not necessary for me to go into a detailed account of our hunt, as Vasquez is now in custody. Sufficient is it for me to say that we did 61 days hard work in the saddle, part of the time in the night, through the darkness, and part of the time through heavy rains, never resting but always on the go. We rode 2,720 miles, searching the southern part of the state from the San Joaquin river to the sea coast, and although we did not succeed in getting our man, yet we did the state a good service in this. We broke up many dens of reputed murderers, and thieves in places where officers had never ventured to go before. I regret one thing very much. It is this, that officers in the upper part of the state, to wit, Santa Clara, should have a feeling of jealousy toward myself and party, and make known my whereabouts and plans through the public prints, and thereby making it more difficult for us to do our work properly. Too much praise cannot be bestowed upon Sheriff Rowland and party for the very able manner in which they carried out their plans, and effected the capture of Vasquez.

One thing I think is quite certain and that is this. We deserve credit for the thoroughness of our search. Had we not been out, Vasquez would still have been at liberty. At least Vasquez told me so himself. He told me the only thing that kept him about Los Angeles was the fear of meeting my party, he thinking that I was still in the southern part of the state.

It is a good deal like hunting a needle in a hay stack, this hunting a man in the mountains. The only way is to do as was done in the present case, to wit, purchase the information that will lead you to the whereabouts of the party sought, the rest is easy.

Hoping to hear from you approving my course in this matter.

> I am Sir,
> Yours Respectfully
> H. N. Morse

While Morse was in the field, Governor Booth had issued a second proclamation increasing the reward on Vasquez to $8,000 if taken alive and $6,000 if captured and delivered dead. All this while Vasquez was hiding on the La Brea Rancho at the house of George Allen, *alias* Greek George, about eight miles northeast of Los Angeles. Thinking it time to stage another robbery, Vasquez sent out a new recruit, one Lebrado Corona, to learn what ranches in the vicinity might be considered likely prospects. Several days later Corona returned with information that Alexander Repetto, an Italian rancher, had recently sold a large consignment of wool for a considerable sum of money. On April 12, 1874, Vasquez left Greek George's in company with Chavez and Corona and rode to Repetto's ranch near San Gabriel. Vasquez himself gave us a good description of this holdup in the interview with Ben Truman:

I had selected Repetto as a good subject. In pursuance of the plan I had adopted, I went to a sheepherder employed on the place, and asked him if he had seen a brown horse which I had lost; inquired if Repetto was at home, took a look at the surroundings and told the man I had to go to the old Mission on some important business, that if he would catch my horse I would give him $10 or $15. I then returned by a roundabout way to my companions on the Arroyo Seco. As soon as it was dark I returned with my men to the neighborhood of Repetto's and camped within a few rods of the house. The next morning about breakfast time we wrapped our guns in our blankets, retaining only our pistols, and I went toward the house, where I met the sheepherder and commenced talking about business. Asked him if Repetto wanted herders or shearers, how many sheep could he shear in a day, etc., speaking in a loud tone, in order to let Repetto hear us and throw him off his guard. I had left my men behind a small fence, and being told that he was at home, I entered the house to see if I could bring the *patron* to terms without killing him. I found him at home, and told him I was an expert sheep shearer, and asked if he wished to employ any shearers; the gentlemen who were out waiting by the fence, were all good shearers, and wanted work. All were invited in, and as they entered surrounded Repetto. I then told him I wanted money. At this he commenced hollering, when I had him securely tied, and told him to give me what money he had in the house. He handed me eighty dollars. I told him that that would not do; that I knew about his affairs; that he had sold nearly $10,000 worth of sheep lately, and that he must have plenty of money buried around the house somewhere. Repetto then protested that he had paid out nearly all the money he had received in the purchase of land; that he had receipts to show for it, etc. I told him that I could read and write and understood accounts; that if he produced his books and receipts, and they balanced according to his statements, I would excuse him. He produced the books, and after examining them carefully, I became convinced that he had told me nearly the truth. I then expressed my regrets for the trouble I had put him to, and offered to compromise. I told him I was in need of money, and that if he would accommodate me with a small sum I would repay him in thirty days with interest at 1½ per cent. He kindly consented to do so and sent a messenger to Los Angeles for the money, being first warned that in the event of treachery or betrayal his life would be forfeit. The messenger returned, not without exciting the suspicions of the authorities, who, as is well known, endeavored at that time to effect my capture but failed.[38]

In describing the "loan" he wished to negotiate with Repetto, Vasquez was simply substituting another word for robbery in a clumsy attempt to excuse his actions. We can be sure he had no intention of paying the money back, much less at interest. If this interview sounds a little polished and sophisticated in tone it is still a reasonably accurate account of the Repetto robbery. We must keep in mind that Vasquez only spoke the words in these interviews. They were written by journalists—in this case Ben Truman—and no doubt many of the words, syntax, and punctuation were inserted by the journalists, and not by Vasquez. When Vasquez mentions the messenger's return with the authorities and their subsequent efforts to capture him, here is what happened. Repetto had sent his nephew with a check for $800 to Temple & Workman's bank in Los Angeles. The nephew had been warned not to notify the authorities. The sum of $800 was the "loan" Vasquez wished to negotiate. Actually it would be more correct to consider it ransom for Repetto's release. Either directly or indirectly,

SHERIFF HARRY MORSE of Alameda County, the intrepid California lawman. From an early photograph.

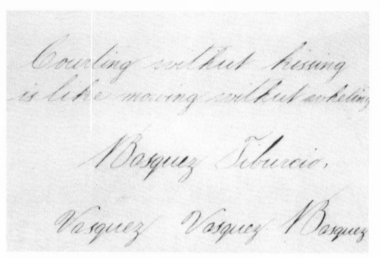

Holograph handwriting specimen of Tiburcio Vasquez. This copy of a poem was made by Vasquez while being held prisoner in jail at San Jose.

SHERIFF'S OFFICE,
County of Santa Clara.

San Jose, March 16 1875.

To A. C. Bassett Esq

SIR.— Pursuant to the Statute in such cases you are hereby invited to be present at the execution of Tiburcio Vasquez, at the Jail of said County, in San Jose, on the 19th day of March, A. D. 1875, at 1:30 o'clock P. M.

J. H. ADAMS, Sheriff.

PRESENT AT JAIL ENTRANCE. , NOT TRANSFERABLE

Facsimile of invitation to the hanging of Tiburcio Vasquez.

the nephew aroused the suspicions of the bank officials, who in turn sent for Sheriff Rowland. Rowland questioned the boy and was satisfied that Vasquez was at the Repetto ranch. In less than thirty minutes Rowland raised a posse and was riding to Repetto's. Vasquez had posted a guard who spotted the posse approaching some three miles distant. The bandits quickly mounted and having the fresher horses outdistanced the posse. Upon reaching the Arroyo Seco, the outlaws met three men in a wagon—Charley Miles, John Osborne, and John Rhoades. Vasquez hailed them to a stop and ordered them to hand over their cash. Miles thought it was a joke, laughed, and was about to drive on when Chavez pointed his rifle at Miles. The trio were robbed just as Sheriff Rowland and the posse appeared on a rise some two miles away. The outlaws disappeared up the Arroyo Seco Canyon with the posse in hot pursuit.

Vasquez had hired a Mexican guide some days before to lead them up the Arroyo Seco and over the summit to the Big Cahuengas Canyon. The guide had not appeared and Vasquez, not knowing the trail, continued up the canyon to the summit where the trail abruptly ended. Beyond them lay a steep canyon, almost impassable, choked with a thick growth of manzanita and chaparral. With the posse behind them there was no choice except to cut through the thicket until they reached the Cahuengas. Eventually they reached the bottom of the canyon and followed it on foot to where it joined the Little Cahuengas, having to abandon their horses in the treacherous terrain. At dusk the posse called off the search and returned to Los Angeles. At the Little Cahuengas, the outlaws separated. Vasquez and Corona crossed a trail to Greek George's and Chavez rode to a Mexican ranch in Soledad Canyon.

At the time of the Repetto robbery, Sheriff Morse was searching Rock Creek Canyon in the Tehachapis. Even so, it was Morse who learned where Vasquez was hiding. At Fort Tejon, Morse received information "for a consideration" that Vasquez was headquartered in the Cahuengas, in an adobe house belonging to Greek George. The informant could have been the Mexican whom Vasquez hired as a guide. Feeling that he should consult with Sheriff Rowland, Morse took the next stage to Los Angeles and presented the information to Rowland, suggesting they organize a joint posse. But Rowland discounted the information, saying he knew the informant and considered him unreliable, and that he had the same information anyway, but there was no truth in it. Morse must have been convinced, for he rode back to Fort Tejon and re-grouped his expedition, returning north to Oakland. Had Morse acted independently on this information he would have captured Vasquez.

Why did Rowland discount the information? It is possible that Rowland believed the information to be false—but if he did when he talked with Morse, something happened to change his mind. For, ten days later, Rowland acted upon the same information and detailed Under-Sheriff Johnston to organize a posse and ride to Greek George's. Rowland himself did not go with the posse because it was thought his absence from Los Angeles would be noticed and communicated to Vasquez. There is always the possibility, not to be denied, that Rowland had his own private reasons for discounting the information, planning all the while to act on it as soon as Morse had gone. Interestingly enough, a few weeks after Vasquez was captured a warrant was drawn for by the State Treasurer in favor of Rowland for the sum of $8,000. George Beers refers to the matter in somewhat couched language:[34]

> Subsequent events warrant the belief that the information brought one hundred and ten miles from Fort Tejon to Los Angeles, April 27, by Harry Morse to Billy Rowland proved correct, notwithstanding the opinion of the latter at the time to the contrary, and that the increased reward led to negotiations with Rowland by the same parties, which led to his betrayal into our hands. Be that as it may, it would be manifestly improper to publish the real facts of the betrayal even if the writer had them at his command, and it only remains for me to describe the modus operandi attending the capture, and to relate subsequent events.

8

ON THE EVENING of May 13, 1874, Under-Sheriff Johnston organized a posse consisting of the following: H. M. Mitchell, special deputy; Emil Harris, detective; F. Hartley, Los Angeles Chief of Police; Sam Bryant, Constable; W. E. Rogers, Los Angeles; George A. Beers, special correspondent to *The San Francisco Chronicle;* and D. K. Smith, Los Angeles, making a total of eight men in all. At dusk the posse rode out of the city and crossed the plains in a northerly direction, entering a canyon on the La Brea Rancho, about one mile east of Greek George's house. The area was kept under observation until noon the next day but because of a thick fog in the canyon no one could know whether Vasquez was at the house. When the fog finally lifted, a man was seen riding away on a white horse. Mitchell thought it might be Vasquez and decided that he and Johnston would follow in pursuit while the rest of the posse surrounded the house.

Just then two Mexicans entered the canyon driving an empty wagon. Stopping them, Hartley asked them to state their business. The Mexicans said they had come to the canyon, as was their habit, to take on a load of wood. The problem of how to approach the house without being seen was subsequently solved by utilizing the wagon and its driver. The posse of six men climbed into the wagon and lay flat on the bed to conceal themselves and instructed the Mexican to drive to the house of Greek George. Johnston told the driver he would be instantly shot if either he or his companion attempted to warn Vasquez. Reporter Beers says that Vasquez noticed the wagon approaching the house, but knowing the driver and wagon, thought nothing unusual of it. When the wagon arrived opposite the south side of the house the posse leaped out and took up positions. They had no orders and each man was to act according to his own judgment. Beers and Bryant were the first to reach the house. Noticing a horse picketed out across the clearing, Beers decided to guard the path leading from the house to where the horse stood. He stationed himself where he might have a clear view of the window which opened upon the path. Vasquez and Corona were inside the house eating their lunch. Just then the wife of Greek George caught sight of the posse and shouted the alarm, at the same moment blocking the doorway. Vasquez made a flying leap through the window as the posse broke into the house. Beers says:[35]

> I stepped into the path leading along the west side of the house, and the next instant the agile form of Vasquez came flying toward me, and I fired. He threw up his hands, at the same instant crying out, "No shoot! No shoot!" and Hartley gave him a charge of buckshot from his double-barrel gun. Johnston and the others closing in upon him immediately, he was led around to the east end of the building. Finding that no more bandits made their appearance, I passed around and found Vasquez and Corona standing side by side against the east end of the building, with the balance of our party standing around watching them, and on the alert for any of the gang that might put in an appearance at the eleventh hour. I went at once to the wounded man and began dressing his wounds. My shot had struck the shoulder, while the buckshot from Hartley's double-barrel gun had struck him in half a dozen places, making painful flesh wounds in the left arm, left forearm and shoulder blade, but none of the shot had penetrated the vitals. Whatever may be thought of this man's courage, he certainly, on that occasion, at least, exhibited astonishing self-possession and command of nerve. There was not the slightest tremor in

his voice, and his heart beat steadily and calmly. He admitted his identity as soon as I began dressing his wounds.

Vasquez is reported as saying to Beers: "You dress my wounds and nurse me careful, you boys get $8,000! If you let me die, you only get six. You get $2,000 for being kind!"[36] He was willing to give the posse credit for the plan which had led to his capture and even congratulated them upon their good fortune. A spring wagon and mattress were brought from the barn and Vasquez was lifted in for the trip to Los Angeles. Corona was allowed to ride with Vasquez in the wagon. At the time of his capture Vasquez was unarmed, although a Henry rifle was found within arms-length of the table where he had been eating.

As the wagon and posse approached Los Angeles, news of the capture leaked out and the whole city was thrown into a pitch of excitement. Several hundred persons had collected in front of the jail to catch a glimpse of the terrible Vasquez. Not the slightest disposition of violence was shown by the group. Vasquez was taken from the wagon and carried into the jail where his wounds were attended to by Dr. Wise. As it turned out, the wounds were not serious and Vasquez was on the mend within the week. During his stay in the Los Angeles jail Vasquez became the center of much attention. An army of newspaper reporters sought to interview him, and the papers of the day were full of articles purporting to be "exclusive interviews." Several interviews were granted by Tiburcio, to Ben Truman, of *The Los Angeles Star,* George Beers, *San Francisco Chronicle,* and to Eugene Sawyer, and the editor of the *Los Angeles Express.* No doubt all this attention pleased Vasquez a good deal. It would not be an exaggeration to say that he even seemed to enjoy the notoriety focused upon him. He insisted at each opportunity that he had never killed a man in his life, and continued to emphasize this throughout his imprisonment. During his stay in the Los Angeles jail he was identified by Charley Miles and Alexander Repetto. Several offers of legal assistance were made. On May 22, 1874, the following item appeared in the *Los Angeles Star:*[37]

TO THE PUBLIC: Wounded, a prisoner, and in the shadow of approaching death, or a more to be dreaded incarceration, an unfortunate and sinful man appeals to the charitable among men, of whatever nation, to contribute to a fund to enable him to place his case fairly before the world and the jury to sit in judgment upon him, hereby asserting his innocence, of the higher crimes imputed to him, and his ability to establish the fact at a fair and impartial trial.

TIBURCIO VASQUEZ

IN JAIL AT LOS ANGELES, May 22, 1874

Whether this notice was written by Vasquez or not is open to some question. In one sense it appears to be the work of some peculiarly ambitious lawyer anxious to get a "finger in the pie." In another sense it is not unthinkable that Vasquez wrote it—or sanctioned it— especially if he thought it would bring in a flow of money. As it turned out, legal arrangements for his defense would be arranged after a change of venue and his transfer to San Jose.

On May 23, in custody of Under-Sheriff Johnston, Vasquez was taken aboard the steamship *Senator* bound for San Francisco. From there he would be taken to Monterey County to be indicted for the murder of Leander Davidson at Tres Pinos. In San Francisco, Vasquez was sought out by a legion of journalists and the curious, talking freely with one and all. Among those who interviewed him was Sheriff Morse, who was interested in fixing certain details of Vasquez' movements when the Morse expedition had been seeking to capture him. On the 27th, Vasquez was turned over to Captain Adams for transport to the jail at Salinas. At each stop along the way large crowds had gathered to catch sight of the famous bandit.

Monterey County had recently been divided by the California legislature to create the new county of San Benito, and Tres Pinos, the scene of the murder for which Vasquez was charged, was now situated in the newly-created San Benito County. There being no adequate jail facilities in that county—nor in Salinas—Vasquez was again moved, this time to San Jose. With the change of venue, Vasquez' case was set for the January term of the District Court of Santa Clara, in San Jose. In the meantime, Corona was tried in Los Angeles for his part in the Repetto robbery and sentenced to seven years in San Quentin.

9

IN THE MONTHS preceding the trial, Vasquez was visited in his cell in San Jose by all sorts of people, mostly women, and given flowers, wines, notions, and various tokens of esteem. Delighted with these attentions, he was courteous and pleasant to one and all. On at least two occasions, he was allowed to pose for photographs. One such portrait was made into a souvenir with a biographical sketch on one side and his picture on the other. Tiburcio sold these to the general public and obliged any number by personally signing them in his meticulous hand. In these days he appeared elegantly clothed, looking more like a *grandee* than a man waiting trial for murder. Two competent lawyers were retained for his defense, P. B. Tully, and a former Judge, W. H. Collins.

On January 5, 1875, the court convened and impaneled the following jury: George Reynolds, Foreman; Tyler Brundage; Frank Hamilton; L. Bomberger; Noah Parr; M. Tobin; George Fitzgerald; J. M. Moorehead; S. T. Woodson; M. Lublines; C. S. Towle, and Hugh O'Rouke. Attorney-General Love and N. C. Briggs served as attorneys for the prosecution. Judge Belden presided over the trial. Principal witnesses for the prosecution were Abdon Leiva,[38] Rosaria Leiva, Captain Adams, Andrew Snyder, John Utzerath, L. C. Smith, F. M. McPhail, Louis Scherrer and others. Leiva's testimony was the foundation for the case of the prosecution. Vasquez was formally charged with the murder of Leander Davidson at Tres Pinos. The courtroom and gallery were filled to capacity and the newspapers reported that Tiburcio "unblushingly bestowed his glances upon the ladies in the gallery."[39] The trial itself lasted four days, most of the testimony being concerned with the details of the robbery at Snyder's Store. Vasquez took the stand in his own defense and on that day, according to the press, "the gallery was filled to overflowing with ladies representing the elite of San Jose."[40] Vasquez insisted again at the trial that he had never killed a man, and that Leiva had been in command of the robbery at Tres Pinos. Closing statements were made by the prosecution and defense. Judge Collins made the statement for the defense and delivered an eloquent, if somewhat bombastic, appeal for mercy. The jury deliberated for two hours. Foreman Reynolds read the verdict: "We, the jury, find the defendant guilty of murder in the first degree, and assign the death penalty." According to reports, "Many of the ladies in the gallery were considerably affected, and brought their handkerchiefs into play." Vasquez received the verdict with his usual composure.

Two weeks later, on January 23rd, Judge Belden delivered the sentence of death by hanging. The sentence is a long-winded and moralistic diatribe in which not a few references are made to expenses incurred by the state in capturing Vasquez. The date of execution was set for Friday, March 18, 1875. A new note of interest occurred some weeks later when a note was found in the Wells Fargo letter box at Hollister:[41]

NOTICE TO THE TOWN OF HOLLISTER

Know you, that in regard to the acts committed by the captain of my company, I say that, finding myself guilty of those acts, I flew to Mexico; but having been informed while there that Vasquez was under sentence of death, I have returned as far as this place with the aim of disclosing the falseness of the evidence sworn against him, and in case Vasquez should be hanged, to quickly mete out a recompense. Because, do not believe that I am in want of resources and lack of sufficient valor to take him, or meet death in the attempt. I wish first to see the result. For this reason I let you know that if Vasquez is hung by his enemies, who, through fear, have turned against him, I will show you I know how to avenge the death of my captain. I do not exact of you to set him free, but do not want him hung, because he was not bloody. I can prove under oath that in time gone by Tom McMahon (a leading citizen of Hollister) will remember that Vasquez and his company saved his life. It was I subsequently who was at the head of the affair at Tres Pinos, in which the murders were committed. Mr. Vasquez was certainly our captain; but on account of Abdon (Leiva) I neglected the orders that Vasquez had imposed upon us. If this is not sufficient, or if by this means Vasquez does not get his sentence appealed, then you will have to suffer as in the times of Joaquin Murietta—the just with the unjust alike will be reached by my revenge. Let him be punished according to the law, then you will never more hear of me in this country or in the State—neither of me or of my company.

If he has mitigation given him, let it be published in the papers. Nothing more.

CLEOVARO CHAVEZ & CO.

Many thought the letter a fraud written by some crank; others believed it genuine. It seems unlikely, however, that a man like Chavez could compose a letter of such rhetoric. It has a journalistic ring and may have been intended to inject a sensational new note into an important news story. Chavez was still at large, however, and a reward of $2,000 was offered for his capture. What eventually happened to him is not clear. One account says he was killed in an attempted holdup, his head cut off and exhibited at San Juan.[42] There is not proof of this. Other versions say he headed a banditti in Inyo County for a time, eventually making his way into Arizona.

As the day of the hanging approached the crowd of visitors to Vasquez' cell grew larger by the day. Judge Collins appealed to the California Supreme Court for a new trial but the motion was denied.

An appeal for clemency was sent to Governor Pacheco but that too was denied. Captain Adams began to make preparations for the execution. San Jose had no gallows so one was borrowed from Sacramento. Adams supplied a curious touch to the affair by having invitations printed which bore the phrase "Not Transferable." At this time Father Serda was a frequent visitor to Vasquez' cell. The good Father may have entertained some notion of extracting repentance from Tiburcio or bringing about a last-minute reform. In any case, two messages purportedly dictated or written by Vasquez appeared at that time making a "clean breast" of everything and asking forgiveness. One begins solemnly "To the Fathers and Mothers of Children" and warns that the young must be protected from "degrading companionship" and asks pardon of all those "I have so ruthlessly trampled upon." It continues to "express gratitude" to Captain Adams for his kindnesses and closes by saying, "Farewell! The end has come!" As another writer has suggested, one can easily detect the influence here of Father Serda and Captain Adams, leaving us to wonder whether Vasquez ever had a hand in its composition. The second message is addressed "To My Former Associates" and assures them that their captain has not disclosed evidence against them, and warns all of them that they should profit by his terrible example and reform while they may. It closes by making reference to the note allegedly signed by Chavez: "The threats which I hear have been made by some of you . . . are foolish and wrong." This message sounds more like Tiburcio but there are still other influences here attempting to say the acceptable thing. Reporter Beers remarked that Vasquez declined to sign the statements but authorized his signature to be attached to them.[43]

The day before the hanging there was a constant press of visitors. Beers wrote: "But this man was in the fullest sense of the word 'equal to the occasion.' For each and every visitor he had a manly, affable and self-possessed reception, replying pleasantly and without bravado to all remarks and inquiries."[44] Vasquez received a number of telegrams throughout the day, one of which was from the famous revivalist, E. P. Hammond, then in San Francisco: "Dear Vasquez. God Bless you. Trust in Jesus. He will be with you and love you. I shall continue to pray for you. P.S. The Governor cannot pardon you, but God can, for Jesus' sake." Upon reading the telegram, Vasquez smiled and said, "Yes, I know. If I have any more hope it is in Jesus!" One of his visitors is reported to have said to Vasquez: "I

Facsimile of the souvenir composite photograph issued and sold in Los Angeles
shortly after the capture of Tiburcio Vasquez.

STATE OF CALIFORNIA,

Executive Department,

Sacramento, *May 3d* 187*4*

Whereas on August 26th, A.D. 1873, near the Town of Hollister, in this State several murders were perpetrated by one *Tiburcio Vasquez* and by men associated with him and supposed to be under his control, and notwithstanding a proclamation offering a large reward for the apprehension of the murderers they are still at large and are engaged in violating the laws and committing crimes in the Southern part of this State:

Now Therefore, revoking the proclamation of $1000 or $2000 reward issued January 24 1874, by virtue of authority in me vested, and in pursuance of a special law enacted for the purpose of arresting and punishing the said criminals, I, *Newton Booth,* Governor of the State of California, do hereby offer

A Reward of Eight Thousand Dollars for the arrest of the said *Tiburcio Vasquez,* payable upon his being *delivered alive* to the Sheriff of the County of *Monterey*; and I do further proclaim that if during an attempt to arrest him he shall make such resistance as to endanger the persons or lives of whomsoever may arrest him, and shall in consequence

Facsimile of the third and final proclamation issued by Governor Newton Booth for the capture of Tiburcio Vasquez. The first proclamation, dated August 27, 1873, offered a reward of $1,000 for the arrest of Vasquez. The second proclamation, dated January 24, 1874, offered a reward of $3,000 for Vasquez if taken alive, and $2,000 if taken dead.

believe implicitly in a future state of existence—in the immortality of the soul. What is your belief on that point?" Vasquez replied: "I hope your belief is correct, for in that case I shall see all my old sweethearts together tomorrow."[45] Shortly before midnight, he chatted with Captain Adams' son, smoked a cigar, then fell into a sound sleep.

On his last morning, Vasquez rose early and ate a good breakfast. At eight o'clock relatives and friends came to see him for the last time. A large crowd had already gathered outside the jailyard beside the gallows. The principal topic of conversation throughout San Jose that day was Vasquez' "courage" and in the saloons bets were being taken on whether he would "die game." Rumors were about that an army of Mexicans was riding on San Jose to rescue Vasquez, but these were obviously stories of fancy intended to add to the excitement. At twelve-thirty, Captain Adams directed that the death warrant be read to Vasquez in his cell, and translated word for word. At the conclusion of the reading, Adams said, "Vasquez, the time has come to march to the scaffold." Tiburcio shook hands with a number of people and said good-bye, and the procession walked to the jailyard, led by two deputies, Vasquez flanked by Captain Adams on one side and Father Serda on the other. Vasquez carried a small crucifix as he mounted the thirteen steps up the scaffold and took his place over the drop. The crowd fell silent as Father Serda and Vasquez performed the final religious ceremony. Vasquez then removed his coat and took off his collar. He was bound with straps about his wrists and ankles. Under-Sheriff Winchell placed the noose around his neck, Vasquez tilting his head so that the noose might be slipped tight. He then gave Winchell a hard, knowing look and said just one word, *"Pronto!"* The black cap was slipped over his head. Captain Adams gave the motion. Then, at one-thirty, the trap was sprung and Tiburcio Vasquez plunged into eternity.

ROBERT GREENWOOD

JANUARY, 1960
LOS GATOS, CALIFORNIA

REFERENCES

1. Truman, Benjamin Cummings. *Life, Adventures, and Capture of Tiburcio Vasquez; the great California bandit and murderer.* Los Angeles, The Los Angeles Star. 1874.
2. Truman, Benjamin. *Occidental Sketches.* San Francisco. San Francisco News Co. 1881. pp.193-194
3. Truman, *Occidental Sketches,* p.193
4. Official Criminal Identification Records. San Jose Landmarks Commission. mission.
5. Truman, *Occidental Sketches,* pp.182-183
6. Beers, George. *Vasquez, or the Hunted Bandits of the San Joaquin.* New York. Robert DeWitt Co., 1875. p.7
7. Sawyer, Eugene T. *Life and Career of Tiburcio Vasquez, the bandit and murderer.* San Jose, 1875. p.4
8. Truman, *Occidental Sketches,* p.194
9. Beers, pp.59-60
10. Beers, p.60
11. Beers, p.62
12. Beers, p.62
13. Sawyer, p.6
14. Beers, p.67
15. Beers, p.62
16. *California's Age of Terror: Murieta and Vasquez.* Hollister, California. The Evening Free Lance. 1927. p.8
17. Jackson, Joseph Henry. *Bad Company.* New York, Harcourt Brace, 1939. p.258
18. Beers, p.69
19. Sawyer, p.12
20. Now known as Paicines. Snyder's Store, no longer standing, stood at the junction of the Pinnacles Road and the Hollister-New Idria road. This spot used to be called Tres Pinos, but when the rail road was built out from Hollister to a point north of the original Tres Pinos, a town grew up there also known as Tres Pinos. The older settlement, where Vasquez made his robbery, came to be called Paicines.
21. *California's Age of Terror.* p.11
22. Sawyer, p.15
23. Beers, p.73
24. Sawyer, p.15
25. Beers, p.74
26. Beers, p.75
27. Beers, p.84
28. Truman, *Life, Adventures, and Capture of Tiburcio Vasquez,*
29. Sawyer, p.23
30. Now a ghost town on the lower banks of the Kings River, 8 miles northwest of Hanford. Kingston was an important stop on the Butterfield Stage Line.
31. Beers, p.91
32. Jackson, *Bad Company,* pp.258-259

33. Truman, *Occidental Sketches,* pp.199-200
34. Beers, p.119
35. Beers, pp.122-123
36. Beers, p.124
37. Beers, p.126
38. Abdon Leiva was released on December 3, 1875. He returned to his native Chile.
39. *San Jose Mercury,* January 6, 1875.
40. *San Jose Mercury,* January 8, 1875.
41. Beers, p.133
42. Sawyer, Eugene T. *History of Santa Clara County.* Los Angeles, Historic Records Co., 1922. p.166
43. Beers, p.137
44. Beers, p.138
45. Beers, p.139

BIBLIOGRAPHY

In addition to the books listed below, material was used from manuscripts located in the California State Archives. The letter by Sheriff Morse, reporting to Governor Booth on the Vasquez expedition, came from this source and is here published for the first time. Numerous references listed in Ramon Adams' *Six Guns & Saddle Leather* were examined but proved either too brief or insignificant for listing here. Other material was located in certain California county histories and in files of old newspapers. Following is a list of major sources:

Adams, Ramon F. *Six Guns & Saddle Leather, a bibliography of books and pamphlets on Western outlaws and gunmen.* Norman, University of Oklahoma Press, 1954.

Beers, George. *Vasquez, or the Hunted Bandits of the San Joaquin.* New York. Robert DeWitt Co., 1875.

California's Age of Terror: Murieta and Vasquez. Hollister, California. Evening Free Lance, 1927.

Jackson, Joseph Henry. *Bad Company.* New York. Harcourt Brace. 1939.

Ridge, John Rollin. *Life and Adventures of Joaquin Murieta.* Norman, University of Oklahoma Press, 1955.

Sawyer, Eugene T. *History of Santa Clara County.* Los Angeles, Historic Records Co. 1922.

Sawyer, Eugene T. *Life and Career of Tiburcio Vasquez, the California bandit and murderer.* San Jose, 1875.

Shinn, Charles Howard. *Graphic Descriptions of Pacific Coast Outlaws,* San Francisco. R. R. Patterson. 1887.

Truman, Benjamin Cummings. *Life, Adventures, and Capture of Tiburcio Vasquez; the great California bandit and murderer.* Los Angeles, The Los Angeles Star. 1874.

Truman, Benjamin Cummings. *Occidental Sketches.* San Francisco, The San Francisco News, 1881.

Walker, Franklin. *San Francisco's Literary Frontier.* New York, Knopf. 1939.

Vasquez; or, The Hunted Bandits of the San Joaquin

VASQUEZ;

OR, THE

HUNTED BANDITS OF THE SAN JOAQUIN.

CONTAINING

THRILLING SCENES AND INCIDENTS

AMONG THE

OUTLAWS AND DESPERADOES OF SOUTHERN CALIFORNIA.

WITH A FULL AND ACCURATE ACCOUNT

OF THE

CAPTURE, TRIAL, AND EXECUTION OF THE NOTED BANDIT.

By GEO. A. BEERS, Esq.

NEW YORK:

ROBERT M. DE WITT, PUBLISHER,

No. 33 Rose Street,

(*Between Duane and Frankfort Streets.*)

Facsimile title page of *Vasquez, or the Hunted Bandits of the San Joaquin,* by George Beers, 1875.

Contents

64

CHAPTER XXVI.

Mr. Beers,
Chronicle Reporter.

GEORGE BEERS, correspondent of *The San Francisco Chronicle*, and member of the posse that captured Tiburcio Vasquez. Beers wrote the best contemporary book on Vasquez, *Vasquez, or, the Hunted Bandits of the San Joaquin*, originally published in 1875.

No. 1.

The Western Union Telegraph Company.

The rules of this Company require that all messages received for transmission, shall be written on the message blanks of the Company, under and subject to the conditions printed thereon, which conditions have been agreed to, by the sender of the following message.

JAS. GAMBLE, General Sup't,}   WILLIAM ORTON, President, } New York.
San Francisco.   O. H. MUMFORD, Secretary. }

Los Angeles Cal May 16 1874

Received at Sacramento,   *May 16 1874 410 P. M.*

To His Excellency Newton Booth

I have the honor to report the capture of Tiburcio Vasquez alias Ricardo Cantoua on the fourteenth inst. In this County I have delayed announcing the Capture until his identification could be more certain. The nature of his wounds fully ascertained and his statement reduced to writing. His wounds are not necessarily serious he has been identified by at least one hundred persons and his Confession places his identity beyond all doubt

I shall proceed to deliver him to the sheriff of Monterey County as soon as his wounds will permit unless you shall otherwise direct I have the honor to remain

Your obedient Servant

Wm R Rowland

Sheriff

—Courtesy California State Archives

Facsimile of the telegram sent by Sheriff William Rowland, of Los Angeles, to Governor Newton Booth, announcing the capture of Vasquez.

Preface

There are several reasons why George Beers' book, *Vasquez, or the Hunted Bandits of the San Joaquin,* should be regarded as the best contemporary source on Tiburcio Vasquez. Beers had the unique experience of being a member of the posse that captured Vasquez at Greek George's near Los Angeles, on May 14, 1874. It was Beers who shot and wounded Vasquez as he leaped through a window and made an unsuccessful bid to escape. And it was George Beers—in his capacity as a reporter for *The San Francisco Chronicle*—who subsequently interviewed Vasquez on several occasions and who covered the trial and hanging in San Jose. As an eye-witness to those events, Reporter Beers wrote from first-hand experience, and no where else can we find so detailed an account of Vasquez from the moment of his capture to the day of his hanging.

The first part of the book is another matter. For information on Vasquez prior to the time of his capture, Beers had to rely on the usual sources, just like anyone else. These sources were newspaper accounts, official records, interviews, and in some cases, the writer's imagination. The first section of the book contains the fanciful story of Vasquez and his childhood sweetheart, Anita. The story is probably fiction, written for two reasons. First, to provide a "love story," and to picture the young Vasquez as a boy not yet wholly committed to evil. But more likely Beers was trying to give us some account—even if fiction—of Vasquez' early life, of which not too much is known. In that case he succeeded well, for the "Anita incident" runs to some sixty pages in length. Once we reach this point, however, the real value of the book commences. Many of the events described thereafter contain authentic data given in no other source.

Beers' book is probably the least known of all the books on Vasquez. Few copies are known to exist and it is of considerable rarity. Other accounts are better known but none of them are so detailed and as authentic. The fact that Beers' book runs to some 140 pages indicates it is a work of considerable scope. Other accounts are only a fraction that size. Two other accounts which appeared the same year as the Beers' work (1875) are more pamphlets than books, and seem to have been written purely to profit from the great public interest in Vasquez at the time.   No doubt that Beers, too, hoped to profit from his book, but in writing it he at least took the trouble to research certain information and to give us the benefit of his observations.   Here we are fortunate for his training as a newspaper reporter.   As it turned out, the book sold very well but he realized only a pittance from it.

The text is here printed in its entirety.   Certain words have been corrected for mis-spelling or typographical errors as printed in the original edition.   No further editing has been thought desirable.   Maps included in this edition have been reproduced from the original.

ROBERT   GREENWOOD

CHAPTER I.—INTRODUCTORY

Southern California—A Paradise for Bandits and a Stamping Ground for Grizzlies—Vasquez's Great Prototype, Joaquin Murieta, "The Marauder of the Mines"—Brief Sketch of Vasquez's Early History, and his first Notable Crime, Committed in Company with his "Tutor," Anastacia Garcia—Wanton Murder of Constable Wm. Hardmount at a Fandango in Monterey—Summary Lynching of Jose Heiguerra.

PROBABLY no portion of the United States presents so fair a field for the operations of freebooters as the Pacific Slope; and no part of the country affords more numerous or better hiding-places for outlaws than Southern California—more especially for those of Mexican or mixed Indian and Mexican blood—as even at the present time much of the country is very thinly settled, and the Mexican refugees from justice can find food and fresh horses, when closely pursued, at every lonely Mexican rancheria in the southern part of the State.

Every one is familiar with the exploits of the famous bandit Joaquin Murieta, who, at the head of a chosen band of followers, ravaged the whole country, and made his name a terror from one end of the State to the other. His capture and death, and the dispersion of his gang of cut-throats by the company sent out on his trail under Captain Harry Love, by the Legislature of 1853, only put a temporary quietus on the outrages of highwaymen in California.

From that day to the present there has been in existence organized bands in different portions of the State engaged either in stealing horses or cattle, or robbing on the highway—murdering without hesitation whenever their victims have ventured to resist their demands.

Within two years after the killing of the bandit chief, Joaquin, a new actor in the bloody drama appears upon the scene, and takes his initiative steps in crime under the apt tutorship of Anastacia Garcia, one of Joaquin's lieutenants, and who had been one of his most desperate adherents.

Garcia's pupil, TIBURICO VASQUEZ, profited so well by the education he received at the hands of his villainous instructor and his associates in crime, as to completely out-Herod his famous, or rather infamous, prototype, and he has since fairly earned the reputation of being one of the most daring and accomplished brigands that ever bade defiance to the law.

Joaquin seems to have been actuated almost wholly by a spirit of malignant, unrelenting revenge for real or fancied wrongs, or by a fiendish delight in violence, cruelty and bloodshed, rather than by a mere love for reckless adventure or a thirst for gold.

Vasquez, on the contrary, evidently took to the "road" partly in obedience to a born impulse to rob and steal; but throughout his eventful career has been actuated principally by cupidity and an inordinate vanity, which impelled him to desperate adventures for the sake of notoriety, as much as for gain.

There is, probably, no good ground for question as to his cool daring and brutality, both natural and acquired, but his "courage" has been so tempered with shrewdness and cunning that, while Joaquin wound up his course within three years after beginning his career as a robber, that of Tiburcio Vasquez has extended over a period of nearly twenty years—albeit ten years of that period he passed within the pitiless walls of San Quentin, the California state prison.

Tiburcio Vasquez was born in Monterey county, in 1838. He was a bright, intelligent lad, and received the rudiments of an English education. As he approached manhood he developed a restless disposition, and became conspicuous for his fondness for adventure. He was an excellent marksman when a mere boy, and was noted for his superb horsemanship; in fact, he excelled in the chase and in all manly sports indulged in by the Mexican population.

He was a great favorite with the senoritas on account of his good looks and graceful deportment, and was the recipient of constant flattery, both from them and his male companions and friends. This fed his inordinate vanity until his head was filled with the most ambitious schemes. Even at that youthful age he indulged the dreams of drawing around him, when he should arrive at manhood, a trusty band of followers, and revolutionizing the entire southern portions of California.

Immediately after the capture and killing of Joaquin Murieta, he formed the acquaintance of Anastacia Garcia, one of the leading members of Joaquin's band, who took a fancy to the lad, and the two became constant companions. Vasquez eagerly drank in each detail of the dark exploits of Joaquin as they fell from the guilty lips of Garcia, and he became infatuated with a desire to rival, and even outdo, the daring deeds of the terrible brigand chief. Garcia did all in his power to cultivate this disposition of his protege, and how well he succeeded the sequel has shown.

Another thing that had a strong influence in seconding the efforts of Garcia was the bitter animosity then existing, and which still exists, between the white settlers and the native or Mexican portion of the population. The native Californians, especially the lower classes, never took kindly to the stars and stripes. Their youth were taught from the very cradle to look upon the American government as that of a foreign nation.

This feeling was greatly intensified by the rough, brutal conduct of the worst class of American settlers, who never missed an opportunity to openly exhibit their contempt for the native Californian or Mexican population—designating them as "d—d Greasers," and treating them like dogs. Add to this the fact that these helpless people were cheated out of their lands and possessions by every subterfuge—in many instances their property being actually wrestled from them by force, and their women debauched whenever practicable—and we can understand very clearly some of the causes which have given to Joaquin, Vasquez, and others of their stripe, the power to call around them at any time all the followers they required, and which secured to them aid and comfort from the Mexican settlers everywhere.

Although of late years; since the country has become more generally settled, courts have been organized, and justice is dealt out to all classes alike, still the dark-skinned highwaymen and murderers impose upon their countrymen by pointing to these old traditions as an excuse for their crimes, and teach each other that to rob or kill a white man or an *Americano,* is a virtue to be practised whenever it can be done without danger to their own necks.

In a land where the climate is so equable and genial, the soil so wonderfully fertile, and game of almost every description so abundant, mere existence is no problem, and little labor is necessary to support it. The Mexicans are, as a class, indolent, and if they exert themselves at all, it is in the way of catching and breaking wild horses, or lassoing cattle, or in hunting wild game on the plains or in the mountains.

A word or two now in regard to the lay of the country in which Vasquez and his coadjutors operated, and so long and so successfully eluded the vigilance of their pursuers, and our eventful story will begin.

A glance at the maps of the United States will show the high mountain range of the Sierra Nevadas, in the eastern portion of the State of California, running from northwest to southeast; in the western portion of the State, near the coast, the Coast Range Mountains, running parallel with the coast, and also from northwest to the southeast.

From El Dorado county, bordering on Nevada, and about a degree north of the center of the State, the Sierra Nevada range gradually leaves the State line as it extends south, and turning west approaches the centre of the State. On the southern border of Kern county a spur of the Sierras turns toward the sea, joining the Coast Range in Los Angeles and San Bernardino counties.

The great basin thus formed between these extensive ranges of mountains is called the Valley of San Joaquin—drained by the San Joaquin river and its tributaries, finding their outlet in San Francisco Bay.

West of the inner Coast Range, and close to the sea, is the Coast Range, variously known as the Santa Cruz, Gavilan, San Lucia, San Rafael Mountains, etc. There are also lesser ranges, generally known as the foot hills.

Between these mountain ranges there are innumerable fertile valleys. At the period of which we write this whole country was very sparsely populated; the settlements in the San Joaquin Valley were few and widely scattered, and the cattle trails were so numerous that it was difficult, in fact, nearly impossible, for the officers of the law to follow the trail of fugitives from justice.

The mountain ranges were almost inaccessible.

Their gorges and gloomy canons constituted a perfect paradise for grizzlies, California lions, and panthers, and a secure retreat for hunted bandits.

When closely pressed, outlaws would take refuge in these mountain fastnesses, where they would be tolerably safe from pursuit.

Near the close of a sultry summer day, in 1854, two horsemen were riding leisurely along a bridle path or trail, skirting a range of low hills in Monterey county. They were mounted on ordinary mustangs, on Spanish saddles, from the horns of which were suspended raw-hide lariats, and behind each saddle was a roll of blankets—the usual outfit of vaqueros.

The two riders presented a striking contrast. They were riding in "single file" along the narrow trail, the one who led the advance being seated sidewise in the saddle, and while he held the reins in his right hand he rested the other on his horse's rump—the rider's face being turned toward that of his companion.

The latter was a mere stripling, apparently not more than sixteen or eighteen years of age. Although slight in figure, he was exceeding well proportioned, with a striking and remarkably prepossessing countenance—not the least attractive feature being his intelligent gray eyes.

Both were evidently of Mexican or native Californian blood. The one in advance was a low-browed, repulsive, though intelligent looking man, with long straight black hair, piercing black eyes, "bull ncek," and of strong muscular development. He was at least fifteen years the senior of his companion.

They were approaching a main travelled road, and the conversation was in reference to their future plans.

"I tell you, Tiburcio," explained the elder of the two, who was riding in advance, "I tell you I'm tired of this dog's life. A vaquero is a slave—a dog! Are we dogs, to slave for these Americanos?"

"Anastacia," was the reply. "I, too, am tired—I want freedom—the freedom of the mountains and the valleys."

"Why, then, idle away more of your youthful years? Why not at once begin the glorious career you have marked out before you? A few bold, shrewd ventures and we may have the means to organize a band that shall strike terror to the hearts of every white household in Southern California. We have a career before us that will make that of Murieta pale into insignificance.

As the speaker concluded this earnest appeal he kept his dark eyes riveted upon those of his youthful companion while awaiting the reply.

Nearly half a minute elapsed, and then suddenly spurring his horse alongside his companion, the young man spoke, in a firm, even tone:

"Well, friend Garcia, the life we have talked about has great attractions, and I have fully determined upon my future course. The only consideration that deters me from at once making a beginning, is the fear that through rashness and inexperience I may make some blunder that will ruin me and bring disgrace upon my parents. It would break my mother's heart; and she has been a good mother to me. I cannot bear to cause her needless sorrow."

"Your mother cannot live always," was the heartless reply, "and you must leave home sometime."

"It is not the leaving home. I have often spent months, and once nearly a whole year from home. The truth is, I do not like all your cold-blooded proposals. While I court adventure, and will shrink from no danger, I do not thirst for human blood; nor do I see any necessity for such reckless slaughter as Joaquin indulged in. It only increases the animosity of the whites against our class, and induces them to arm and otherwise guard against robbery."

"Carrajo! Your blood is altogether too thin, amigo. You'll soon get over all that squeamishness. A few adventures on the road, and you'll overcome all such merciful scruples, and be as ready with the knife and revolver as the oldest hand at the business."

The young man's eye was lighted with a strange fire as he replied: "You'll find me as ready *now* in the use of those weapons as the 'oldest hand at the business,' when the occasion arrives for their use. But it is their reckless use that I deprecate. Strategy, in my opinion, is quite as important an element in emergencies as mere courage or brutality. Recklessness can, in the end, only result in confusion and disaster to those who yield to the impulse, or follow its dictation."

"Damnation, Tiburcio! do you know more than men nearly twice your age? What would Joaquin have ever accomplished but for his reckless daring on all occasions?"

"Rather, what might he not have accomplished but for that same recklessness? What did he accomplish? His own destruction and the dispersion of his gang after a bloody history of three years."

"Carrambo! You are incorrigible, and we won't argue. I think I know what the trouble is with you."

"What trouble?"

"Tiburcio, you need not disguise it—you are in love. That is what thins your blood; it is not your squeamishness about taking life, nor yet your regard for your mother—though I dare say you have a proper affection for the old lady."

The young man knitted his brows as he replied, "My love affairs are my own, and I allow no man to interfere with them."

"Ha, ha, ha!" laughed Garcia, with a fiendish chuckle. "I thought the fair Anita had something to do with your damnable hesitation. But you need not get angry, amigo; I do not wish to interfere with your amours; I only want you to act the man, and make good your pledges."

"I propose to violate no pledges. I have declared my willingness, nay, eagerness, to take to the road with you, but I am my own master and can bide my time."

"But you give no good reason, and I attribute your delay, as I've a right to do, simply to your amours with the lovely Anita."

"Be that as it may, when the time comes I shall act. You well know the dreams I have for the future. If I go upon the highway as a common robber, it is only because I have no other resource to raise the funds I need to carry out my great scheme."

"You had better be content, Tiburcio, with the rollicking life of a freebooter. If you start in with me now, in a few years—perhaps within a year or two—you may find yourself at the head of as fine a band of adventurers as ever rode in the saddle. But your scheme to revolutionize Southern California—as the Americanos would say, to 'buck' against the present government—is as wild as any of the hairbrained schemes of the famous Don Quixote."

"Nevertheless," was the firm reply, "it shall be the object of my life, wild and visionary though it may appear."

Vasquez fell behind, and Garcia, resuming his position in the saddle, the two applied the spurs to their jaded animals and loped on along the trail for the next half hour in silence.

The day had been hot and oppressive, but now the sun was low down in the west, and a gentle breeze cooled the heated air and refreshed the travellers and their weary animals.

Turning with the trail from the base of the mountain, a few minutes' ride, almost directly west into the valley, brought the two vaqueros to the banks of the San Benito, here but an insignificant stream. Crossing to the western bank they dismounted, removed their saddles, and after watering their horses, picketed the animals near by, where there was a luxuriant growth of alfilirea—a sort of wild clover—and made preparations for a lunch.

The meal consisted simply of cold meat and bread, and *pinole*— a universal article of diet among the Mexicans when travelling in this way, and which is simply parched corn ground. Simple as it is, it is a most nutritious and stimulating article of diet, and one of the most valuable to the hunter or the traveller who has to camp out and carry with him his own provisions.

As they were about to sit down Garcia untied his blankets from the saddle, and unrolling the bundle, produced a quart bottle of aguadiente—the Mexican substitute for the American's whiskey, and quite as fiery in its effects.

Handing the bottle to Tiburcio, the young man swallowed a copious draught of the seductive liquid; Garcia applied his lips to the bottle more cautiously, and then joined his companion at his meal, which was devoured pretty much in silence.

During the repast the dark eyes of Garcia were intently watching every motion of his companion, and an expression of fiendish satisfaction rested upon his features as he noted symptoms of the exhilarating or rather exciting effect of the strong potation he had imbibed.

At the conclusion of the meal the bottle was once more passed, and again the boy, for he was scarcely yet more than a stripling, indulged in a "heavy" drink, for he was feverish and internally excited by the emotions awakened in his bosom by the solicitations and taunts of his companion.

"Well," he exclaimed, rising to his feet, and lighting a cigaretto, "I suppose our horses are rested, and now that we've taken our refresco, suppose we saddle and move on, for the sun is just setting."

"We need not hurry on that account," replied Garcia, "for there is a full moon tonight. It is already above the horizon, although we cannot yet see it."

"All right then; but we have a good ways to go yet, and might better move on."

"The horses need more rest, and besides, amigo, I've a piece of news to impart to you."

"Ah! I hope it's good news. It will be the first I've heard for some time."

"I hope you will deem it good news, Tiburcio, for it's a matter I have taken considerable pains to bring about."

"Well, out with it," was the impatient response; "I am eager to hear what your mysterious news can be."

"I only hope you'll be as eager to act upon it as you are to hear it. Do you recollect the short, thick-set old man we saw in Monterey about a month ago—the man who wanted to buy sheep?"

"Yes, I remember him."

"Well, I have kept track of him. He is still buying sheep, and is now on his way to some ranches on the Salinas River for that purpose. The main road is only about a fourth of a mile ahead, on this trail. If I have not miscalculated, he will pass along here between this and nine o'clock tonight. It is possible he may have stopped at the last ranch below here, but I do not think he has. At all events we will soon know. He has money with him to the amount of at least four hundred dollars, and I mean to rob him."

The speaker narrowly watched the effect of this unexpected announcement upon his youthful companion.

Tiburcio heard the communication in silence, turned on his heel, and walked slowly to the bank of the river, where he stood with his head bowed upon his bosom in deep thought, for several minutes.

Then he roused himself suddenly, and returning with a brisk, eager step to his tempter, he said:

"Garcia, this is not fair. You should have forewarned me. However, it might as well be now as hereafter. I will show you that I am not behind you in courage. Garcia, I want you to let me do the job."

The robber signified his intense gratification at this sudden conversion of his obstinate pupil by an expressive grasp of the hand.

"Good," he said; "you are a man at heart, after all, if not a man of years."

"You will let me do the job, then?" asked Vasquez, eagerly.

"No," was the quick reply; "you watch me, and then you will know how to do this afterwards;" and leading the way to the main thoroughfare, both adventurers were soon hidden in the dense thicket that skirted the roadside.

The sun went down, and the delicious night wind blew freshly from the mountains. The full moon flooded the whole valley with a silvery, softened light; the dark shadows of the trees blended with the thick foliage of the chapparal, or were sharply outlined on the bare earth; while the shrill notes of the night bird mingling with the mournful cry of the owl, contributed to the weird and ghostly character of the scene.

They had not long to wait, for within half an hour after making their ambush the innocent and unsuspecting old man came jogging along the road toward them.

As he neared the fatal ambuscade both Garcia and Vasquez examined their revolvers, and as he came up, Garcia stepped out, and presenting his pistol, called out in Spanish:

"Halt, and dismount!"

Startled at the sudden advent of the robber, the horse sprang clear from the road and landed in the chapparal on the lower side. Finding his horse hopelessly entangled in the brush, the old man drew a revolver from its holster, but before he could use it, a bullet from Garcia's pistol crashed through his brain, and he fell lifeless from his horse.

With two bounds Vasquez cleared the road, and seizing the horse by the bridle, led him back, and secured him to the limb of a tree.

"It won't do to stay here," exclaimed the murderer; "we must drag the body so far from the road and trail that it will not be discovered, at least, until we are far out of the way."

The body was taken several hundred yards from the road and about the same distance from the trail, where the robbers found a place on the margin of a stream where the earth had been washed out during the rainy season, and after securing the money-belt, which contained $350 in gold and silver, they threw the body into the excavation, and with broken limbs of trees, which they used for digging away the earth from the margin of the hole, they managed to cover the body sufficiently, they thought, to prevent immediate decomposition—or, at least, to neutralize any smell that might attract attention to the spot.

Returning to the road, they removed the saddle and bridle from the horse and hid them in the chapparal, some distance from the road. Letting the horse go where he would, the robbers returned to the river, saddled their own horses, and finishing the contents of Garcia's bottle, left the spot, going in the direction of Monterey.

They rode in silence until midnight, when they once more unsaddled their horses, and after picketing their animals, spread their blankets and laid down to rest.

Early next morning the ill-gotten booty was divided, and the robber and his pupil pushed on towards Monterey. During the journey but little conversation took place. Garcia was moody and taciturn, while Vasquez was a prey to conflicting emotions.

Although not guilty of shedding the blood of the lone traveller, or even of having intentionally aided or abetted Garcia in the murder, yet he felt a strange sense of oppression that he could not shake off.

He could not forget, and never did forget, that moonlight picture— the ruthless killing of that inoffensive old man. He had willingly consented to the robbery, and the murder was the legitimate result of the plan. He felt safe from discovery, but realized that the bloody transaction cast the die, and that henceforth his lot was among desperadoes and cut-throats.

On reaching the vicinity of Monterey, the two criminals turned aside from the main road and remained for two or three days at the ranch of a relative of Garcia's, when, hearing that a dance was to take place at a fandango house near the suburbs of the town, they resolved to be present and join in the festivities.

Vasquez had been restless as a caged lion since the robbery, and was in a condition to do anything desperate that came to hand. A conference was held between Garcia and Vasquez, and thinking it probable that they would meet two or three desperadoes of Garcia's acquaintance at the ball, they resolved to try and enlist them in a lawless expedition into the San Joaquin Valley.

It is a sufficient description of a fandango to characterize it as a sort of free and easy Mexican ball, at which the handsome senoritas and their dark-skinned admirers mingle together in the graceful mazes of Mexican dances, wine and aguadiente flow like water, and not unfrequently the knife and pistol are called into requisition to settle disputed points, or satisfy the jealousy of some half-drunken "Greaser."

The early portion of the evening, until near 11 o'clock, passed off very much as such affairs usually do; mirth and hilarity abounded, and there were no difficulties of any moment until Garcia, who was half drunk, in a fit of jealousy struck one of the guests a fearful blow on the head with a water pitcher.

In an instant all was confusion and uproar, and in the midst of the melee a constable of the town, William Hardmount, who had been sent for by the friends of the man whom Garcia had struck, entered the room to quell the disturbance.

Hardmount approached Garcia to arrest him. The latter instantly drew a revolver and ordered him to stand back. Vasquez and a desperado named Jose Heiguerra, and another named Feliz, all of whom were half drunk on aguadiente, sprang to Garcia's side and drew their weapons, and while the unfortunate officer was endeavoring to persuade Garcia to put up his weapon, one of the party—either Garcia or one of his three backers—deliberately shot him dead.

Alarmed for their safety, Vasquez, Garcia and Feliz instantly left the room, and mounting upon their horses, effected their escape. Heiguerra was seized and hung within an hour after the homicide.

CHAPTER II.

CONSTABLE HARDMOUNT had long been a very efficient officer in
Monterey, and was beloved by every one for his generous and many
qualities; and his wanton murder created the utmost excitement and
indignation throughout the whole county. The prejudice existing
against the native Mexican or Creole population was increased a hundred per cent, and for several days scarcely a "Greaser" ventured to
move.

A large concourse of excited citizens assembled early on the morning succeeding the murder, and acting in the capacity of "Vigilantes,"
appointed a committee of energetic men, to take the affair in hand
and mete out justice to the murderers.

After several stirring harangues by some of the leading citizens of
Monterey, in which the importance of making a wholesome example of
the miscreants was set forth, and summary vengeance called down
upon their heads, a committee was appointed and the business of
investigating the circumstances of the homicide was placed in their
hands.

They were instructed to examine into the affair, decide as to who
the guilty parties were, and then to take measures to secure their apprehension. Money was pledged by wealthy citizens to enable the
committee to fit out parties and prosecute the search until some one, or
all, of the murderers were hunted down and brought to justice.

The investigation occupied nearly the whole of one day, and
although it did not definitely appear who fired the fatal shot, the
testimony was so conflicting, yet enough was proven to show conclusively that Garcia, Vasquez, Jose Heiguerra, and Feliz, acted in
concert, and were equally guilty of resisting the officer. The fact that
the survivors had taken flight together was enough of itself to establish
their guilt in the minds of the committee and of the entire community.

Two of the witnesses, a senorita and a lad about twelve years of
age, who was present, testified before the committee, that when Hard-

mount approached Garcia, who was pointing a cocked revolver towards him, Vasquez took another pistol from the hands of Jose Heiguerra, and firing under the extended arm of Garcia, killed the brave officer on the spot. The preponderance of the testimony, however, went to show that the four men were side by side in the attitude of defiance, and with drawn weapons were ordering the officer to leave the fandango house; and that when Hardmount made a final move to seize Garcia, the latter shot him dead in his tracks.

The committee formally pronounced all four of the Mexicans guilty of wanton murder, and sentenced the survivors to be hanged whenever caught within the limits of the county.

Three scouting parties were promptly organized, and any holes or cover in the county and near its borders were scoured for weeks, but without finding any traces of the red-handed outlaws.

Meanwhile the three miscreants had travelled night and day until they had gained a secure retreat in a little secluded valley hidden away in the Panoche range of mountains in the southern portion of Santa Clara county, about fifty miles south-east from Gilroy, called Saucilito.

It was a hiding place to which Joaquin Murieta and his gang had often retired to recruit and to evade pursuit, and was known at that time only to men of that class, to a few adventurous hunters, who had explored the region, but who, however, had no idea of the character of the men who sought refuge in the lonesome place.

There were three Mexican adobe buildings in the valley, situated about half a mile apart, and there was plenty of luxuriant grass for horses. The trail leading to the lonesome place was very indistinct, and a portion of the route was crossed and recrossed in every conceivable direction by cattle and sheep trails, rendering it impossible for the most experienced trail-hunter to find the way without a guide thoroughly familiar with the mountains.

The three fugitives reached the place, Garcia as guide, in a worn-out, half-famished condition, and their horses were well-nigh exhausted by the hurried journey, during the progress of which they had hardly been allowed to stop long enough to slake their thirst at the streams they crossed.

The animals were at once picketed out in the abundant pasturage, while the murderers, after a hearty meal of mutton and tortillas, washed down with liberal potations of aguadiente, stowed themselves away, rolled up in their "mantas" or blankets, to sleep off the fatigue of their hurried journey.

Stopping at one of the adobe houses were three desperadoes who had been members of Murieta's band, and at the house where Garcia, Vasquez and Feliz took up their quarters, were two others, and as soon as the murderers of poor William Hardmount had recovered from the fatigue of their hurried flight from the infuriated populace of Monterey, a drunken carousal was inaugurated, which was kept up for several days.

It must be borne in mind by the reader that in collecting the facts in regard to this and other murderous transactions which occurred so long ago, and which have never been subjected to a legal investigation, it is a difficult matter to get at the exact truth, there being so many different versions of these affairs handed down from the date of their occurrence, and subject to the prejudices or whims of those who tell the stories.

The writer believes the above unvarnished account of the murder of William Hardmount to be as nearly correct as it is possible now to get it. Subjoined, however, is an account of the murder taken from a recent number of the Salinas City *Index:*

"About the year 1854, when Tiburcio Vasquez was no more than fifteen or sixteen years of age, he, in company with Anastacia Garcia and one Heiguerra, were at a ball given at a Spanish dancehouse in Monterey City. Garcia was so drunk, noisy, and insolent, that complaint was made to Constable William Hardmount, who attempted to arrest Garcia, but was shot dead by Vasquez. Vasquez left at once, but Garcia and Heiguerra remained. Ned Lyons, who was Sheriff, attempted to arrest Garcia, but was deterred by a pistol held by the latter in a threatening manner. While parleying, Jack Robinson came into the room with a shot-gun, and Garcia fled—Heiguerra opening the door to facilitate his escape. Robinson put a charge of buckshot into Heiguerra on the instant, and pursued Garcia, and shot him as he ran, one buckshot entering his wrist, causing him to drop his pistol, but he got away. The next morning an indignant populace took Heiguerra, wounded as he was, and hanged him in the porch of the house where Hardmount was murdered. Subsequently Garcia came and gave himself up, and was examined on a charge of murdering Hardmount, during which it was proven by a number of witnesses, that Tiburcio Vasquez fired the fatal shot. Garcia was discharged, but no indictment was ever made out against Vasquez for this murder, although there are witnesses of the affair living at this day. Tiburcio has never appeared openly in Monterey since, but, associating freely with Garcia, he commenced a career of crime which is probably unequalled in this or any other country."

Following is Tiburcio Vasquez's own version of the affair (all he chose to say about it), as given to the writer in Los Angeles, on the 20th of May, 1874. The relation was given in Spanish, General Baldwin, deputy sheriff of Los Angeles County, acting as interpreter:

"About the year 1852, myself and friends were in the habit of giving little balls among ourselves. These balls were frequently interrupted, and the participants rudely insulted and outraged by parties calling themselves native Americans. Whatever their nationality, they were a low order of men.

"From these insults arose my inclination to play the part which I have since acted. The events I allude to transpired in the county of Monterey, and resulted in one or two personal collisions, which, however, passed off without bloodshed.

"At this time I was also charged with having assisted Anastacia Garcia in a difficulty which took place in a ball-room, in which Garcia killed an employe of the sheriff. This imputation arose from the fact that on the day succeeding the affair, Garcia called on me at my mother's house, and we went off together throughout the country.

"Garcia was afterwards arrested in Los Angeles county and taken to Monterey, where he was lynched by a mob."

As stated above, several days were spent by the murderers in debauchery at their retreat, during which several quarrels took place among them, but which did not result in bloodshed.

At last the outlaws began laying plans for future robberies, and for several days various propositions were under discussion. Vasquez, now fully identified with the desperadoes, entered into the discussion of these plans with great eagerness, and his co-conspirators discovered that although he was a boy in years, he possessed an acute intellect and the shrewd judgment of an old hand at the business.

It was also discovered that he had a will of his own, and was not easily led against the dictates of his judgment. He combatted successfully every proposition made by Garcia, and so plainly pointed out the weak points in the plans he presented, as to completely neutralize Garcia's power over the others as a leader, and the whole party, with the sole exception of Garcia, signified their desire that Vasquez, young and inexperienced though he was, should lead them forth to plunder, declaring their full confidence in his judgment and courage.

This, of course, was gall and wormwood to Garcia, and he did not even make an effort to conceal his vexation and chagrin. But when Vasquez, at their solicitation, unfolded his plans, and laid his programme before them, they were dumbfounded by the bold, romantic, and apparently rash and impracticable schemes which emanated from his fervid and self-confident brain, and the result was that no agreement could be effected between them, and for a time each went on private expeditions of their own, sallying out from their retreat singly for the purpose of "adventure," and returning to the common rendezvous for safety and relaxation, and to recruit their horses—occasionally bringing in animals they had stolen.

Tired of inactivity, and dissatisfied with his companions, after nearly a month of quiet at Saucilito rendezvous, and feeling a strong desire also to visit a beautiful girl whose affections he had won (the girl hinted at by Garcia, in his conversation with Tiburcio, as related in our first chapter), Vasquez determined to emerge from his hiding place, visit Anita, have a parting interview with his mother, and then enter boldly and systematically upon the manner of life he had voluntarily chosen.

Bidding his companions a friendly "adios," he left the Saucilito valley, and crossing the Panoche Mountains, re-entered Monterey county.

He well knew that he was treading upon dangerous ground, but in the mood he was in the very danger had a strange fascination for him which he did not try to resist. He was starving for excitement, and eager for adventure.

Near nightfall of the third day after leaving the rendezvous, the young and desperate adventurer, while descending a hillside near the road between Hollister and the city of Monterey, saw approaching a solitary horseman, and he instantly resolved to waylay and rob him.

Securing his horse in a thicket at a convenient point near the roadside, he carefully examined his pistols, and seating himself on a rock from which he could see without being seen, he patiently awaited the approach of his victim.

As the traveller approached, Vasquez coolly stepped into the highway and in Spanish ordered the traveller to halt, dismount and hand over his valuables.

As the man apparently did not understand the orders, Vasquez translated it into intelligible English, when as quick as thought the stranger presented a revolver and fired.

The rash act sealed his doom, for Vasquez was not in a mood to bear trifling with. The smoke of the discharge had not begun to rise, when a bullet from the pistol of the robber entered his heart and he sank to the earth in the agonies of death.

Vasquez sprang forward and seized the horse, which he led some distance from the road and secured from the observation of passers-by, and returning dragged the body of the murdered man to where he had fastened his own horse.

Secured in a buck-skin belt around the body, the robber found $1,200 in gold coin, and nearly $100 in the various pockets in gold and silver coin. In the saddle-bags, affixed to the saddle, he found $800 in gold and silver. He also secured two splendid Colt's revolvers.

Fearing that the horse of the murdered man, a splendid animal, might lead to his detection if he undertook to dispose of it, and fearing the same result if he allowed it to go at liberty, he removed the saddle and trappings, and hid them away in the bushes, and stepping up to the noble animal, deliberately shot it through the head with one of its dead master's weapons.

After his bloody work was finished, he secured the plunder about his person, and not even taking the precaution to bury the body, but merely concealing it with leaves, he remounted and resumed his journey.

On the following day toward nightfall, he reached the vicinity of the ranch where his sweetheart, a beautiful Spanish girl, whom we will call Anita (but whose real name it is proper to omit, as her relatives, people of the highest respectability, still reside in the county), and stopping at a neighboring ranch, the proprietor of which was a friend of Garcia, and with whom he knew he would be safe from exposure, he waited for the shadows of evening to make a visit to the confiding girl, whose pure love he had won.

From the ranchero he learned with some consternation, although he had anticipated such a state of affairs, the intense excitement which had been caused by the killing of Hardmount; the sentence which had been pronounced against him and his comrades in crime by the avenging Vigilance Committee, and the expeditions which had been fitted out against them.

His judgment, however, was that in all probability the search had by this time been already abandoned, and that the committee, doubtless supposing that the murderers had succeeded in getting out of the county, and little dreaming that any of them would have the temerity or the apparent foolhardiness to venture within the county limits so soon, had ceased their efforts to bring them to justice. He therefore apprehended little danger in seeking an interview with Anita. Once in her society, he knew that such was her love for him, and her thorough confidence in his manliness and integrity, he would have no difficulty in convincing her of his entire innocence of the crimes imputed to him.

The love affair between Vasquez and Anita was disapproved by the girl's parents, but they had no idea how thoroughly infatuated Anita had become with the dashing young highwayman. Reports of his connection with the murder of Constable Hardmount had reached the household, and as day after day had passed without the usual visit from her lover, the unfortunate girl was filled with grief and the direst forebodings, and was in the depths of the profoundest despair. It was next to impossible for her to believe in his guilt; yet the fact that he had fled the country, without seeing her, or sending her a letter or even a verbal message, seemed almost incontrovertible proof of his guilt, and she sank day after day under her weight of sorrow, until she had become but a mere shadow of her former self.

The friend with whom he was stopping knew something of this, and communicated his knowledge to Vasquez, who, despite the cold, heartless mood his crime had produced, heard the communication not without a genuine twinge of conscience; and he shuddered when he speculated upon the probable effect of his conduct upon Anita and upon his doting mother.

Not daring to visit Anita openly, he resolved to prepare the way for a clandestine meeting by sending her a brief note, assuring her of his entire innocence of any intentional connection with the murder, and of his ability to fully vindicate himself whenever the excitement should die away, and he could be certain of a fair and impartial investigation of the circumstances. He accordingly prepared the way for the meeting he desired by inditing the following note, in Spanish:

Dearest Anita: Forgive me for my long silence—imposed by the cruel suspicions of those whose prejudice against our race led them to condemn me without a hearing, and from whom I was compelled to flee for my life. When the present excitement has subsided, I will be able to prove my innocence before the whole world. Meanwhile I have plans which I wish to lay before you, and I have ventured here at the risk of my life to prove to you my innocence of any crime, as well as my undying devotion to you. It will not do for me to be seen at present, but I must see you tomorrow. Can you not walk to the Willows—the place where we last parted—at 9 o'clock tomorrow morning? Let me know by him who hands you this letter.

This note safely reached the hand of the fair Anita, and the heart of the young girl beat wildly as she ran her eager eyes rapidly over the lines and comprehended their meaning. She could scarcely indite a legible reply, so overwhelming were her emotions; but after a strong effort she controlled herself sufficiently to write a brief note to her lover, promising to comply with his request, and meet him at the old trysting place.

The morning was cloudless, and the sun rose bright and beautiful over as fair a landscape as lies beneath the skies. Anita's heart beat gladly and her eye beamed brightly with fond hope as the hour drew near at which she was to repair to the Willows to meet her lover, where she had so often met him when no clouds intervened between them and their pictures of future happiness.

The young robber repaired early to the trysting place, and throwing himself upon the greensward, impatiently awaited the arrival of Anita. As the hour approached, the fair girl appeared—coming with graceful, eager steps—and entering the thicket of willows, she looked wistfully and anxiously on every side for her lover.

In her dainty mouth she held a pure white rose; her eye was bright with new hope, and her cheeks flushed with pleasure. She had removed her hat, setting free a wealth of dark, curling tresses—as lovely a picture of maiden beauty as the sun ever shone upon.

As her lover stepped from his place of concealment, her quick ear caught the sound of his stealthy footsteps, and turning towards him, she uttered an exclamation of joy, and bounding forward to where he stood, with arms outstretched and a smile of glad welcome upon his handsome features, she fell upon his bosom and sobbed convulsively for several minutes.

When she had given free vent to her pent-up emotions, the soothing influence of his caresses and exclamations of endearment aroused her from the wild and almost hysterical mood she had yielded to, and she dried her tears and so far succeeded in controlling her emotions, as to be able to converse with her lover.

Seating themselves on the grass beneath the overhanging foliage of a graceful willow, they canvassed the situation and discussed that ever difficult problem to lovers who are oppressed by stern parents— what to do next. Reclining in her lover's embrace, Anita listened to his plausible version of his presence at the fandango, and his accidental connection with the murder of the constable.

"Ah! Tiburcio, why do you go in company with that bad man, Garcia? My father says he is a robber by profession, and he is suspected of many murders."

"I do not associate with him, my dear," replied the hypocritical lover; "I have been in his company, but never heard him talk of robbery, or propose any crime."

"Oh! I'm so sorry you ever had anything to do with him. How will you ever overcome the disgrace? Can you ever walk abroad again in Monterey county a free man?"

A tear glistened in her anxious eye, as she turned an appealing glance upon the face of her lover.

"Anita, I will not only recover my good name from the disgrace which now covers it, but I will yet show the members of that Vigilance Committee that they were dealing with the wrong man when they charged me with murder, and threatened me with the rope."

Anita shrank involuntarily from the stern gaze of Vasquez, as he muttered this threat beneath his set teeth.

"Tiburcio," she replied, with great earnestness, "pray give up your wild schemes of military glory, and settle down to some quiet avocation."

"Have you no pride, Anita—no ambition for yourself, no pride in my future?"

"Oh, how can you ask such a question, Tiburcio? For you, indeed, I have pride and high hopes for your future. For myself, no ambition but to be happy with you, to live with you."

"Anita, I am going to leave this part of the State, and settle in Los Angeles county. Will you go with me?"

"How can I? My parents will not even permit you to visit me now. To even ask their permission for us to marry would be even worse than folly. It would transform my home into a prison."

The young girl bowed her head upon her hands and wept long and bitterly.

"As we know they will never consent," replied Vasquez, "what is there in the future for us? There is but one course for us to pursue, if we would be true to our mutual pledges. Fly with me to Los Angeles county, where we can be united by a priest of our church. Your parents will soon reconcile themselves to the situation, and I can soon build up a home and a fortune for us."

"But you have no money, Tiburcio—no means with which to commence life with, and I would only be a burden on your hands."

"Forgive me Anita," replied her tempter, "if I have deceived you in that respect. I have money—more than enough for all our immediate wants, and amply sufficient to commence in some respectable business."

Vasquez removed the money-belt which he had taken from the murdered traveller, and poured a glittering heap of gold into her lap.

Anita uttered a cry of astonishment.

"This gold, Anita," continued her lover, in an eager, convincing manner, "I have been patiently saving for years. I have saved it for this hour, for this very emergency, which I foresaw."

"But how, Tiburcio, how have you been able to accumulate all this gold?"

"By saving all my earnings; by buying and selling horses; by trading horses; by the constant increase of a flock of sheep I have owned for four years, without the knowledge of a single one of my relatives. My mother has also saved money, and made me a present of all she could save."

Long and earnestly did the desperate man argue and plead with Anita to elope with him and share his fortunes; but he could not get her consent to go with him. She willingly agreed, however, to meet him at the same hour on the following morning at the Willows; and after an affectionate parting, the young girl turned toward home, while Vasquez returned to the ranch of his friend.

At nightfall, he saddled his horse, mounted and rode to his mother's house. Leaving his horse picketed some distance from the dwelling, he first carefully reconnoitered the premises, and after satisfying himself that no enemies were lurking about, he cautiously approached the adobe building, and tapped gently at the door.

The next moment he was in his mother's arms.

For several minutes the poor woman, whose heart had for several days been filled with anguish and weighted down with fears and anxiety over the fate of her wayward son, was so overcome by her emotions that she was unable to speak.

Hurriedly Tiburcio assured her of his innocence.

"Mother," he said, "I am innocent of any crime; I only happened, by accident, to be standing near Garcia, when the affair happened. But such is the animosity of the Americanos against our race that I knew in the excitement following the murder, my life would be sacrificed to the angry passions of the mob. I therefore fled the county, and have risked my life in returning, solely to crave your blessing. With that I shall leave this portion of the State. When the excitement has died away, I shall return here and court an investigation, confident of my ability to prove to the world my entire innocence of this crime, or any voluntary connection with it."

"Oh, my son! do not leave and go among strangers. You can remain quiet here, and no one need to know of your presence."

"I must go, mother. I will go to some quiet locality in the southern portion of the State, and I will write to you often, and also communicate with a lawyer here, and when the proper time comes I will return and vindicate my character from the foul stain that now covers it with obliquity."

"You will stay, and see your father and brothers—they will be home within an hour?"

"Mother, I must not stay a moment. I have far to ride tonight, and besides I am not safe here; at any moment parties may visit the house in quest of me. I only crave your blessing, mother, and then with a strong heart and willing hands I will go forth from your presence to battle with the world."

"My blessing you have, my son, with all my heart. And, oh, do not, Tiburcio, forget the many instructions I have given you. In the name of God, my boy, avoid evil companions, and their evil ways. The recent events have almost broken my heart, but I know my son is innocent."

"Before God, mother, I am an innocent man. And now, dear mother, goodbye!"

"Good-bye, my son," faltered the sorrow-stricken mother, as her arms enfolded the recreant in a last fond embrace; "good-bye, and may God bless you!"

CHAPTER III.

CRUEL ABDUCTION OF THE GIRL, ANITA—THE FLIGHT ACROSS THE MOUNTAINS—TREACHERY OF THE VILLAIN GARCIA—HIS ATTEMPT TO STEAL THE GIRL FROM VASQUEZ—SANGUINARY END OF PONCHO RICARDO AT THE HANDS OF ANITA.

As THE YOUNG HIGHWAYMAN rode in the starlight along the trail which led to the ranch of the friend at whose house he rendezvoused, he threw aside, by a strong effort of the will, the feeling of depression and sadness which had stolen over him as he received his mother's last tender embrace, and witnessed her deep sorrow, and her weight of anxiety for his present safety and future welfare, and strove to bend all the powers of his mind upon the future.

The immediate business on his hands was his love affairs with Anita, and as he urged his horse along the trail, he pondered long and deeply on how to overcome her scruples against the elopement he had proposed to her. He did not meditate any harm to the girl. He loved her as honestly and truly as it was in his depraved nature to love. Loved her as the hunter loves a rare specimen of a hunting dog, or a pet horse. He coveted her with a selfish desire to have her all his own, and her own personal welfare scarcely entered his mind.

The result of his deliberations was the resolution to take her with him to Los Angeles—with her own consent, if it could be obtained; if not, why then he would forcibly abduct her. Settled in this determination, as soon as he reached his friend's place, he at once selected from the numerous horses in the ranch an animal that had been well broken, and which had been trained as a saddle horse for ladies; paying the round sum (in those days) of $250 in gold for the horse, a side-saddle, blankets, saddle-bags, etc., the entire outfit necessary for Anita's comfort on the journey.

This purchase effected, Vasquez next turned his attention to preparing and laying in a stock of provisions for the trip. Everything was in readiness, and the robber was preparing for bed, when the clattering of horses' hoofs was heard approaching the house, followed by a peculiar rapping at the door. When the door was opened in response to the mysterious summons, to Vasquez's infinite surprise, Garcia himself crossed the threshold.

He, too, had grown restless at the narrow limits of the rendezvous, and had ventured upon the forbidden and dangerous territory of Monterey county in quest of "adventure"—that is, in search of some one to rob and murder.

Notwithstanding his growing aversion to the man, and the fear that his thirst for blood, and his habitual rashness, might again bring him into trouble, Vasquez witnessed his arrival with undisguised satisfaction.

To abduct Anita alone, he knew would be a difficult, if not an impossible, undertaking, but with Garcia's assistance, he felt that the scheme would be entirely feasible.

So he seized the burly outlaw by the hand and welcomed him with his sweetest smiles and the most flattering and exaggerated expressions of gratification, all of which the murderous villain received with much complacency. As soon as he had eaten his supper, Vasquez drew him aside, and explaining his nefarious scheme, requested his assistance in carrying it into execution.

Garcia replied to the proposition with many sneers, denouncing the proposed scheme of abduction, not on any moral or humane grounds, but as an act that would only add to the already intense feeling against him throughout the county, and be sure to inaugurate a determined and thorough search for him throughout the State.

Vasquez, however, was determined to carry out the programme he had decided upon, and had plausible replies for each of the arguments presented by Garcia. He also assured him that he should exert all his powers of persuasive eloquence to induce Anita to accompany him voluntarily, and promised him if he would aid him in case his eloquence proved unavailing, and it became necessary to secure possession of the girl by stratagem and carry her away by force, that when they had once got her to a place of safety, he would, in return, co-operate with him in any adventurous undertaking he might inaugurate.

Garcia finally consented to take part in the adventure, and assist Vasquez in case it became necessary to abduct the girl, and accompany him with her on the proposed journey to Los Angeles county.

The matter thus being determined upon, it only remained for them to agree upon the modus operandi of the abduction. It was arranged that the two confederates should proceed with their horses, taking with them the horse prepared for Anita, before daylight, and picket them in the thicket of the copse, where they would be free from observation; and that when the appointed hour, 9 o'clock, arrived, Vasquez would step out to receive Anita, while Garcia should remain concealed with the horses until a signal should announce to him that Vasquez's persuasive powers had failed, and that his co-operation was required to effect the abduction.

These preliminaries being satisfactorily arranged, the two worthies separated to seek a few hours' slumber.

By daylight of the following morning, Vasquez and Garcia were so securely hidden in the willow thicket, that one might have passed within ten feet of them and their horses, without discovering any indications of their presence.

Pending the hour of nine o'clock, they whiled away the time in discussing various plans for the future. Garcia had been informed by his whilom protege, that he had ample funds for the purposes of the trip to Southern California, and was not a little curious to know from what source he had obtained the money; but Vasquez, although inwardly giving himself much credit for the "courageous" adventure which had replenished his purse, chose to be reticent on the subject towards Garcia, not thinking it a wise policy to put himself unnecessarily in his or any other man's power. He knew that the robber had proved treacherous towards others, and he reasoned very naturally, that if an occasion was presented in which, through disaffection or self-interest, the temptation arose in Garcia's breast to betray him, he would doubtless yield to it.

To all of his inquiries, therefore, in regard to how he had come into possession of the money, he returned vague and unsatisfactory replies.

Although outwardly Vasquez was perfectly tranquil, and his countenance betrayed no anxiety or trepidation in regard to the adventure before him, yet inwardly he was a seething volcano—a prey to the most torturing anxiety and impatience.

At length, to his infinite relief, Anita appeared, and springing forward, with smiles and expressions of endearment, he welcomed her and enfolded her in his arms. Taking her beyond ear-shot of his concealed confederate, Vasquez pleaded long and earnestly, with all his impassioned eloquence, for Anita to accompany him at once—severing all connection with her friends and the home of her girlhood.

To all of his arguments, however, she replied firmly, and with tears and impassioned protestations and appeals to his better nature, besought him to abandon the idea as wild and chimerical, and unworthy of a true man. The look of mingled surprise and sorrow with which she regarded him as he continued to urge her to fly with him like a thief in the night, gradually changed to a look of indignation as he began to upbraid her for her very virtue, and as he grew more and more emphatic in his language, and began to hint at using force instead of argument, an expression of horror stole over her features, and suddenly realizing to the full and awful reality the utter helplessness of her situation, she uttered one wailing appeal for mercy, and fell senseless at the feet of her brutal lover.

Further signal was unnecessary. As Anita's agonizing cry rang out on the morning air, Garcia sprang from his secret lair, and in a moment was at Vasquez's side.

Together they dragged the helpless form to where the horses were tethered. It was several minutes before they succeeded in restoring her to consciousness, but at length she opened her eyes, and fixed them with a mournful, inquiring expression on the face of her lover. She did not at first comprehend the situation, but as the recollection of the recent conversation flashed across her mind, and with it a full realization of her perilous situation, the blood began to course like lightning through her veins, and springing to her feet, she turned to flee, only to find herself face to face with the villain Garcia. As she caught the sinister gleam of his malignant eye, the terrified girl shrank back appalled.

Laying a hand heavily on her shoulder, and looking upon her with a stern regard, Vasquez addressed her:

"Anita, everything is in readiness for our flight. This friend, Senor Romero, a gentleman whom we can trust implicitly, will accompany and protect us. Will you submit to an inexorable fate, or will you compel me to use force?"

"Oh, my God, Tiburcio!" replied Anita, in tremulous accents, as the hot flush of indignation on her cheeks gave place to the deathly pallor of despair. "Oh, my god! is this your love—your tender regard for me? Oh, I see it all, now. You are indeed the guilty wretch—the monster which they told me you were. Would to God that I had died before making this appalling discovery!"

Although visibly affected by her distress, and himself as pale as the fragile being whose fate he held in his hands, no sign of relenting could she detect upon his stern and impassive features, and no word of mercy fell from his bloodless lips.

Garcia had led forward the horse prepared for the girl's use, and Vasquez, lifting her from the ground, where she had fallen upon her knees to implore their mercy, placed her in the saddle. Vaulting into his own saddle, he directed her to follow, and requesting Garcia to bring up the rear, he guided his horse along the bed of a shallow stream on the banks of which grew the tangled thicket of willows and alder bushes.

For Anita there was simply no alternative, and she submitted passively to the inexorable fate, almost hoping that it was all a horrible dream. Now that her lover had thrown aside his mask, and appeared in his true character, she was filled with the utmost dread. But notwithstanding her lively fears, she knew that to supplicate would be of no avail, and allowing her horse to follow its leader, she looked neither to the right or left, but bowing her head in sorrow upon her bosom, breathed a prayer to Heaven for deliverance.

The arroyo, or rivulet down which they were moving, wound among low hills for several miles, where it mingled its waters with the San Benito river. Its banks were fringed for nearly the entire distance with willows, alders, and sycamores, so that the party were well shielded from observation.

On nearing the San Benito, at a point not far distant from the scene of the moonlight murder, recorded in our first chapter, the party were halted, the horses unsaddled and picketed in the grass, while Vasquez and Garcia prepared supper.

No attempt was made by either to cheer up the spirits of their prisoner, for they felt instinctively that it would be useless. To their surprise, however, she made an effort to partake of the food set before her, which consisted of bread and honey, and cold meat, and a bottle of milk. She had resolved to keep up her strength and her courage, hoping that the efforts of her friends or some fortunate accident, perhaps her own exertions, might yet restore her to liberty.

The minds of her abductors were fully occupied with their plans in regard to the trip. Vasquez thought that the whole county would be aroused as soon as it became known that Anita was missing, and that it would require all his cunning and finesse to avoid capture. He had counted confidently on the girl's infatuated love for him, but he found that he had mistaken her nature, and he was forced to admit to himself that he could not hope for her submission.

He felt that he had lost both her love and respect, and consequently any power that he had possessed over her.

He felt humiliated and angry, and already began to hate the girl whom he was wronging, and to curse himself for his rashness in tearing her from her home.

Suggesting to Anita the advisability of her trying to get a little sleep, and spreading her blankets for her, Vasquez rolled himself in his own blanket to seek necessary repose, bidding Garcia, who was to watch, to wake him at sundown.

Tired with the ride, which to her had been a very fatiguing one, as the journey had been made along the bed of the arroyo, and she had been compelled almost every moment to bow her head to her horse's neck to avoid the depending branches of the trees, she felt grateful for even the small favor of being allowed to rest, and she reclined on the blankets spread for her—not to sleep, for she had not the slightest inclination to, but to rest, and to speculate upon the future.

Her position was a most trying one; but Anita had strength of character far beyond her years, and now that circumstances were bringing the powers of her mind into action, she felt conscious of a fortitude and strength of will that surprised even herself.

She now fully believed in the guilt of her lover in connection with the murder of Hardmount, and shrewdly divined that the man who now watched over her while Vasquez slept, and whom the latter had called Romero, was none other than the notorious villain, Anastacia Garcia.

As she stole a glance at his repulsive features, on which years of crime had graven their record in lines as plain and ineffacable as the epitaph on a tombstone—in every lineament of which the word *treachery* could be read in letter italicized—she withdrew her gaze with a shudder, and felt that, criminal though he was, at the present it was Vasquez himself to whom she must look for protection from that man.

Although she had been subjected to the terrible outrage of being forcibly abducted from her home, no further indignity had been offered; and the reflection that Vasquez had taken that step solely through his intense passion for her, she had faith to hope that if the journey was safely made to Los Angeles, she would find some way of regaining her liberty. She resolved to avoid giving Garcia reason to suspect her great aversion to him, and to be as conciliatory in her conduct toward Vasquez as was consistent with maintaining an attitude of firmness against voluntarily remaining in his society.

The journey was resumed as soon as it had grown dark, and was continued without any notable incident until the following evening, when the two robbers and their victims arrived in the Saucilito rendezvous.

Anita was so exhausted by the continued anxiety, and the fatigue of the trip, that she was scarcely able to stand. It was with grateful feelings, therefore, as she crossed the threshold of an adobe house, that she found herself confronted by one of her own sex, who stepped forward, and taking her kindly by the hand, led her to a private apartment, aloof from the rough crowd who were gathered in the first room and outside near the door.

As soon as they were alone together, the woman cautiously inquired of Anita as to her name and destination, and when the poor girl related to her the circumstances under which she had been abducted from her home, and that she was being taken to the "Lower Country" against her will, the woman's indignation was apparently aroused, and embracing Anita tenderly, she bade her cheer up, and to have hope—promising to do everything in her power to mitigate the unpleasant features of her surroundings, and that if an opportunity presented, to assist her to the best of her ability in an effort to escape from her thraldom.

Refreshments were brought her, and after a half-hour's conversation with her new-found friend, the tired girl retired to rest.

Meanwhile, the mysterious departure of Anita from her home had filled the hearts of the household with consternation. Her mother was frantic with grief, and insisted that her father and brothers should at once institute a search, and use every possible endeavor to unravel the terrible mystery.

They did mount and ride in every direction but the right one, carefully examining the ground for a trail that might indicate the direction she had taken, but returned to the house after a day's fruitless search.

The night was spent in a futile discussion as to the course best to be pursued. Although Anita had been a dutiful child, and was without reproach, yet her attachment to the handsome Vasquez had not been concealed; and when her parents had pre-emptorily forbidden her to meet him, she had declared to them that she should not refuse to see him, and would bide her time, and when she should arrive at an age which placed her beyond their control, would marry him.

It was not strange, therefore, that her family came to the conclusion that Vasquez had found some way to meet her, and had succeeded in inducing her to elope with him. To avoid scandal, they resolved to forego all search or inquiry in regard to her, and it was given out by the self-deceived family that Anita had gone to visit some relatives, living in a distant part of the State.

Far from even dreaming that such an interpretation of her absence could have been entertained by her relatives, Anita clung to the hope that they would bend every energy to the task of hunting for her.

But no help came.

Nearly a week of most disagreeable life was spent at the rendezvous, relieved only by the assiduous attentions of Margarita, Anita's kind and sympathizing female companion.

During the time Vasquez had made two attempts to regain the love of the stolen girl, and to induce her to become reconciled to her situation; but his appeals had no effect except to render it still more apparent to him that he had overrated the influence he once possessed over her.

Notwithstanding his bitter disappointment, he had no thought of giving over the idea of finally triumphing.

He treated her with great kindness, and allowed her all the liberty possible, without giving her an opportunity to escape.

Finally, preparations were made for the southern journey, and late one evening Anita was informed that the start was to be made early next morning.

The unwelcome announcement was tempered by the promise that Margarita was to accompany her on the trip.

Meanwhile, Garcia had watched the affairs closely, and divined the state of Anita's feelings toward Vasquez. He had agreed to accompany the party to Los Angeles county, and doubtless intended to do so when making the promise; but his brutal passions had full sway, his nature was treacherous as that of a serpent, and coveting passion of the girl, he resolved to play false to his pledges with Vasquez, and if possible to steal her away from the rendezvous before the hour fixed for starting on the southern expedition.

For the last three days Garcia had been plotting, but Vasquez himself was so vigilant, that it seemed impossible to carry the devilish scheme into execution. Garcia had studied the character of Vasquez pretty thoroughly, and knew that it would never do to be even suspected by him of treachery in this matter.

He therefore resolved to trust the execution of the first part of his plans to a subordinate, named Poncho Ricardo, a horse-thief and highwaymen, with whom he had been involved in numberless crimes.

The plan was to have the girl abducted by Ricardo, and removed from the valley by a different road from that over which she had been brought to the rendezvous.

As though the Fates were propitious, Vasquez left the adobe house where Anita was lodged, just before dark, to visit a ranchero on the opposite side of the valley, informing Garcia that he did not intend returning until late—probably about midnight.

This was Garcia's opportunity, and he resolved to take advantage of it, and laid his plans instantly and with shrewdness.

Coward that he was, he resolved to employ one of his satellites to effect the abduction, so that in case of failure and discovery he would not be suspected by Vasquez, whose determined character he did not wish unnecessarily to put to test.

So Poncho Ricardo, a half Indian, who would cut a white man's or woman's throat for a ten cent piece or a glass of aguadiente, was entrusted with the "job."

Anita had embraced Margarita at ten o'clock that night, and retired to her couch, but found it impossible to sleep. Tomorrow she was to resume her journey in company with her captor, and a thousand wild fancies ran through her brain, and in vain she tried to compose herself.

At midnight she detected the sound of a muffled footfall in the hallway opposite her bedroom door, and after the lapse of a few moments she heard some one tampering with the lock of the door.

Her heart beat wildly, but she summoned all her resolution.

It may be, she reasoned, a friend, who has sought me out, and is now seeking to communicate or rescue me. She did not believe it to be Vasquez, for he had never sought to intrude upon her privacy, and she did not deem it probable that he had suddenly changed his tactics.

Her suspicion fell instantly upon Garcia, and her fears took a definite shape.

Margarita had procured for her a pair of derringer pistols, as a means of defence in an emergency like this, and she at once decided upon her course of action.

Slipping quietly from the bed she hastily dressed, and throwing about her person a manteleta she seized the pistols and concealing them in its folds, she approached the door, and with courage awaited the movements of the midnight prowler.

At length there was a low knock at the door.

"Who knocks?" she demanded, in as firm a voice as she could command.

"A friend, senorita, who comes from Tiburcio," was the response, whispered through the key-hole.

She replied aloud, "What does the wretch want at this unreasonable hour?"

"You are to accompany me at once, senorita, where he awaits you."

"I do not believe you," she answered, lighting a lamp; "and I will not go. If he has sent for me, where is Margarita, who was to accompany me?"

There was no response, but the next moment the window sash was suddenly pried from its fastening and shoved aside, and turning quickly at the sound, the terrified girl beheld the burly form of Poncho Ricardo in the act of entering the room through the open window.

"Fuera! Begone, villain," she exclaimed, springing to the centre of the room. "Advance one step at your peril!"

With an oath, Poncho sprang from the window towards her, with arms outstretched to seize her.

Involuntarily shrinking backward, she threw aside her mantle, and quickly raising one of the derringers to a level with the repulsive countenance of the intruder, she pulled the trigger, and the wretch fell lifeless at her feet.

The bullet had passed entirely through the brain.

The concussion had extinguished the lamp, and Anita sank to the floor with a scream of terror, which resounded through the building, and penetrated the apartment of Margarita, who instantly sprang from bed, and throwing on a wrapper, lighted a candle and hastened to the scene of the tragedy.

CHAPTER IV.

UNCEREMONIOUS BURIAL OF PONCHO RICARDO—COMMENCEMENT OF THE JOURNEY TO LOS ANGELES—DARK DESIGN OF GARCIA—ANITA'S SCHEME FOR COMMUNICATING WITH HER FRIENDS—VASQUEZ'S PRECAUTIONS AGAINST GARCIA'S POSSIBLE TREACHERY, ETC.

GARCIA had calculated on Anita's complying without remonstrance with the pretended order of Vasquez, and did not doubt that she would at once respond to the summons, and accompany Poncho, whom he had agreed to join at a point about two miles distant.

He had repaired to the rendezvous agreed upon, but so great was his impatience, that he could not remain there. He had accordingly obeyed an instinct, and returning to the valley, had lurked in the vicinity of the building in which the girl was housed, and had kept a vigilant eye on the movements of Poncho.

Just as his patience had become nearly exhausted, he discovered Poncho at Anita's window, and with intense anxiety awaited the result of his forced entrance.

When the loud report of the pistol rang out upon the night air, Garcia sprang forward in time to see the fall of his confederate, and almost simultaneously with the villain's death came the sound of horses' hoofs coming towards the building.

Vasquez was returning.

Like lightning Garcia flew to where his own horse was tethered, and hurriedly vaulting into the saddle, spurred the animal to the corral, and in a twinkling removed its trappings and turned it loose.

Then he returned to his room, removed his spurs and all traces of preparation for a journey, and curled up in his blankets.

Vasquez had heard the explosion of the brave girl's pistol, and alarmed at the shot at that late hour of the night, put his horse to its highest speed until he reached the house.

Throwing himself from the saddle, he rushed to Anita's apartment, where he found Margarita had placed the senseless form of the girl upon the bed, and was bathing her temples and trying various means to restore her to consciousness.

Spurning the inanimate form of Poncho with his foot, Vasquez stepped to the bedside, and bidding Margarita to stand aside, bent over Anita and anxiously sought for wounds, or any traces of injury or violence.

Satisfying himself that she was only in a fainting fit, and that she had suffered no violence, he next examined Poncho, whom he found stone dead.

The dead body was dragged from the room, and left in the open air.

Bidding Margarita to pay every possible attention to her charge, Vasquez strode hurriedly to the apartment occupied by Garcia, whom he strongly suspected of having a hand in the attempted treachery which had cost the wretch Poncho Ricardo his life.

To his surprise he found Garcia apparently plunged in the depths of a profound slumber, and his suspicions were at once dispelled.

He placed a hand on the sleeper's shoulder, and shook him until he stopped snoring, yawned, rubbed his eyes, and asked: "What's up?

"Get up! Garcia, get up!" was the response. "Some hell-hound burst into Anita's room during my absence, and the girl has killed him."

"Caspita! Wonderful! What a brave little woman. Who is the man?"

"Poncho Ricardo, I think, but his face is so besmeared with blood and the other contents of his skull, that I am by no means certain."

Garcia slid out of bed, hastily dressed, and the two robbers hastened to view the dead body that Vasquez had dragged from the house, and left lying with its ghastly face upturned to the moonlight.

A brief examination resulted in their fully identifying the body as that of Ricardo, and Vasquez wondered not a little that the low-born villain had ventured to undertake the carrying out of such an impulse.

His idea was that the creole had entered Anita's apartment to compel her to submit to his embraces, and that the girl had managed to obtain possession of his pistol, and in self-defense had taken his wretched life.

Garcia suggested that he had probably desired to abduct her, and carry her off into the mountains.

Vasquez scouted the idea as altogether improbable, but to satisfy himself, asked Garcia to accompany him to the corral.

Poncho's horse was not there, nor was his saddle, bridle, nor any other portion of his outfit in their accustomed place.

A thorough search was made about the premises, and the horse, saddled and bridled, was soon found concealed in a little clump of pepper trees, near a spring, but a short distance from the house.

Vasquez was satisfied then that Ricardo had intended to carry the girl off by force, and he exulted in the failure that had resulted in his deserved killing.

The two robbers now hastened to the house.

They found Anita fully restored to consciousness, and though her face was still somewhat flushed from the recent excitement, her eye and voice were calm and self-possessed.

She had emerged from the terrible ordeal none the worse for the trial to her nerves.

She was, in fact, a stronger, braver woman than ever before, in her own estimation, as well as that of those with whom she was surrounded.

Both Vasquez and Garcia were profuse in their expressions of admiration at her courage and presence of mind.

Vasquez assured her that he would take precautions that would render it impossible for her to be ever again subjected to such danger while under his protection.

Anita volunteered no thanks for the assurance, simply replying that, inasmuch as he had taken her from her natural and lawful protectors, he was bound to shield her from violence and from want. She added, however, that she would feel grateful if he would leave her altogether, and let her find her way back to her relatives as best she could.

Vasquez made no direct reply to this request, but informed her that his preparations for a journey to Los Angeles county were complete, and that she must be in readiness to accompany him and Garcia at 9 o'clock.

Vasquez had ceased to disguise the identity of his companion in crime by calling him "Romero," and now addressed him in Anita's presence as Garcia.

Vasquez and Garcia now withdrew, and as soon as the door was closed which rid her of their unwelcome presence, Anita threw herself into the arms of Margarita, exclaiming:

"Oh, my dear friend! must I go still further from my childhood's home, and my old friends? Can we not take some provisions and flee from the valley, hide ourselves away in the thick chapparal, and on foot seek for assistance at some honest ranch? My friends are wealthy, and will amply reward you for any help you can give me."

"It would be useless," replied Margarita. "I do not know even the route by which I, myself, entered this valley, nor do I think I could find it. Indeed, there are only two trails by which the valley can be entered or departed from; and each of them passes through defiles so narrow that two persons cannot walk abreast. We should most certainly be overtaken, and if we luckily escaped that, the chances are that we would either be destroyed by the wild beasts which infest the mountains, or starve to death before we could reach a friendly ranch."

"There is, then," rejoined Anita, "no alternative but to get ready for the journey."

"Try and get some sleep, my friend," said Margarita, "for the journey will be a trying one, and you will need all your strength and nerve."

"As you are to accompany me," replied Anita, "I shall feel better reconciled to the fate; and oh! pray do not desert me if an opportunity presents for escape!"

"I am as much myself in the power of these men as you are," was the reply. "Indeed, dear Anita, I am in greater danger than you can be. For do I not know all the secrets of these guilty men—of Garcia and his associates in crime? One word from me—one single act that gave him reason to expect treachery on my part, or a design to assist you to escape—and my life would pay the forfeit."

"And do you know of crimes committed by Vasquez—him to whom I gave my honest love, and whom I almost worshipped as the very incarnation of all that was noble, and manly, and generous?"

"Alas, my dear friend, I can say no more. You know how he is wronging you. Can you doubt that such a man would not hesitate at highway robbery or even the taking of human life, or the betrayal of a friend, to carry out any scheme that might engage his soul?"

"No; indeed, I cannot doubt that," replied the heart-broken girl. "I have seen enough to convince me that he would hesitate at nothing that stood in the way of his will."

"Nothing remains, therefore," said Margarita, "but to quietly get ready for the journey. I will accompany you, and it is probable that your apparent submission will deceive both Garcia and Vasquez, and quiet any suspicion they may have entertained that you will try to escape, and appeal to strangers for protection. Vasquez's suspicions once allayed he will relax his vigilance, and we may find an opportunity to escape when we least expect it."

And she added, looking the girl earnestly in the eye, "Rest assured, dear Anita, that I will do all in my power to help you. I have determined, notwithstanding the great danger if I am retaken—nay, the absolute certainty that my life would be forfeited in that contingency—to accompany you when you do endeavor to escape, and share your every peril. Indeed, you cannot now doubt my devotion, for have I not proved it at a fearful risk? Did Vasquez have presence of mind enough to seek to ascertain how you came to be armed when Poncho entered your room, and found that you had my pistols, he would probably have shot me down like a dog. He undoubtedly thinks you got possession of Poncho's pistol."

"Should he seek to know, I will pretend," replied Anita, "that I had the pistols with me when he took me from home."

"It will not do to make that pretence," replied her companion, "for both he and Garcia know the weapons to be mine. Conceal them about your person, and do not let either of them see them."

It was four o'clock in the morning, and daylight was just appearing, when the girls separated to seek a little repose before starting.

Vasquez arose at seven o'clock.

His first business was to get the loathsome carcass of Ricardo out of sight.

Giving a two-and-a-half gold piece to a half-breed who loafed about the place, he directed the man to bury the body at the foot of the nearest hill.

The half-breed fastened one end of a lariat around the body, and hitching a mule to the other, dragged the remains to the point indicated, and after removing all the clothing, being of an economical disposition, proceeded to inter the cadaver.

A hole in the ground about two feet in depth was deemed amply sufficient for the purpose. The body was rolled in, and the earth replaced.

The dead malefactor received about as unceremonious a burial as the San Francisco paupers used to under the economical administration of Coroner Rice, in cases where they took their departure so suddenly as to require an investigation into the cause of their sudden "taking off."

This matter attended to, the half-breed returned to Vasquez for further orders, for he was to accompany the robbers on their southern journey, with pack mules on which to carry provisions, blankets, etc.

He was ordered to get his breakfast, and then to pack the mules and start out on the trail that led in the direction of the New Idria Quicksilver Mines, and the Arroyo Cantua.

Those who have read the life of Joaquin Murieta, will remember that the Cantua canon was his principal hiding place and rendezvous.

To this day it is a sort of house of refuge for criminals. It is difficult of access, and easily defended, while the vicinity affords abundant feed for herds of horses.

The southern journey was commenced soon after nine-o'clock that morning.

On leaving the valley, Garcia guided the party on a trail leading to New Idria Quicksilver Mines, some sixty miles distant.

Margarita rode next; Anita followed, while Vasquez brought up the rear. All were mounted on fleet and hardy mustangs, who are most serviceable in climbing and descending precipitous mountain trails.

Pedro, the half-breed, had started on ahead with his pack animals, three in number, loaded with barley for the horses, provisions for the riders, a good supply of blankets, and a tent large enough to afford shelter for all.

Anita was an enthusiastic lover of the picturesque, wild and grand scenery of mountainous districts, and every turn in the trail disclosed a fresh view which engaged her attention and prevented her from unnecessarily brooding over her unfortunate predicament.

About six miles from the starting point Pedro was overtaken urging his pack animals over the trail, and the party passed on, Garcia giving the half-breed minute directions how to find the place where he intended to camp for the night—a spot where feed and water were abundant, some thirty miles from the rendezvous they had left. It was a little canon in the inner coast range of mountains, about three-fourths of a mile from the line of the trail which they were following.

Whenever the nature of the ground over which they were travelling permitted, Anita and her companion rode side by side, and Vasquez frequently spurred his horse to Garcia's side, to ask for information in regard to the country and its inhabitants.

Anita's education had not been neglected, although the region in which she had passed her days since early childhood afforded no facilities for acquiring anything more than a "common school education."

She had acquired sufficient knowledge of the English language to be able to converse quite fluently, and to write a tolerably grammatical letter in that language.

"Necessity is the mother of invention," the old adage says. It is true. Adversity sharpens the wits. While waiting at the rendezvous, to all intents and purposes a close prisoner, Anita had revolved in her mind a thousand plans of escape, and a thousand expedients to facilitate the escape.

It seemed to her most important to convey information of her exact situation to her friends at home.

As the time had drawn near for her to leave the rendezvous at Saucilito, and no one came near her whom she could trust to carry a message to her friends, she saw that her only opportunity for sending such intelligence would probably be a chance meeting with some stranger while en route through the mountains and plains to Los Angeles.

She knew, however, that even if the party accidently encountered any strangers on the road, Vasquez would allow her no opportunity of conversing with them alone, and she felt that the chances were that the strangers so met, unless they were numerically superior, and were armed, would be robbed and, perhaps, murdered by Vasquez and Garcia.

She had, therefore, carefully prepared a letter, both in Spanish and English, stating that she was a prisoner, and detailing the circumstances under which she had been abducted from her home.

In this letter she besought whoever should find it to either make an effort to release her from the hands of her captors, or to lose no time in conveying the intelligence of her unfortunate situation to her friends, in the county of Monterey, promising a liberal reward for the undertaking.

This letter she carefully placed in her bosom, and she concealed its existence even from her friend Margarita, trusting to chance or a kind Providence for an opportunity to place it in the hands of the first stranger she met whom she dared to trust with it.

On the day before she started with her captors for the southern country, she made several copies of the letter, so that if one should fall into the wrong hands, she would still be able to hope for a more favorable result with the others.

The precious missives, her dernier resort, she now carried hopefully in her bosom.

She had reloaded the pistol with which she had defended herself against the assault of the villain Ricardo, and both the derringers presented her by Margarita she now carried in convenient pockets she had prepared in her over-skirt expressly for them.

The possession of these weapons gave her confidence in her ability to protect herself from violence and outrage, either at the hands of the men who had captured her, or from evil disposed strangers, should she fall into the hands of such, while the consciousness of possessing the letters which might prove the means of releasing her from irksome bondage, filled her with hope, and so raised her spirits that she felt almost cheerful, and answered all questions or remarks addressed to her by Vasquez in a manner that astonished him considerably.

He began to believe that her entire submission was only a question of time, and he congratulated himself upon her apparently tractable disposition.

Soon after twelve o'clock Garcia suddenly reined in his horse, and made a gesture of silence to those behind.

They were just rounding the base of a low hill thickly covered with chapparal, and were entering upon a plain of several miles extent.

On looking in the direction indicated by Garcia, a herd of half a dozen antelopes were observed by the party. The animals were leaving the valley and moving toward the trail and the hill in a direction that would strike the trail perpendicularly within fair rifle shot of where the party were halted.

A strong breeze was blowing from the valley directly in the face of the travellers, and the animals did not scent their presence.

Garcia and Vasquez hastily dismounted, and bending low so as to conceal their movements, cautiously moved forward to a position that would give them a good shot, and when the antelopes reached the trail, both men discharged their rifles simultaneously, and brought down two fine specimens, while the balance of the herd sprang off and were instantly hidden in the brush.

The game was quickly flayed, and the choicest portions of the carcasses cut off; and securing the meat behind their saddles, the robbers remounted, and the party pushed on toward the spot selected by Garcia for their first night's camping-ground.

They arrived about four o'clock in the afternoon at the point where the trail must be abandoned to reach the camping-ground.

Halting long enough to break some twigs from the manzanita bushes through which the trail passed, and drawing a line on the ground to indicate to Pedro, when he should reach the spot, what directions they had taken, the party moved toward the mountain, and in half an hour reached the luxurious pasturage where they were to camp for the night.

They had ridden some thirty miles with scarcely a halt for the entire distance, and the females were considerably fatigued by the journey.

The camping place was selected under a spreading live-oak, and the horses, after being watered at an adjacent spring, were picketed near by in the abundant grass.

Garcia and Vasquez busied themselves for half an hour in collecting fuel to supply a camp-fire during the night, and while they were away from the spot, Anita confided to her companion the secret of the letters she had prepared, and gave her two of the documents, with instructions to conceal them in her bosom, and in case of any failure on her own part to place one of them if possible in the hands of the first friendly stranger they should encounter.

It was fully two hours before Pedro with his slow-moving pack-animals arrived in camp.

The loads were at once removed from the mules, and the tent pitched for the accommodation of the party. A blanket was stretched across the inside of the tent, separating the space into two apartments.

The females were assigned the rear room, but remained at the fire in front of the tent until supper was over.

The long, weary ride had given them all good appetites, and the savory antelope steaks, broiled on the coals, were devoured with a relish known only to them whose appetites have been sharpened by hard exercise and the invigorating life-giving atmosphere of Southern California.

Supper disposed of, the fire was allowed to die away, and the females and their escort retired to rest, Vasquez pretending to not deem a guard necessary.

Anita, now that she had a definite plan in view, though it did not promise immediate results, found her anxiety greatly allayed, and she dropped into a profound slumber almost immediately after wrapping her blankets about her, and slept soundly until morning, awaking greatly refreshed and eager to resume the journey, for she felt that every step would take her nearer deliverance.

Vasquez noted her cheerful mood with satisfaction, but Garcia viewed it with inward suspicion. His keen eye did not fail to detect the silent sympathy between the two women, and he divined correctly that there was a mutual agreement between them on a plan of action looking to the escape of Anita from their clutches.

The youth and inexperience of Vasquez led Garcia to underestimate his natural shrewdness; and while fully resolved to obtain possession of the girl by force or stratagem—if necessary, even to kill Vasquez to accomplish his object, he was so far from dreaming that the youth mistrusted his intentions that he took no note of the latter's watchful eye and quiet, wary movements; nor did he note the fact that Pedro had preferred the open air to the tent during the night.

The half-breed had rolled himself up in his blankets, and remained in the rear of the tent wide awake during the entire night, constantly alert for any suspicious movements inside the tent, or the approach of hostile parties to the camp.

This was in pursuance of an agreement between Vasquez and Pedro before the journey was commenced. Vasquez agreed to remain awake every alternate night, while the half-breed, in consideration of a liberal donation of coin from the embryo bandit, agreed to alternate with him during the entire journey.

CHAPTER V.

The ride to Cantua Canon—Hostile reception of Garcia at the Mexican house—His plot with Jose Sanchez—A surprise—Unexpected meeting with a party of Americans—Major Baldwin, "Rocky" Pettingill and One-eyed Jim—Anita's plan of escape.

When Anita stepped from the tent after a night of most refreshing sleep, the sun was just peeping over the mountains, and the morning air was filled with the grateful fragrance of wild-flowers, and resonant with the joyous carol of the birds.   No one who has not visited the State can form a just conception of the transcendant glory of a sunrise in the peculiarly favored climate of Southern California after the winter rains have ceased, and all nature is springing into fresh life with a magical vigor known to no other climate under the sky.

Anita gazed upon the glorious scene with soul filled with rapture. The golden sunlight illumining the clear sky, and warming the green foliage of the trees and the magnificent carpet of wild grass, bedecked with flowers of a thousand hues; the birds of gay plumage, warbling their sweetest notes in glad ecstacy, charming every sense, and so entranced her, that she did not note the call of her captors to the morning meal, until Margarita laid a hand lightly on her arm.

She drew a deep sigh, and slowly and reluctantly accompanied her companion to the frugal but ample breakfast rudely prepared for them.

Half an hour afterward, the horses were saddled and bridled, the pack-mules loaded, and the cavalcade was on its way to resume the southern trail.

Cantua Canon was their destination for the day, and when they reached the trail, Garcia informed them that they had thirty-eight miles to travel before going into camp; but that as they had some three hours earlier start than on the previous day, they would strike camp without fast riding, quite as early, and if no accident detained them, even earlier than they had the night before.

A brief halt was made at noon to rest the horses, and to refresh themselves with lunch, and then the journey was resumed.

Garcia, for reasons of his own, wished to avoid New Idria, and so made a wide detour, and reached Cantua Canon without meeting any strangers or acquaintances.

The mouth of this canon is a narrow defile, so easily defended, that two or three men ensconced behind the rocks, and well supplied with arms and ammunition, could prevent the passage of a regiment of men.

Some distance above, the canon widens into a broad valley or basin, dotted with spreading oaks, and the stream which wound through it, was fringed with a luxuriant growth of sycamores and willows.   On the banks of the stream were two or three Mexican houses, occupied by horse and cattle thieves.

The camp was pitched in the willow thicket near the stream, about five hundred yards distant from a Mexican house.

Pedro had not yet arrived with the tent and blankets.   Immediately after a hasty dinner, Garcia left the party, saying that he wished to hunt up an acquaintance, and make some inquiries in regard to the route southward.

Garcia went directly to the house, where he found half-a-dozen long-haired swarthy, low-browed Mexicans lounging about the place, smoking cigarettas.

As he approached the place, three or four villainous looking dogs came bounding towards him with angry and ominous growls, neither of the men making the slightest attempt to keep them off the stranger.

Garcia steadily advanced, and as the dogs approached, coolly drew one of his revolvers and deliberately shot the most demonstrative animal through the head.

The loungers suddenly exhibited some symptoms of life, and one of them had the presence of mind to whistle to the dogs and call them in.

The Mexicans drew their pistols and awaited the arrival of the stranger.

Garcia strode up to the party with a determined tread, and wearing an ominous scowl upon his face.

"Hell's furies!" he exclaimed, "do you allow your dogs to eat up every stranger who happens this way?"

"In the fiend's name," replied the foremost man in the group, a broad-shouldered, sinister-looking ruffian, cocking his revolver, and striding towards Garcia, "who are you that comes from God knows where, armed to the teeth, and shooting down other people's animals?"

As he spoke he raised his revolver, but before he could pull the trigger, the robber fired and laid him prostrate on the ground.

There was an instant clicking of revolvers, but Garcia, with a cocked revolver in each hand, exclaimed:

"Hold, you fools! I am Anastacia Garcia. Do you not know me? The next man who raises a hand will get a bullet through his brain!"

There was an instant cessation of hostile demonstrations. Pistols were replaced, and one of the party, a tall man of herculean proportions and piercing black eyes, advanced, and proffering his right hand to the robber, addressed him as follows:

"My God! Anastacia, did you drop from the skies? Indeed, we did not know you. A thousand pardons for the mistake."

"It is of no consequence, I think, was the surly reply, "except, perhaps, to your friend there,"—accepting the proffered hand, and pointing to the prostrate form of the man he had shot down.

It was found that the man was only wounded and stunned, the ball having grazed the left side of the temple, and after shaking hands with all the party, Garcia took the man whom he had first addressed one side, and the two held a long conference together.

The man's name was Jose Sanchez, a treacherous, bloodthirsty villain, who although he did not possess sufficient courage to join any organized expedition for robbery and murder, was always ready to profit by the robberies of others, and help to secrete outlaws from justice.

He had committed many robberies on his own hook, but had seldom joined with others. Being by nature treacherous himself, he committed his depredations generally with the sly cunning of the fox, and unseen by other eyes. He and Garcia had long been acquainted, and when the latter had detailed to him his connection with Vasquez, and the particulars of the abduction of Anita, a plan was agreed upon between them to steal away the girl from her infatuated lover.

In consideration of his assistance, Garcia promised to reward him well with the possession of the girl, Margarita, and a division of the proceeds of future robberies.

Sanchez held Garcia somewhat in dread, partly because the robber possessed secrets, the revelation of which would be fatal to him, and partly because of his revengeful and bloodthirsty disposition.

Anastacia was an own cousin of Manuel Garcia, *alias* Three-fingered Jack, whose bloody career under Joaquin Murieta stands in bold relief on the criminal annals of the Pacific coast.

Anastacia, who was several years younger than Manuel, had not made quite so "brilliant" a record, but was regarded as even a more dangerous foe than Three-Fingered Jack had been, for the reason that he was equally prompt with the knife and pistol, and possessed better judgment and far excelled his cousin in the art of strategy.

Since the killing of Three-fingered Jack, Anastacia had grown more bloodthirsty and relentless.

Sanchez entered with apparent eagerness and enthusiasm into the scheme proposed, which was to follow closely upon the party when it should leave Cantua Canon, and camp each night in the vicinity of Vasquez and Garcia, and after night-fall stealthily approach the camp and by a signal—the bark of a coyote—inform the latter of his presence, so that they could meet and form a plan of action.

Sanchez was to take with him one man in the undertaking.

Garcia, after suggesting to Sanchez the propriety of hinting to his friends that a visit from them to the party at the tent would not be welcome to its occupants, returned to his party.

It was nearly dark when he reached camp, and Pedro, the half-breed, had just got in.

The tent was pitched among the willows, and the tired party was soon in the arms of Morpheus—all except Vasquez, whose turn it was, in pursuance with his agreement with the half-breed, to keep awake.

He rolled himself up in the blankets, however, as usual, lying down inside of the tent as though to sleep. He listened vigilantly to every sound during the night, but nothing disturbed him.

Bright and early next morning, they were on their way to Fire-baugh's Ferry, some thirty odd miles distant, on the San Joaquin river.

The ride was monotonous after leaving the mountains and striking out on the plains, and nothing occurred to the travellers of any moment, until about two o'clock in the afternoon.

They had a gulch to cross, and as they came to the brink, they found a party of three Americans encamped by the trail beside the sluggish arroyo or creek which ran through the gully.

Anita could scarcely repress her emotions at the sudden appearance of the party, and she thought possibly an opportunity would occur to give them one of the letters she had prepared for such a chance meeting.

Garcia and Vasquez were thoroughly surprised. Since leaving the canon, they had constantly had a fair view of the plain ahead and on either side, unobstructed by timber, and had kept a vigilant outlook. Herds of cattle and wild horses had been seen, but no signs of human beings greeted their vision.

To find themselves thus suddenly and unexpectedly in the presence of an armed party of Americans, who outnumbered them, was unpleasant, to say the least.

They were startled and confused.

Garcia reined his horse suddenly back on his haunches, placing a hand on one of his pistols.

Vasquez was by his side and followed suit, while the women awaited further developments with no little trepidation.

The advent of the travellers was received by the Americans with characteristic sang froid. They were not in the least surprised. In fact, although themselves hidden from view by the gulch or little ravine in which they were resting, and in fact hidden, by whose banks they had reached the spot, they had paid frequent visits to the top of the banks, and exposing only heads and shoulders, had examined the plain in every direction for the appearance of travelers, and had detected the approach of the robbers a good hour before their arrival.

It was a characteristic frontier scene.

The Americans had picketed their horses close by the stream, among the herbage which grew there in wild luxuriance. The saddles and blankets had been removed and laid underneath a small cottonwood, the upper branches of which scarcely showed above the level of the plain.

The blankets had been spread upon the grass in the shade of the cottonwood, and using their Spanish saddles for pillows, were lounging in careless and easy attitudes. Two of them were puffing lazily at their pipes, while the third was engaged in writing.

Each man had a navy revolver and a large hunting-knife in his belt, and within easy reach a Henry rifle lying upon the ground. They were similarly attired—trousers of Kentucky jean, "butternut" color, dark woolen shirts, and brown sack coats—each wearing a broad-brimmed slouch hat of felt.

The one engaged in writing was a handsome man in spite of his unkempt hair and beard, and his uncouth attire. He was apparently about thirty-four years of age, tall and lithely built, with intelligent grey eyes, thin lips and a determined cast of features. He was known to his companions as Major Baldwin.

Laying next to him on his blanket, with hat drawn down so as to entirely conceal his brow, lazily puffing a short "dudheen," which constant use had brought to the highest possible degree of perfection in point of color, and had left nothing further to be desired in the quality of strength, was a short thick-set individual, with red shocky hair, pug nose, and short grizzly beard. His name was James Murphy, a native of Erin, but commonly known among hunters and miners as "Grizzly Jim," or "One-eye Jim"—these aliases having been bestowed upon him as memorials of a desperate encounter he once had in the mountains in Inyo county with a grizzly bear, in which he had lost an eye, but "got away" with the varmit after all.

It was the right eye, and now a hideous, unsightly scar had taken its place. To render his visage still more striking, the left eye was so horribly "crossed" that tears from that organ would flow down the right cheek.

The third individual was a long, lean and lank specimen of a New England Yankee, with sharp, intelligent, good-natured eyes, a nose of extraordinary length and sharpness, and, as One-eyed Jim characterized them, ears like a hound.

Although Major Baldwin was the junior member of his party, he was its leader. He was born in Central New York, and had graduated at the early age of eighteen at Hamilton College. Political influence had secured him the appointment of a cadet at the West Point Military Academy, and he had graduated at that institution with honor, and was now captain and brevet major in the engineer corps.

Some ten years of his life had been passed in arduous services on the plains, in a cavalry regiment, and shortly after his transfer to the engineers he had been granted an extended leave of absence. Tiring of society at home, and desiring to visit California, he had organized an adventurous party at New Orleans, and started overland, passing through Texas, New Mexico, and Arizona.

Before reaching Santa Fe the party, numbering originally twenty-two men, had been reduced by sickness and death, and through fights with hostile Indians, to ten men.

In a fight with the Apaches, in Arizona, near the present site of Prescott, in which the brave little band were greatly outnumbered, the entire party, with the exception of its leader, were killed. Baldwin alone escaped to the nearest military post.

He there fell in with "Grizzly Jim" and the eccentric Yankee above described, who was known throughout Arizona and Colorado as one of the best hunters and sagacious, intrepid Indian fighters in those territories. Joe Pettingill was his name, sometimes familiarly addressed as Joe, but commonly known among the hunters as "Rocky Pettingill"—and by his most intimate and privileged chums, "Rocky," for short.

He was an adept at following an Indian trail, or any other trail, full of strategical talent, and noted for his presence of mind and intrepid nerve in emergencies.

In his early youth he had received an excellent education, but an unfortunate love affair had soured and embittered him against society, and he had buried himself from its sight in the wilds of the Far West, in search of adventure.

After the close of the Mexican war, in which he took part, in a Tennessee regiment, he had spent some two years in the land of the

Montezumas, during which he had mastered the Spanish language as well as the vulgar idiom of the "Greasers," and acquired a thorough knowledge of the peculiarities of the peculiar race.

After a series of adventures in Arizona, the trio were moving hither and thither through Southern California, and on the day in which we introduce them to our readers, they were on their way from Visalia, on the eastern side of Tulare Valley, to Monterey, on the Pacific coast.

When Vasquez and his party appeared on the brink of the gulch, Baldwin completed the sentence he was inditing in his daily journal, closed the book, then arose from his recumbent posture, taking up his rifle, stepped forward a pace or two, and courteously addressed the newcomers in English.

There being no response, he hailed them in Spanish.

The salutation was responded to by Vasquez, who at once rode down the side of the gulch, followed by the rest of his party.

As the Mexicans crossed the narrow stream to the spot where Major Baldwin was standing, "Rocky" Pettingill and "One-eyed Jim," arose and sauntered towards the party.

The sharp eyes of "Rocky" scanned the features of the Mexicans and their female companions with a keenness which rendered the former somewhat uneasy, and filled the bosom of Anita with no little excitement.

Unconsciously, almost, she instinctively divined his character. In those searching eyes she read wonderful intelligence and shrewdness, and in the sharp lines of his face she found tenacity of purpose, and saw honor marked in indelible characters on his bronzed features.

Her eyes rested but for a single moment upon the striking visage of One-eyed Jim, and then she encountered the glance of the Major. She was pleased with his handsome, manly features, and his noble and courteous bearing.

Her heart beat tumultuously with hope, and it required an almost superhuman effort of the will to conceal her agitation. As she was not immediately addressed by either of the strangers, she had time to fully recover from her agitation before Major Baldwin politely invited the party to dismount and camp with him for the night, at the same time giving Anita an inquiring glance, and courteously asking if she was not fatigued with the journey.

Anita gracefully replied to the kind invitation, and signified her desire to accept it, acknowledging that she was indeed fatigued, and would gladly halt and rest.

Vasquez, by nature polite, affable and gentlemanly in his deportment among either friends or strangers, also responded courteously, and dismounting from his horse, removed the saddle and secured the animal with a lariat to a small sapling; saying, that although they could not camp there for the night, they would rest for an hour and then resume their journey.

He then assisted Anita and Margarita to alight, and picketed their horses, while Garcia looked on with a sullen scowl. He was evidently displeased and angered at the arrangement.

Pettingill had divined the true character of the robbers at a glance, and he had not failed to note the agitation of Anita.

He felt, instinctively, that something was wrong. Both he and the Major noticed that Anita was ill at ease with her companions.

Vasquez had no reason to think that the Americans had any suspicion of his true errand, and felt at his ease among them. He was an acute judge of character for one so youthful, and he saw nothing in the manly countenances of Baldwin or Rocky to give him any uneasiness.

The grotesque visage of One-eyed Jim simply amused him, and somewhat excited his curiosity.

He entered into conversation with Baldwin, and won the good opinion of him as well as of Rocky and the scarfaced Irishman, who took no part in the conversation.

Garcia only spoke in monosyllables, but kept an eye on everything that took place.

Rocky noticed the robber's watchfulness, and felt an intense desire to unravel the mystery of his connection with so fine a looking young man as Vasquez and his handsome female companions; for although several years older than Anita, Margarita possessed more than the average share of female beauty.

Yielding to his strong desire to penetrate the mystery of Garcia's watchfulness, he made a pretence of looking after his horse and left the group, giving a quiet signal to One-eyed Jim to follow.

In a few moments the Irishman joined him, and he at once communicated his suspicions and a plan he had devised to separate the two Mexicans from the women.

His plan was to manage some way to get Vasquez's and Garcia's horses stampeded, and he asked One-eyed Jim to exercise his wits to that end.

"Divil take me," said Jim, "if I see how it's to be done without bein' seen be that murdering thafe that looks for all the wurruld as if he'd ought to be strung up to the nearest saplin'. His snaky eyes watch everythin'."

"Well," replied the Yankee, "you can go on down the stream, until you are out of sight beyond the bend. Then you can climb up out of the gulch, and sneak up opposite the horses, and get clear to the bank above them without being seen. Then, seems to me, while I get the ugly looking devil into conversation you can slip down and cut the lariats so nearly in two that the slightest pull will break them. Then return up the bank, and fire your rifle, or if needs be you can come tumbling over the bank as though by accident. Be careful to keep your face concealed from the animals until you have weakened the lariats, for I think that a sudden view of that all-fired scar of yours would frighten them into conniption fits."

With a grunt of disapproval of this shallow attempt at witticism at the expense of his features, One-eyed Jim assented to the proposition, and at once entered upon the execution of the delicate job, while Rocky Pettingill sauntered back to the party and engaged Garcia in conversation, by asking him for information in regard to the route to Monterey, and the camping places in the intervening mountains.

So artless was the cunning Yankee, so apparently free from guile, that the robber's reserve wore off rapidly, and he was soon conversing almost as freely as Vasquez was with the Major. The women had withdrawn to a shady spot several yards distant, leaving the four men in conversation between them and the horses.

Rocky had produced a jack-knife from his pocket, and as the conversation progressed, he whittled away most industriously on a piece of tough cottonwood, adroitly managing to get the Mexican's back turned from where their horses were feeding.

Happening to refer to some locality in Mexico where he had been, Garcia became so interested that his whole attention was absorbed, and he plied the willing Yankee with innumerable questions.

Rocky plunged at once into the midst of a most thrilling account of a pretended adventure of his with some brigands in the state of Chihuahua.

CHAPTER VI.

THE MACHINATIONS OF GARCIA—PLOTS AND COUNTERPLOTS—HIS INTERVIEW WITH SANCHEZ—A STARLIGHT TRAGEDY ON THE TULARE PLAINS—GARCIA AND VASQUEZ SURPRISED AND CAPTURED—BLOODY DEATH OF SANCHEZ AND PEDRO, THE HALF-BREED.

THE MAJOR, who did not have the slightest inkling of the game his subordinates were playing, listened with amazement to the blood-curdling yarn which was holding the Mexicans as though they were spellbound.

Just as Rocky had brought his fictitious story to its most exciting climax, and the Mexicans were listening with intense interest, his thrilling narrative was rudely interrupted by a most unearthly scream or yell of anguish, that startled the group as though a 15-inch shell had exploded in their midst.

The Mexicans were for a moment fairly paralyzed by the suddenness of the alarm; Major Baldwin's surprise was thorough. Hastily grasping his rifle, he sprang in the direction of the sound, followed by Rocky.

The terrified females, clasped in each other's arms, added to the confusion by their shrill screams, while the horses of Vasquez and Garcia, mad with terror, broke their lariats, and plunged snorting up the canon, at the height of their speed.

Springing forward to where the horses had been tied, One-eyed Jim was discovered writhing and twisting about on the grass at the foot of the bank, emitting groans and cries of anguish, and indulging in a series of agonizing facial contortions, that almost made the straight black hairs of the Mexicans to stand erect, and filled Major Baldwin with alarm.

"For God's sake, Jimmy!" he howled, "what's the matter?"

"Howly mither of Moses!" howled Jimmy, "Captain, but I'm kilt entirely. It's stung be a rattlesnake I am; bad coss to the day I iver left the ould sod, and came to this thavin' country. Och, hone! Captain, dear, can't ye do nothing for me?"

"Where are you bitten, man?" demanded the Major.

"In me leg, captain; jist here in me ankle," answered One-eyed Jim, clasping his left ankle convulsively, and howling with pain.

The Major and Rocky bent over the prostrate form, and while the Major was endeavoring to remove the boot, Rocky contrived to post him on the fact that the Irishman was only playing a part.

Although he could not understand their object, the Major had sufficient confidence in his two companions to believe that their purpose was a laudable one, and he assisted Rocky to carry the supposed dying man back to the spot where the group had been camping when the yells of the Irishman had so suddenly broken in upon their conversation.

The Major and Rocky busied themselves apparently in ministering to One-eyed Jim.

The Mexicans followed them, and were for a few moments at a loss what to do.

Rocky at once tendered them the use of horses to follow those stampeded; but Vasquez politely declined the offer, saying that they could use the horses ridden by Anita and her companion.

The Major said he would render them any assistance in his power, were it not that the condition of One-eyed Jim demanded the immediate and constant attention of both himself and Rocky.

Garcia did not at all like the idea of leaving the females, and giving Anita perhaps an opportunity to inform the Americans of her situation and implore their assistance.

But he had full confidence in the loyalty of Margarita, and believed the Major and the Yankee to be gentlemen who would not seek to meddle with the women.

So he and Vasquez saddled the horses of the women and followed the trail of their fleeing animals.

The two Mexicans had no sooner disappeared than Rocky hastened to Anita and her companion.

He found them pale and trembling with anxiety, and hastened to explain to them the nature of the sudden alarm, and inform them of the escape of the horses, and the absence of Vasquez and Garcia in their pursuit.

As Anita began to comprehend the situation, her eye brightened, and she resolved to at once throw herself upon the protection of the strangers.

With an imploring and tearful gaze into the honest countenance of the intrepid ranger, she appealed to him for assistance.

"Senor," she said, "I am in trouble. Can you not—you and your friends—can you not help me?"

"I thought as much," replied Rocky, "and I am not often mistaken. It was to give you an opportunity to speak to us, that I planned the stampede of the horses."

"Oh, senor, thanks—a thousand thanks for your kindness! I am, indeed, in trouble. I am a prisoner, torn from my home, and compelled to travel against my will. God only knows to what fate I may be subjected if you cannot aid me."

"Rest assured, senorita," replied Rocky, "you are among brave hearts and true, and you may rely upon our protection."

"Lest we be interrupted," replied Anita, "here is a letter I had prepared, that in case of a chance meeting with strangers and no opportunity, such as this, occurred, that I could speak, I might, at least, contrive to hand them the writing. It gives my name, and that of my parents in Monterey county, and the name of the man who has thus abducted me."

Rocky seized the letter and placed it in his pocket.

"What do you think we had better do?" he said. "Shall we take you now, and on the return of the villains bid them begone?"

Here Margarita interposed.

"I have been thinking, senor," she said, "and I have some suggestions."

"Let us have them, dear Margarita," replied Anita, "for you are doubtless wiser than I, and better know the dangers that surround us."

"Well," replied the girl, "should the Americanos rescue us now, it would be impossible for them to return directly to Monterey county. The country is infested with desperadoes, and though they are not now organized under any one leader, they are men who will temporarily co-operate in any villainous enterprise. Should Vasquez and Garcia return here and find us in the hands of the Americanos, and that these brave men were determined to restore you to your friends, within twelve hours they would raise a force that would retake us, and they would murder the Americanos, and perhaps ourselves, as mercilessly as they would kill a coyote."

"What can we do, then?" rejoined Rocky—"what do you propose?"

"I hardly know," replied Anita; "but if it is possible to follow our trail, and by strategy separate us from our captors, and effect our escape to some town without giving them any clue to the direction we have taken, I think it would be best."

One-Eyed Jim now made his appearance and put an end to the conversation. He had ascended to the plain, was now returning to inform them that Vasquez and Garcia had recovered their horses and were returning, and were now only about a quarter of a mile distant.

Rocky bade the women be of good cheer, assuring them that a most determined attempt would be made to rescue them from their captors.

He then, himself, laid all the facts before Major Baldwin, and together they opened and perused the letter indited by Anita.

While they were reading the letter Anita came hurriedly up to them, and handed Rocky two other copies of the writing; one for the Major and the other for One-Eyed Jim, saying that, in case any casualty should separate the Americans, each would possess the record of her name and residence, and the particulars of her abduction.

She then retired to her friend, Margarita, so as to excite no suspicion in the minds of her captors.

In a few moments the Mexicans returned with their horses, and as considerable time had been wasted in their capture, Vasquez insisted on camping where they were for the night.

In cutting the riatas or lariats, One-eyed Jim had ingeniously mutilated them in such a way that the Mexicans had no idea that a knife had been employed, or that the stampede had been the result of deliberate design.

Garcia was opposed to camping with the Americans, but finally allowed himself to be over-ruled, and yielding a reluctant consent, unsaddled his horse, and busied himself with mending the broken lariat.

Vasquez dismounted, and after paying a brief visit to the women to see that they were provided for, remounted his horse and struck out on the trail they had passed over in the morning, to meet Pedro with his pack mules, expressing a fear that he might have experienced some difficulty in following the trail, on account of the many cattle trails and trails of wild mustangs, which ran in every conceivable direction.

He met Pedro some three miles back on the trail, and returned with him to camp.

On the way Pedro informed his master that he suspected the party was being followed. About half an hour before the arrival of Vasquez he had discerned two horsemen coming in the direction of the Cantua Canon.

Vasquez could find nothing in that circumstance particularly suspicious, though he enjoined the utmost vigilance upon Pedro, whose turn it was that night to keep awake and watch.

Pedro was subjected to the same rigid scrutiny that Rocky had bestowed upon his predecessors, but the Yankee could not penetrate the stolid countenance of the half-breed, or make a satisfactory mental analysis.

Major Baldwin took a lively interest in the intrigue, and had determined to exercise the utmost vigilance in guarding against any attempt at a treacherous surprise on the part of the Mexicans, and, if possible, to outwit them, and release the prisoners.

After the supper was over he held a quiet consultation with his two companions, and the result was that One-eyed Jim was directed to remain awake during the entire night, and promptly give the alarm should the Mexicans make any suspicious demonstrations.

The Mexicans, with the two women, retired, as usual, to the tent, Pedro alone remaining outside, rolled up in his blankets, apparently to sleep, but in reality to watch.

The Americans camped a few rods distant, One-eyed Jim lying down by the side of the others, rolled up in his blankets as though to sleep.

And so, though each was to all appearances profoundly sleeping, and the camp wholly without a guard, in reality each party had a most efficient sentinel.

About midnight the ominous hooting of an owl was heard some distance down the gulch.

Pedro thought nothing of the familiar cry, and made no note of it.

The quick ear of One-eyed Jim, however, accustomed to all the voices of nature, and familiar with the various ruses incident to frontier life, detected the skillful counterfeit in an instant, and cautiously waking the Major, who lay next to him, bade him listen.

The cry was repeated, and the Major, in turn, called the attention of Rocky to the sound.

The precaution was unnecessary, for Rocky was already awake, and had also detected the fraudulent imitation of the night bird.

The three Americans were now on the alert, and with breathless interest awaited the result.

There was no moon, but the sky was cloudless, and the starlight, shining down through an atmosphere of wonderful clearness, relieved the gloom sufficiently to enable sharp eyes to discern the outlines of objects in the canon, and to reveal any movement that might be made.

Anita remained awake for a long time, tossing to and fro with anxiety, but finally the demands of nature became inexorable, and the wearied girl fell asleep.

In less than a minute after the signal had been given, the vigilant eye of Grizzly Jim detected a movement at the tent, and called the attention of his comrades to the phenomenon.

A human form was seen to slowly emerge into the starlight, and peeping cautiously about, glide silently and stealthily from the spot and disappear in the shadow of the opposite bank.

A moment later the form appeared revealed against the sky, crawling snake-like over the bank, and disappearing on the plain.

The instant the midnight prowler vanished from the view of those who were watching his movements with such curious interest, One-eyed Jim began to detach himself from his blankets to follow his trail, but was stopped in the very first motion he made, by the hand of Rocky Pettingill laid heavily on his arm.

"Hist!" cautioned Rocky, in a low, earnest whisper. "Don't move yet. That black devil that lay outside the tent has just unrolled himself from the blankets, and is crawling after the man who left the tent. Wait until he gets up the bank, and then follow."

A moment later, Pedro appeared on the bank, and then vanished precisely as Garcia, whose movements he was shadowing, had done before him.

Then One-eyed Jim left his companions, and swiftly and silently followed.

So quietly had all these movements been made, that even the horses tethered only a few yards distant, did not detect them, and the supreme silence had been unbroken by the slightest sound.

Crawling a rod or two from the bank, Garcia arose to his feet, listened for a moment, and then gave the answering signal.

It was responded to immediately, when Garcia, having now got the exact direction from which the signal had been given, cautiously moved that way.

Pedro followed his movements as closely as he dared, while One-eyed Jim, who did not care to watch the motions of Pedro further than to keep posted as to his whereabouts, so that he might avoid a collision, now certain of the general direction Garcia was taking, made something of a circuit, and soon gained a position almost opposite the robber, and quite as near to him as Pedro, who was following on his heels.

There was little difficulty in avoiding discovery, as the plain was tolerably thickly covered with the growth of greasewood, a shrub something like the sage brush of the alkali plains, and which here grew to a height of from two to four feet.

Bending low to prevent detection, and keeping almost opposite him, One-eyed Jim proceeded carefully for about twenty rods, when Garcia halted, and looking cautiously on all sides, emitted a low, peculiar whistle, which was responded to almost instantly by some one concealed in the brush just ahead.

Dropping on all fours, the wily Irishman wormed his way through the brush in time to hear the first salutations between Garcia and Sanchez—for it was Sanchez and his confederate whom Pedro had seen following the trail the day before, and who were now on hand according to the compact entered into with the treacherous robber, whom he had signalled for the purpose of holding a consultation.

Garcia lost no time in useless circumlocution, but immediately posted Sanchez on the present situation. The latter did not at all like the presence of the white men, and expressed his unqualified disapprobation of the want of caution shown in camping with them.

He suggested that an attempt be made immediately to gag and bind Vasquez, and leaving him to be liberated by the Americans in the morning, to also gag and bind the girls and silently carry them from the spot.

Garcia placed an unqualified veto on this proposition, denouncing it as entirely impracticable as well as foolhardy. He said that it would be utterly impossible to get the horses out of the canon without alarming the Americans, who would doubtless interfere with their movements.

Besides these imperative considerations, he insisted that the attempt should be made in such a way as not to involve himself, in case of failure, in a quarrel with Vasquez. He wanted the affairs so adroitly managed as to give his fellow robbers and pupil the impression that the work was undertaken by outside parties.

After a thorough interchange of opinions, it was finally agreed that Sanchez should proceed up the canon or gulch some distance, cross over and taking the trail go on ahead and camp at a point near Firebaugh's Ferry on the San Joaquin River.

Garcia would return and sleep until morning, when the party would leave the Americans and follow the trail. He agreed to lead the party directly into the camp of Sanchez. While *en route* he would devise some plan to induce Vasquez to accompany him away from the camp on the following morning, and trust the women in the safekeeping of Sanchez and his man until their return.

This arrangement having been mutually agreed upon as the most feasible plan that could be adopted under the circumstance, Garcia started on his return.

One-eyed Jim witnessed the parting, and not choosing to precede the robber to the camp lay perdu until he began to think the coast was clear for his return, when his attention was arrested by the singular movements of the spy, Pedro.

Instead of following the wake of Garcia, that individual was actually moving cautiously toward the spot where Sanchez and his man were adjusting their saddles and making preparations for a start.

One-eyed Jim watched his proceedings with curious interest.

Pedro evidently intended either mischief to the thief Sanchez or treachery to Vasquez.

The Irishman cautiously drew nearer so as to lose no incident in the drama or tragedy about to be enacted.

Pedro disappeared suddenly from view, as though he had sank silently into the earth.

Sanchez was tightening the circha, or saddle-girth, preparatory to mounting, when the figure of the half-breed suddenly arose from the ground behind him. There was a flash of glittering steel as Pedro lifted a long sharp knife in the starlight, and in a twinkling the brawny arm descended like lightning, and Sanchez fell with a gurgling moan to earth; with a wild snort of terror the frightened horse sprang off across the plain.

Sanchez's assistant, only twenty feet distant, was in the act of mounting when his master fell. Startled by the snort of the dead man's horse, he withdrew his foot from the stirrup, and instantly turned his head, and just in time to see Pedro, the reeking knife in hand, springing toward him with tremendous bounds.

His horse sprang away, as he drew his knife to meet the onslaught.

Pedro's first blow laid open the whole left side of the stranger's face with a terrible gash, and the two instantly engaged in deadly combat.

One-eyed Jim rushed from his covert, regardless of danger to himself, so absorbed was he in the affray.

Blow after blow from each of the combatants, followed in swift succession, until at length the blows of each grew weaker and weaker.

At last the knives were dropped, and the desperate men staggered apart, and fell to the earth and expired almost at the same moment.

One-eyed Jim hastily examined the prostrate forms.

That of Pedro was already lifeless, the last blow having penetrated the heart.

The stranger gasped once or twice, and clutched wildly at the surrounding brush, and with an almost inarticulate imprecation on his lips, gave up the ghost.

On examining the body of Sanchez, it was found that the knife had entered the chest, just behind the right collar bone, and had probably severed the aorta, or penetrated the heart-sack, or the heart itself.

His death had been almost instantaneous.

One-eyed Jim was too familiar with scenes of carnage and bloodshed to be much startled at the terrible tragedy, and having fully satisfied himself that the two men were thoroughly dead, and that there were no survivors left, he hastened to report to his companions.

He returned to the camp as silently as he had left it, and communicated the bloody details to the Major and his companion, Rocky.

The affair changed the whole aspect of the situation, and the Americans saw in the death of Pedro and the two strangers a sort of providential opportunity of effecting the return of the women at once.

As they lay in their blankets they cautiously interchanged views and considered various plans of operation.

They finally came to the unanimous conclusion to rescue the women soon after daylight.

One-eyed Jim, whom nothing delighted so much as a skirmmage, advocated moving upon the enemy's works at once, arguing that the "murdherin' villains," as he called them, ought to be wiped out on general principles.

The cautious Yankee advised, when requested by Baldwin to suggest a plan of operations, that as soon as the Mexicans began to stir in the morning, at a signal to be given by himself, Vasquez and Garcia should be disarmed and made prisoners.

That important part of the programme successfully accomplished, it would be time enough to decide as to what disposition should be made of them.

It was now nearly four o'clock, and the next hour was devoted to sleep by the tired adventurers.

Shortly after daybreak the Americans were astir, the Irishman making the morning air resound with the notes of a comical Irish ditty.

His hoarse voice soon aroused the Mexicans, and in a few moments Garcia emerged from the tent, and sauntering sullenly to where the Americans were starting a fire for the morning meal, bade them "Good morning" in a gruff tone, and spread out his hands with the palms towards the flames, to warm them.

Rocky was beside him, and One-eyed Jim in a position where a single step would bring him directly in his rear.

The opportunity was a more favorable one than the Americans had expected to obtain, and Baldwin instantly gave the signal to the two men, and not stopping to witness the affair, strode quickly and as silently as possible to the vicinity of the tent.

On the alert for the signal, One-eyed Jim comprehended it instantly, and stepping in a careless manner behind the robber, still humming his ditty, he suddenly threw his left arm around Garcia's neck, at the same instant seizing his right wrist, and tripping him, drew him backward to the ground.

With a herculean effort the astonished bandit struggled to his knees with the Irishman, but the latter, although his inferior in build, was his master in strength, and in a moment had him prostrate again, this time laying him face downward.

It was the work of but a moment to disarm and pinion him securely.

Rocky hastened to the side of the Major, and the moment Vasquez stepped from the tent, he felt the cold muzzle of a cocked revolver pressed against each temple, and before he could recover his self-command One-eyed Jim had securely pinioned his arms behind, and removed his weapons.

CHAPTER VII.

Impotent rage of the captured Bandit Garcia—Extraordinary coolness of Vasquez—He takes the place of Pedro—Release of the captured robber, and restoration of Anita to her friends.

The conduct of the surprised Mexicans was as dissimilar as the actions of two men could possibly be, and afforded a good index to their characters—or rather their dispositions.

Whatever of surprise and chagrin Vasquez might have felt inwardly, his outward equanimity was scarcely disturbed. There was a momentary knitting of the brows, and a flash of fire from his gray eyes, but this manifestation was only momentary.

His self-possession was complete, and it served him well in gaining him the respect of his captors, who could not avoid a sort of feeling of admiration and of good will towards a man who could be thus cool and collected in such an exciting emergency.

When his arms and ankles were being pinioned, he simply remarked, with a quiet smile:

"You are taking unnecessary trouble, it appears to me, gentlemen. You have my weapons, and I am too small a man to contend against you even if allowed free use of my limbs; you have me in your power completely, without tying me up like a dog."

"You will not be ill-treated," replied Baldwin, "nor will you be deprived of your liberty longer than we deem it necessary."

The insane fury of Garcia knew no bounds. He howled like a madman, cursing and raving as only a demon ripe for hell could curse and rave, cursing the Americans as cowards, and calling down the direst maledictions on their heads.

He was conveyed to a clump of sycamores some distance from the tent, and lashed to a sapling.

A few moments later the cords that bound Vasquez's ankles were removed, and then he was bidden to accompany One-eyed Jim and Rocky. Jim led the way to the plain above where lay the ghastly remains of Sanchez and his man and Pedro.

On viewing the corpse of the halfbreed, Vasquez gave an involuntary start, and gazed inquiringly at his captors, turning a shade paler, and exhibiting a degree of nervousness in striking contrast with the coolness he had exhibited when the cold muzzles of the revolvers were pressed against his temples.

He listened intently as One-eyed Jim narrated the events which had taken place during the night, and as the sanguinary narrative progressed in broken Spanish, a look of intelligence gradually settled upon his countenance, and his equanimity was again restored.

"I fully comprehend the transaction," he said as the story was concluded; "but at present I have nothing to say further than that Pedro, who lies here murdered, doubtless lost his life in my service. I see I have secret enemies. Perhaps it is to my personal advantage that I have fallen into your hands."

His remarks were repeated to Major Baldwin when the three men had returned to camp.

Daring their visit of inspection to the dead bodies, Anita and her companion had left the tent, awakened from their troubled dreams by the fierce maledictions of Garcia, fearing and wondering what had happened to so arouse his ire.

They were informed of the tragic events of the preceding night, and of the summary arrest of Vasquez and Garcia, and that they were now liberated and would be kindly and courteously provided for, and if necessary guarded by the Americans to their homes.

Margarita signified her desire to accompany Anita to Monterey county, and the latter was eager to accept the proposal, and with soul overflowing with gratitude she poured out her thanks to her friend for her devotion, and to the Americans for their prompt interference in her behalf and their generous offer to guard her to the home of her kindred.

The girls at once began preparations for cooking breakfast for the entire party.

While this was being done Baldwin and Rocky visited Garcia, untied his ankles, liberated him from the tree and took him up to the plain.

As they turned and followed in the very footsteps he had taken at midnight, his face assumed a look of blank astonishment.

But when he came suddenly upon the dead bodies of Sanchez and his confederate, and the gory corpse of Pedro, he was struck dumb with surprise and fear.

He jumped to the conclusion that in some way the Americans had discovered his plans, and had ambushed Sanchez; but how Pedro came to be there, and why he himself had been missed or purposely allowed to escape, were problems he was in no way able to solve.

He fully expected that the Americans intended to massacre him on the spot, and his face became livid with terror.

Rocky divined something of the emotions that were agitating the robber, and after allowing him to view the sickening spectacle for a few moments, led him back to the camp, and once more secured him to the tree.

He indicated a wish to speak with Vasquez, but was not allowed the privilege.

Baldwin had a long and earnest conversation with Anita in regard to the manner in which she had been treated since her capture, and in what manner she wished the Mexicans disposed of.

No true woman wishes harm to the man whom she had once truly and fondly loved. Though she no longer loved Vasquez, she could not find it in her heart to consent to any steps being taken to have him tried and punished for the crime of abducting her from her home.

Baldwin was surprised at her evident desire to shield Vasquez from the punishment he so richly merited; but the ingenuous girl fully and satisfactorily explained her motives.

In the first place she acknowledged her former love for Vasquez, and the betrothal to which her parents had objected, and assured the Major that Vasquez had not offered her the slightest indignity since the abduction, but had treated her most kindly. She said she did not doubt that he had torn her from her home in a sudden fit of impatience at the delay occasioned by the opposition of her parents, and that he did so in the hope that in time she would forgive him for the wrong, and finally consent to the marriage without the permission of her parents.

In fact, she attributed to Garcia the first suggestion of the daring deed, and said that probably but for his evil influence, Vasquez would never have thought of committing such an act. The attempt at Sauci- lito to steal her from the protection of Vasquez she also attributed to his scheming. She detailed the circumstances attending the murder of Constable Hardmount, but did not choose to connect Vasquez with the deed, though in her own heart she could not doubt his complicity in the crime.

She further said there was another consideration which had weight with her in desiring that no effort be made to bring Vasquez to punish- ment. She knew him to be possessed of a most indomitable will, and did not doubt that punishment would arouse in his breast a desire for revenge that would never let him rest until he had gratified it. She wanted to leave no cause for his seeking to revenge himself either upon her or her rescuers. What became of Garcia she cared not.

Immediately after this conversation with Anita, the Major took Vasquez aside and frankly told him what he intended to do.

The young robber was in a conversational mood, and did not seek to deny the abduction, justifying himself on the ground that Anita was pledged to him, and that according to her own statement, she was subjected to the surveilance of her relatives, and by them, in a certain sense, deprived of her liberty. He claimed that his own honor and manhood demanded that he should free the girl from the durance in which she had been held; saying that when he resolved on the steps he had taken, he supposed that Anita's love would overcome her scruples, and cause her to consent to a marriage as soon as they had arrived in Los Angeles county.

Baldwin assured him that the girl was inexorable in her determination to return to her home.

Vasquez replied that he was now fully satisfied of the folly of the step he had taken, and should make no further effort to alter her determination.

Baldwin felt favorably disposed toward the young adventurer, and finally informed him that he should take both him and Garcia along with the women until the party arrived at Santa Clara county, and that if they made no trouble on the route he would there set them at liberty.

Vasquez's wrists were freed on his solemn agreement to make no attempt to scheme further against the liberty of Anita, nor attempt to escape from his captors, nor attempt to liberate Garcia.

The cords were removed from his wrists, and he was allowed the free use of his limbs, nor were his movements about camp restricted. His arms, of course, were retained by the Americans, as well as those of Garcia.

The hardened robber was kept a close prisoner, and Vasquez was forbidden to speak with him.

The young Mexican did not, however, regard this as much of a hardship, for he had grown to distrust his elder in crime; and in fact shrewdly suspected that he had meditated treachery in regard to the girl. He suspected that the events of the preceding night, in which Pedro, his own confidant, had been slain, were in some way connected with Garcia, though exactly how he could not understand.

It was a strange mystery to him that the half-breed should have left the canon. He presumed that he had heard the approach of the strangers, and in endeavoring to spy out their purpose had been discovered, and in the desperate encounter that ensued all three had met their death.

Shortly after his conversation with Baldwin, Vasquez discovered a horse peering over the bank into the canon, and calling the attention of the Major to the animal, was allowed to try and capture it.

On reaching the plain Vasquez found both the horses of Sanchez and that of his confederate, and succeeded in capturing both of them, and brought them into camp.

They were stolen horses, and Vasquez instantly recognized them by the brands as horses he had seen picketed in Cantua Canon. He had now no doubt that the riders had followed his party for the purpose of stealing away the women, and when he remembered that Garcia had absented himself from the party on the night it camped in the Cantua, he at once felt his suspicions in regard to the robber's treachery confirmed.

The entire party camped that night in the vicinity of Firebaugh's Ferry, on the San Joaquin river.

Next morning, bright and early, they were on their way to Pacheco Pass.

Baldwin had decided that it would be dangerous, if not entirely impracticable, to attempt to reach Monterey county by the trail which led through Cantua Canon and the mountains, through which the captive women had been brought by their abductors.

It was, therefore, decided to move through the Pacheco Pass to Gilroy, in Santa Clara county, thence south again through San Juan, in Monterey county, to the home of Anita's parents.

The day passed without any adventure worthy of note.

Garcia rode in sullen silence.

Vasquez was moody and taciturn, but occasionally responded to remarks addressed him by Baldwin and his two comrades.

The joy which gladdened the heart of Anita at her unlooked-for liberation, and the prospect of a speedy re-union with her beloved parents, was somewhat tempered by the knowledge that many long and weary miles still lay between her and the home of her childhood, and that many contingencies might yet arise to prevent her return.

The country was traversed in every direction by desperadoes of Garcia's type, and there was no calculating at what unlucky moment the little cavalcade might encounter a gang of Garcia's own acquaintances or confederates, who, if they recognized the captive, as they could not fail to do, would, without doubt, attempt a rescue.

In that event, what could Baldwin's small force of three men do against odds?

And then, too, she thought, even if a direct and open attack should not be made, much of the route could be easily ambuscaded.

So, in spite of the cheering assurances of Baldwin, and the efforts of Margarita to quiet her feelings by pleasant conversation, Anita felt down-hearted, serious, and ill at ease.

What to do with the captured bandits, was a problem that puzzled Baldwin more than anything else.

Anita was stubborn in her opposition to Baldwin's proposition to seek to punish her persecutors by a public prosecution, and Baldwin felt bound to respect her wishes on that point.

They camped that night, after a ride of some thirty miles, in the valley, some four miles distant from the pass, a strict guard being kept over the two robbers, and especially over Garcia.

Early next morning, after consultation with Rocky and One-eyed Jim, Baldwin decided to liberate Garcia and Vasquez.

He at once made known his decision to the robbers, and demanded a promise, "on honor," that they would make no effort to recapture the females, nor in any other way seek to molest or injure the party.

Garcia was not a little surprised at this leniency, and readily made the required promise, for he knew that if taken on to Gilroy, he would without doubt there be recognized and swung from a limb of the nearest tree for crimes that he had committed at that post.

Vasquez was permitted to retain his weapons, two formidable pistols and a rifle, while Garcia's weapons were retained by Major Baldwin, who agreed to leave them at an express office in Gilroy, to the address of "Manuel Carlos."

The two robbers then took their departure in a southerly direction, at right-angles with the route pursued by Baldwin, who pushed on with his little party through the Pacheco Pass, and camping that night in Santa Clara county, near the road leading from Gilroy to San Juan, in Monterey county.

Meanwhile, the sudden and mysterious disappearance of Anita from her home had carried dismay to all the household.

Her father and brother had been for days in the saddle, scouring the mountains and plains looking for traces of the lost one, but as days had passed into weeks without the slightest trace being discerned, a profound gloom settled upon the hearts of all, and the search was abandoned.

As stated in chapter three, Anita's relatives had concluded that she had been persuaded by Vasquez to elope, and to save the family's good name, they had foregone all search for the missing girl after the first day, and had given out that she had gone to visit some relatives in a distant portion of the State.

It had not been difficult to keep the affair from the public, as at that time the whole county was sparsely settled, the houses or cabins of the rancheros were miles apart, and visits between the families were of rare occurrence.

And so the afflicted family had borne their misfortune without the aid of a "sympathising" public.

The brother was the only one of the household who obstinately refused to accept the theory that Anita had voluntarily left her home.

The more profoundly he reflected upon her previous character and upon the circumstances surrounding the case, the more he inclined to the opinion that she had been abducted by force.

Toward the close of the second day, after dismissing Vasquez and Garcia, Baldwin's little party neared the vicinity of the scene of Anita's abduction.

All fear of being retaken had now left Anita's mind, and her heart beat high with fond anticipation of the joy her return would carry to a sorrowing household.

At her request the place was approached by the party moving in single file up the bed of the stream, down which she had been taken by Vasquez and Garcia.

When they had reached the spot where Vasquez had placed her upon the horse, the party halted, and Anita, giving him the necessary directions, the Major galloped forward to the adobe building in which the family lived, to break the news of Anita's return.

The advent of a stranger at the ranch was an unusual occurrence, and the clatter of the horse's hoofs upon the hard ground as Baldwin's neared the house, brought the entire family to the door.

The Major dismounting, stepped forward toward the group, which stood expectantly awaiting the announcement of his errand.

Naturally, his announcement that Anita had been rescued from her captors, and was even now at the Willows, sent a thrill of joy through the hearts of all.

The glad mother could scarcely speak from emotion, but amid tears and sobs, poured out her thanks to the brave Americans who had restored her daughter to her arms.

The brother flew toward the Willows to meet the cavalcade. The meeting between brother and sister may be better imagined than described.

In a few moments the happy girl was clasped in her mother's fond embrace, and during the evening she detailed to her indignant relatives each event that had transpired to her from the date of her abduction down to the moment of her arrival home.

There was very little sleep in the house that night.

The affair was discussed over and over again, and held up to the light in every attitude.

The question whether an attempt to retake the girl would be made, or to take revenge by an attack on the household was discussed thoroughly, and the conclusion was unanimous that in all probability, even if Vasquez should have no hand in the outrage, Garcia would seek to gratify his revengeful disposition either by abducting Anita, or murdering one of the Americans, and perhaps burning the roof over the family, or setting fire to their stacks of grain.

The Americans readily agreed to remain at the ranch for a few weeks and help to guard the family from the threatened danger.

The following day was spent in the rest so necessary to both animals and men after the hard journey.

Margarita, whose devotion to Anita was feelingly portrayed by the grateful girl, was received with open arms by the household, and she was soon made to feel perfectly at home among her newfound friends.

Baldwin had originally started for Monterey county for the purpose of thoroughly exploring the region with a view of locating there; and Anita's brother volunteered to pilot him during the investigation.

Day after day, Baldwin and the young man rode here and there throughout the county, leaving the balance of the party at the ranch to guard the females and property.

Some ten days had elapsed since the restoration of Anita to her friends, and although the utmost watchfulness had been exercised, especially at nights, not the slightest incident occurred to excite apprehension or alarm.

Constant guard was kept—"six hours on and six hours off"—the "tricks" being divided between "Rocky" and One-eyed Jim; and when the Major and Anita's brother were at home from their trips of inspection of lands through the county they stood their hours and relieved the Yankee and his Irish *companero*.

The continued immunity from molestation created a feeling of security in the hearts of all except Anita.

While she regretted the hardships imposed upon her American friends of exercising such constant vigilance, and standing guard every night, still she could not shake off the fear that had taken possession of her.

She felt sure that Garcia would seek revenge. As he had not scrupled to undertake a treacherous part towards his own comrade,

Vasquez, in order to steal her away, she felt almost certain that, soon as he thought everything was quiet about the ranch, and the far felt secure, he would make his appearance and work them an inju.,.

On his return from a visit to Monterey, one day, Major Baldwin sought her out, with the intention of allaying her fears, if possible, but the interview, instead of convincing Anita of the groundlessness of her apprehensions, resulted in impressing the Major himself with the imminence of the danger, and so sensible were the reasons offered by Anita for expecting and fearing a visit from Garcia, that the Major fully justified her in the position she had taken.

Accordingly he communicated his views to his subordinates, and they finally came to the same conclusion, namely, that there was greater danger now than when the party first arrived at the ranch.

The outlaws would naturally wait for time to lull the household into fancied security, and it would also require a little time to organize a party to suit their purposes.

On the evening after this consultation was held, the Major and Rocky were hunting game some distance from the house, and in sight of the house which Vasquez had made his rendezvous prior to the abduction.

As they stepped upon a slight eminence, Rocky made a sudden exclamation, and the Major, with his eyes, followed the direction in which the Yankee was pointing, just in time to see a human form, about the size and proportion of Garcia, pass swiftly into the covert of willows skirting the stream between the two ravines.

CHAPTER VIII.

VASQUEZ AND GARCIA RETURN TO SAUCILITO RENDEZVOUS—ANOTHER MARAUDING EXPEDITION TO MONTEREY—ROBBERY OF THE SAN JUAN STAGE—ROBBERY OF CAPTAIN BALDWIN AT MONTEREY—VASQUEZ'S INHUMAN MURDER OF THE POOR INDIAN BOY—MIDNIGHT ATTACK UPON THE RANCHERO'S CABIN—EXPLOIT OF ONE-EYED JIM.

WE LEFT Vasquez and Garcia skirting the hills in the direction of the New Idria Quicksilver Mines,—or rather of Cantua Canon, for they would have to pass through the Cantua to reach that point.

Garcia had started nearly twenty minutes before Vasquez, but the latter soon overtook the robber, and the two rode south a long distance in silence.

While Vasquez's previous suspicion of treachery on the part of

Garcia had been confirmed by the revelations made on the night of the starlight tragedy during which Pedro had met his death, still, under the present circumstances, he did not think proper to let Garcia know that he had made the discovery.

He had not, thanks to the courageous watchfulness of One-eyed Jim, been outwitted by the robber, and chose now to retain his connection with him for the purpose of hastening a thorough acquaintance with the desperadoes whom he aspired to command.

They fell into conversation after awhile, and Garcia manifested strong determination to seek revenge on the Americans.

Vasquez was disposed to let them alone, as they had treated him with great leniency; and he tried to induce Garcia to forego his revengeful scheme, and join him in a plan to effect a heavy robbery, the proceeds of which would put them in possession of ample funds.

Many plans were discussed by the two desperadoes as they rode along together, but they had agreed upon nothing when they arrived in the Cantua Canon, in the neighborhood of the spot where they had encamped with the captive women, and where Garcia had "put up" the "job" against Vasquez.

They remained here one night. Vasquez was introduced to a number of swarthy, greasy-looking horse and cattle thieves, but found none of the description that would suit his preconceived romantic ideas as to the material he would like to command.

Some inquiries were made in regard to Sanchez, but neither of our adventurers cared to enlighten the company as to his fate and that of his companion; and as it had been no unusual thing for those worthies to leave their companions for days and sometimes even months without giving any warning of their intended departure, nor deigning to give any satisfactory account of the adventures they had undergone during their absence, little anxiety was manifested as to their present whereabouts, or ultimate fortune and fate.

The next night found the two desperate adventurers snugly ensconced at the old rendezvous at Saucilito—the little secluded valley in Panoche Mountains, where Poncho Ricardo met his death while attempting to outrage the captive girl Anita.

Here they rested and plotted for several days, a good portion of the time being spent in wild debauchery.

During this time, Vasquez was introduced to, and made acquaintance of, some of the most noted desperadoes of the time, some of whom had figured with Joaquin, and have since met with sanguinary deaths; some languish now in the State Prison at San Quentin, and some of them are still at large, preying upon the public.

Prominent among these new acquaintances, was an overgrown creole, of mixed Indian and Mexican blood, named Juan Soto. He was just about the age of Vasquez, but would weigh nearly twice as many pounds. His features were brutal and repulsive, and cruelty was marked in every lineament of them.

Although not yet twenty years of age, this wretch had already embrued his hands in the blood of several white men, and even the "Greasers" with whom he associated were in wholesome dread of him, as they had a right to be, for he was as unscrupulous as a hyena, and had no more conscience than a South Sea Island cannibal.

Garcia seemed determined to make one more expedition into Monterey county, partly to get revenge upon the brave Americans who had rescued the captive women; partly to effect another robbery, and last, but not least, to get the woman whom he called his wife, and who possessed most of his secrets, and who was as ruthless in the pursuit of plunder as himself, and who had always proved true to him in the most trying emergencies, and with her remove to the southern portion of the State.

This woman lived in a lonely adobe cabin, on the Tuche Rancho, on the Salinas river, twelve miles from Monterey.

The final plan adopted was this:—Garcia, taking Soto and two older hands at the business, would form one party, while Vasquez with the others would constitute another.

They were not to co-operate in Monterey county, but each selecting his own plan of operation, they agreed to rob and plunder for the space of six weeks, and on a given day, meet at San Emedio, in Kern county, and from there proceed to Los Angeles county, joining their forces, and making a new organization for their future operations.

This plan was of Vasquez's own devising, as he did not wish to again put himself in the hands of the people of Monterey, nor did he wish to rouse the indignation of the people of that county by perpetrating further outrages in the vicinity of his boyhood home. He preferred, as Mark Twain would express it, to make it "sultry" for other neighborhoods, and then return and enjoy the fruits of his adventures among his old associates.

"Whom the gods wish to destroy," however, "they first make mad."

No sooner was everything in readiness for the two parties to move, than Vasquez so far modified his plans as to signify his willingness to take his men to the vicinity of Monterey, and co-operate with Garcia in one or two robberies before trying new fields.

They accordingly emerged from Saucilito and moved in the direction of Monterey. On their way thither they robbed the stage between Gilroy and San Juan, near the latter—getting some eight hundred dollars in coin, three gold, and one silver watch, besides some other jewelry. The lives of the driver and passengers were spared.

They then divided the spoils and separated, Vasquez taking his party to a secure hiding place, only a short distance from Monterey, while Garcia and his party selected as a headquarters the ranch before used as a base of operations at the time of the abduction.

The two leaders made an appointment for the night following their arrival, the meeting to take place at a low Mexican house in the outskirts of Monterey.

Shortly after dark they met as agreed upon, and discussed the situation.

There was a gentleman then living in Monterey named Baldwin, commonly called Captain Baldwin, who usually had considerable money on hand, and him the confederates resolved to rob.

They thought it the best policy to effect the transfer of Baldwin's coin to their own coffers, if possible, without spilling his blood.

Baldwin had an Indian boy for body servant, and Vasquez had been quite intimate with the lad, and assured Garcia they could trust John with the knowledge of their presence without fear of his betraying them, and he had no doubt he could induce him to rob his master and bring the money to them.

Disguising himself as thoroughly as possible, Vasquez sauntered into the town, and soon encountered Indian John on the street, and made himself known to him.

The young Indian had always entertained strong liking for Tiburcio, and the latter now had no difficulty in inducing the boy to accompany him to the house where he had left his confederate, Garcia.

Both the robbers then used all their persuasive powers to induce the Indian boy to rob his master and join them in the glorious career they had marked out.

Captivated by their specious and eloquent arguments, the dishonest little cur consented to the scheme, and signified his readiness to undertake the job that very night, as his master was attending a meeting of a secret order to which he belonged, and would not return home probably until quite late.

He left the robbers, and in less than an hour returned with a bag containing seventeen hundred dollars in coin, which he had taken from Captain Baldwin's trunk, after forcing the lock. He was eager to accompany the robbers and place himself beyond pursuit.

This, however, was no part of their plan. They told him it would not do, as it would only fasten the crime upon him. They insisted that he should return at once and injure the lock of Baldwin's room, so as to let it appear that the room had been forced open, and if charged with the robbery, to strenuously deny all knowledge of it.

They would not even allow him to retain a dollar of the money, telling him that he would be searched, and that if any money should be found upon him which he could not account for, he would be strung up to the nearest lamp or signpost.

They assured him that if he would be patient for a few days, until all suspicion had been averted from him, he could leave his master and join them, and then he should receive his proportion of the ill-gotten booty.

The boy was forced to submit to this arrangement.

When Baldwin returned from the lodge and discovered his loss, his suspicions at once rested on the Indian boy, but when he found him apparently sleeping soundly in his accustomed place, and a vigorous search failed to reveal any money on his person, or other evidence, either in his stolid demeanor, or about his clothes or room, to implicate him in the transaction, the Captain thought he had done the aborigine an injustice, and the mystery was placed in the category of those things which are "hard for a fellah to find out."

Garcia found it impossible to induce Vasquez to join him in an attack on the Americans who were guarding Anita's home, so the money stolen by the Indian boy was divided, and the two men separated, to meet in Los Angeles county.

Vasquez made immediate preparations for leaving Monterey county. He foresaw that Garcia's determination to seek revenge of the Americans would result in the discomfiture of the bandit, and he did not wish to be involved in the calamity.

Having communicated his intentions to his followers, he disguised himself as on the previous occasion, and entered Monterey for the purpose of seeing one or two old companions, whom he could trust with a knowledge of his presence, and whom he wished to convey a message to his mother.

He had scarcely entered the town, however, before he became aware that his footsteps were being dogged, and the discovery gave him a chill of alarm.

Turning down a dark alley, and threading his way among piles of rubbish, he suddenly wheeled at the sound of footsteps, and was about to fire upon the pursuer, when his hand was arrested by the familiar voice of Indian John, who spoke in a low tone, calling him by name.

The young desperado felt a momentary relief on finding that it was only his dupe that had been dogging him, and putting up his pistol, he asked the boy what he wanted.

"Me want money," replied the Indian.

"I have none to give you now," replied the robber. "As soon as the affair blows over, and it is safe to do so, you shall have your share," he added, in a surly tone.

"You lie!" rejoined the boy. "Me no believe you. Me stay with you; me go 'long with you now, till me get money."

Here was a dilemma quite unlooked for, and the robber could see no way to shake off the boy.

Without replying to his last threat, he turned and retraced his footsteps in the direction of his camp.

The boy was as good as his word, and followed close upon his heels.

At the edge of the town Vasquez stopped, and turning toward the boy, said:

"You had better remain quiet and do as I say. When you can safely leave I will come for you, and you shall join me and share the money."

"Me want money now. If you no give me money, me go tell."

At this moment the moon, which had been obscured by clouds, suddenly shone down bright and clear, rendering it almost as light as day.

The black, piercing eyes of the young Indian glittered like diamonds in the moonlight, and Vasquez read in his dusky features a look of unalterable determination.

"You are a foolish boy," said the robber; "but I suppose you have a right to the money, so here it is."

Vasquez lifted a purse from the depths of one of his pockets, and held it toward the boy.

As the latter reached out both hands in his eagerness to clutch the prize he had risked so much for, it slipped from the robber's grasp and fell to the ground.

The boy stooped down quickly, when swift as a lightning flash the treacherous, inhuman monster drew a keen, glittering knife from his belt, and seizing the doomed Indian by the scalp-lock, drove the cruel blade to the hilt again and again into the stooping form.

The first touch of Vasquez's hand upon the Indian's head instantly revealed to the poor wretch the full horror and helplessness of his situation, and almost before the knife descended, he emitted a despairing shriek for mercy that nearly paralyzed the murderer's arm.

The spirit of murder had full possession of him, however, and he thrust the remorseless blade again and again into the vitals of his victim, long after the soul had fled.

Then spurning the body with his foot, he picked up the purse.

It was saturated with gore.

Fearing that the dying cry of the Indian might have been heard in the town, the murderer hastened to his horse, which was tethered in some bushes about an eighth of a mile distant, and hurriedly mounting, he hastened to rejoin his party.

He had no inclination to sleep. Callous by nature, and already hardened as he was by his sanguinary crimes, yet the agonizing death-cry of the poor Indian boy, the victim of his remorseless treachery, still rang in his ears, and penetrated to the innermost recesses of his dark soul.

Could he ever sleep peacefully again?

Yes. "Human nature" can descend to any depth, and conscience can be completely stifled, but retribution is inevitable.

But there was no sleep for Vasquez that night.

He laid himself down, and rolled up in his blankets, but almost immediately arose and replenished the camp-fire.

Then he thought of the bloody purse, and by the lurid light of the camp-fire he examined his clothes, and found tell-tale marks of blood.

He spent the night in obliterating these bloody reminders of the dark crime.

At early daylight he aroused his followers, and bade them prepare for the southern journey.

After breakfast, he gave his men $200 apiece in gold, the party mounted, and started for New Idria by way of the old rendezvous.

Where this money was procured, the men could not imagine. They had been growing restive, and in fact were on the point of leaving their beardless leader altogether; but the jingle of his coin reassured them and they now followed him without a murmur.

The last chapter closed with the incident of Major Baldwin and Rocky discovering a human form bearing a striking resemblance to that of Garcia gliding into the willow thicket that had been the scene of the love passages between Vasquez and Anita, and from which her abduction had been effected.

The Major was for rushing forward and giving chase to the kidnapper, but Rocky interposed decided objections.

"Let us at once move leisurely to the house," he urged, "and not give the slightest sign that we have seen the reptile. To enter the thicket would probably be to rush into an ambuscade. Even if that should not prove to be the case, we could never catch up with him, or get a shot at him."

There was no denying the truth of these common sense suggestions, and the Major reluctantly accompanied Rocky to the house, where the inmates were at once informed of the occurrence.

Neither the Major nor Rocky had the slightest doubt that the man seen was Garcia, and all felt certain that mischief was intended.

Preparations were made accordingly to give him and his gang a warm reception, and the household remained up throughout the night, except Anita's mother and the girl Margarita.

The night passed, however, without further alarm, and soon after breakfast the Americans and Anita's father went to bed, to seek sleep and refresh themselves after their all night vigils, the brother remaining up to give warning in case strangers approached the dwelling.

Anita also sought her couch.

The day passed slowly away without incident, and at nightfall all were on the alert again.

One-eyed Jim was detailed by the Major to leave the building and scout about the ranch on foot, and that worthy, as soon as he emerged from the dwelling, wended his way by a circuitous route to the vicinity of the Willows.

Arrived within perhaps one hundred and fifty yards of the old trysting place, One-eyed Jim dropped upon his hands and knees and moved cautiously forward, picking his way with the utmost care so as to create no alarm.

He had arrived at a point within about twenty rods of the thicket, when he detected the sound of horses' footsteps plashing in the water and striking upon the ground and rocks in the bed of the stream.

He paused and listening intently, could hear the sound of voices in earnest discussion.

Dropping on his belly he crawled along snakelike, as close to the spot where the horseman had halted as he could without alarming the horses or rendering discovery by the riders imminent, when he again paused and listened.

To his intense satisfaction he found that he was within earshot. In fact, he could hear every word uttered.

The words spoken were few but important.

The speaker was Garcia and he was giving instructions to Soto and his other sattelite in regard to an attack upon the house about to be undertaken.

One-eyed Jim noticed a fourth horse, saddled and bridled and provided with cartiras (saddle bags for provisions) and a roll of blankets strapped behind the saddle, but no rider.

He was at no loss to understand for whose accommodation this extra animal was intended.

The horses were all tied to the willows, and the desperadoes came out from the canes, and passing within twenty feet of the prostrate and silent form of One-eyed Jim, moved stealthily in the direction of the house.

Their plan, as overheard by the scout was to enter the dwelling silently, if possible, bind and gag Anita and take her from the place. Nothing was said as to the ultimate intention in regard to her—what her proposed fate or prospective destination; nor was anything said in regard to Margarita.

In case they were discovered and interfered with by the Americans, the latter were to be shot or cut down without mercy.

In case they got away with the girl without creating an alarm, the prisoner was to be brought to the Willows, left securely bound, and the desperadoes were to return and set fire to the kitchen part of the dwelling-house, which was of wood, and as quickly as possible set fire to three adjacent stacks of grain. If practical, shoot down the inmates of the building as they emerged, and then returning to the Willows, bind Anita upon the horse provided for her, and then, mounting their own horses, make a hurried flight from the county.

One-eyed Jim was nonplussed. It was simply impossible for him to return and give the alarm. He could not reach the house without exposing himself first to the brigands, and giving them the alarm.

He felt a strong inclination to shoot down Garcia on the spot; but a moonlight aim is somewhat uncertain, and as the moon was only a little way above the horizon, it gave but a feeble light.

However, he felt pretty certain that his friends would not be found napping, and he resolved to do the very best he could do under the circumstances, and that was to wait until the desperadoes had got fairly out of ear-shot, and then remove their horses to another part of the ranch.

Accordingly, after the lapse of some ten minutes, One-eyed Jim arose from his recumbent position, and advancing to the willows, untied the horses one by one, and mounting upon one of them, led the balance by a circuitous route to a point on the opposite side of the dwelling, and about two hundred yards distant, where there was a corral known as the "Line Corral"—so called from the fact that the enclosure was formed by a line of closely planted willows, originally intended as a hedge, but which had been allowed to grow up into straggling trees.

He had made much better time with the horses than the villain Garcia and his comrades had on foot, and had turned all four of the animals into the corral, where his own, Baldwin's and Rocky's horses were, and secured the gate before the first note of alarm was given.

He had closed the gate and was springing with rapid bounds toward the house, when he saw a flash in that direction, followed by the sharp crack of a rifle.

This was followed by a half a dozen shots in rapid succession, and he redoubled his speed, exerting every nerve to lessen the distance between himself and his friends.

As soon as One-eyed Jim had left the party at the house at the direction of Major Baldwin, a brief consultation was held, as to the best plan of disposing of the remaining force.

The rear of the house commanded a more extended view of the surrounding grounds; one man was considered sufficient as a sentinel there, while the rest could guard the front.

Anita's brother was directed to go to the rear of the dwelling, and keep a vigilant watch, while the Major, Rocky Petingill, and the old man would move a little distance from the front of the building, and separating right and left so as to watch all the approaches, keep guard there until something should be heard from One-eyed Jim.

About the time this individual had secured the horses he had captured from the enemy, and had closed and fastened the gate of the corral, as above described, the young man who was guarding the rear, detected the stealthy footfalls of the approaching marauders.

There was no way to inform those in front of the building without giving a general alarm, so he possessed his soul in patience until, bending down and moving forward a few yards, he suddenly caught sight of the three forms of the robbers stealing toward the house.

They were moving nearly abreast, and only a few feet apart.

It was the first time the Mexican youth had ever been placed in a similar position, and he trembled in every limb. His arms shook as with an ague, and he could scarcely hold his rifle. It was not cowardice that unnerved him; it was something like the phenomenon usually exhibited in the case of boys, and not unfrequently of grown men, when they have their first shot at a deer or bear.

The boy was not conscious of a feeling of cowardice, but was filled with shame and a feeling of exasperation at his inexplicable weakness at such a critical moment.

With a desperate and partially successful effort to conquer his nervous weakness, he raised his rifle and taking careful an aim as he could, fired at one of the approaching objects.

Garcia, thus surprised when he thought the coast clear, gave a yell of rage and disappointment, and raising his rifle fired and shouted to his companions to open fire on the house.

CHAPTER IX.

GARCIA AND SOTO ATTACK THE AMERICANS AND ARE REPULSED— ASSASSINATION OF WARREN WILLIAMSON BY GARCIA—THE SHERIFF'S PARTY ATTACK GARCIA AT HIS CABIN ON THE TUCHE RANCHO—DEATH OF JOAQUIN DELATORE—WOUNDING OF CLAYTON, AND ESCAPE OF GARCIA—HIS ARREST IN LOS ANGELES, RETURN TO MONTEREY, AND SUMMARY EXECUTION BY THE VIGILANCE COMMITTEE.

AT THE SOUND of the rifle shots, the Major and Rocky rushed to the assistance of the boy, Baldwin directing the old gentleman to remain on guard at the front.

As they reached the side of the youth, Garcia was just ordering a charge, not knowing of the proximity of the Americans, and hoping to find the place guarded by only one man.

As soon as Baldwin and Rocky, however, opened a rapid fire with their Henry rifles, he saw his mistake and ordered a retreat.

Pouring a final volley into the little group of defenders, the discomfited bandits turned to flee in the direction of their horses—or rather where they had left the animals securely tethered in the Willows, and where they supposed them still to be.

Baldwin's party promptly returned the parting volley of the bandits, and the latter had not fled a dozen yards before One-eyed Jim put in an appearance, coming as on the winds of the wind; and in order that his friends might not mistake him for one of the foe and fire upon him, as he halted to take aim at the demoralized outlaws, he gave vent to an unearthly war-whoop, which echoed and re-echoed through the valley like the shrill scream of a locomotive whistle.

At the same instant he sank on one knee, and taking a quick but certain aim, drew the trigger, and one of the fleeing desperadoes fell to the earth.

The appalling war-whoop of One-eyed Jim, and the fall of one of their number, acted like magic on the nerves of Garcia and Soto, and they fairly flew in the direction of the Willows, where they expected to regain their horses and make good their escape.

One-eyed Jim lost no time in informing his companions of his feat in stealing the robbers' horses, and was eager to follow up the advantage.

Baldwin, however, would not listen to the idea for a moment. He called attention to the self-evident fact that to leave the house and attempt the capture of the bandits during the night would be worse than folly—it would, he said, be sheer madness; for wherever they might stop on the ranch they would hold the attacking party at a fearful disadvantage—the same advantage precisely which the Americans had just had over them when they made the attack upon the house.

The bandits were therefore left to make their retreat as best they could.

The body of the fallen desperado was visited, and it was found that the fatal bullet had passed through his heart.

Next morning the corpse was dragged to the margin of a swamp a mile or two distant, and after removing $150 in coin from the clothing, it was buried without even the formality of a coroner's jury, and left to moulder into forgotten dust.

This unpleasant job attended to, the Major left Rocky and One-eyed Jim to guard the house, while he mounted his horse and hastened in the direction of Monterey, to inform the authorities of the recent occurrences at the ranch, and to rouse out the Vigilantes in pursuit of Garcia and Soto.

After the fall of their comrade, the two robbers strained every nerve to reach the Willows.

On arriving there and finding their horses gone their consternation and wrath knew no bounds. Muttering deep and terrible curses on the heads of the Americans, they plunged on in the direction of the ranch, which had been their rendezvous.

They felt safe from the pursuit until daylight, but at once woke up their host and demanded a pair of his best horses.

The ranchero protested against this forced loan, but Garcia was inexorable, and he was compelled to furnish saddles also, and blankets.

Partaking of a hasty breakfast, the outlaws were mounted before daylight.

Garcia ordered Soto to leave the county and at once, and proceed to the Saucilito rendezvous, and await his appearance there, which he promised would be within a day or two.

Garcia himself rode in the direction of Monterey. He did not intend, in fact, did not dare, to enter the town. He wanted to visit his own cabin on the Tuche Rancho, some twelve miles from Monterey on the Salinas river. The route from where he started would lead him within a mile and a half of the town.

Garcia started in the direction of Monterey some two hours in advance of Major Baldwin.

As the robber arrived at the brow of a hill within sight of Monterey, and not more than five miles distant, he saw a horseman approaching, and desiring to avoid recognition he wheeled his horse from the roadside and spurred the animal into the chapparal, until both horse and rider were completely hidden.

Dismounting and hitching the horse to the brush, he returned to the roadside, and, still keeping concealed, he took up a position which commanded a good view of the road.

As the horseman approached, he recognized a prominent citizen of Monterey, named Warren Williamson, with whom he had had a difficulty, and against whom he had a causeless spite.

He instantly determined to assassinate him.

As the unsuspecting traveller drew near, the heartless assassin deliberately brought his rifle to his eye, and taking fatal aim, fired.

The terrified horse wheeled suddenly, and his unfortunate master, desperately wounded, was thrown to the ground.

Garcia sprang forward to finish his murderous work.

The dying man rose to his knees and attempted to draw his pistol, but received a bullet through the head from the murderer's pistol, and expired without a groan.

The wretch then explored the pockets and found eighty dollars as a reward for the brutal job.

Without any attempt to hide the body the wretch remounted and continued his journey, urging his horse forward at the top of his speed, until the trail was reached which led to the Tuche Rancho.

After getting a mile or so on the way to his destination, he allowed the jaded animal to slacken its speed.

The terrified horse of the murdered man had galloped a short distance down the road, and then stopped and neighed for several minutes, looking anxiously up the road, and on every side, as though expecting its fallen master to make his appearance.

An hour and a half later, Major Baldwin, coming over the hill on his way to the town, reined up suddenly at sight of the bloody spectacle.

The horse was standing over the corpse, and neighed piteously at sight of the new comer, but when the Major, recovering from his momentary astonishment, spurred forward and dismounted to examine the body, the dead mans' horse fled affrighted to the town, and went directly to his master's stables.

Baldwin spent but a single moment in looking at the dead body of Williamson—long enough to be able to describe his features, and to note the significant fact that all the pockets were turned inside out—when he remounted and went to Monterey at the height of his horse's speed.

He rode at once to the sheriff's office, and reporting what he had seen, procured a fresh horse, and rode out with the sheriff and several citizens to the scene of the murder.

Before going out the sheriff ordered a spring wagon to follow, in order to bring in the body.

On arriving at the spot the body was instantly recognized as that of Warren Williamson, one of the most highly respected and universally beloved citizens of Monterey.

The body was placed in the wagon, and as the mournful cavalcade entered town, and the news spread on every side that Williamson had been found murdered on the highway, the excitement throughout the community was most intense.

On the way Major Baldwin had informed Sheriff Keating of the attack made upon his party at the ranch the night before by Garcia, and the killing of one of his men by One-eyed Jim. As this information spread, the excitement became still greater, and volunteers to hunt Garcia to the death came from all quarters.

The sheriff dispatched a party of eight men to the scene of the attack the night before, with instructions to disinter the body of the slain bandit, and bring it into town for the purpose of identifying it, if possible.

A posse of twelve or fourteen men was then organized to search for Garcia. Major Baldwin volunteered his services, which were gladly accepted, and shortly after noon Sheriff Keating and his posse started for Tuche Rancho, where it was thought Garcia would be found, for not a doubt existed but that the unfortunate Williamson had met his death at the desperado's hands.

Arriving within a mile and a half of the house in which Garcia's wife lived, the posse was divided into three divisions. Four men, led by Major Baldwin, were directed to make a wide detour and approach the building from the rear; Charles Clayton, one of Sheriff Keating's deputies, with three men, was ordered to take up a position on the left of the house; while the sheriff himself was to lead the balance of the party to a position on the right.

This programme was carried out without any casualities; but when Clayton got his men into the designated position, his zeal led him to exceed orders.

He was first to reach his position, and anxious to win distinction, he instantly made a rush for the house.

The result proved the rashness of the move. One of his men, Joaquin Delatore by name, gained a side door, and attempted to kick it in when a chance directed shot from Garcia's rifle through a panel of the door, laid the brave fellow dead upon the spot.

The next instant Clayton himself received a severe wound, and fell by his side.

The two survivors sprang forward, and picking up the prostrate form of their leader, bore it out of reach, and awaited further orders from the sheriff.

The sheriff's party next reached their position, and at once opened fire upon the cabin, directing their aim at the windows and doors.

Garcia kept up such a rapid fire in return, that it was thought he had at least one or more confederates with him, and the sheriff did not think it prudent to make an assault. His plan was to keep up a tolerably brisk fire at the weak points until night, and then, if possible, drive out the inmates by bringing hay from a neighboring stack, and piling it up to the eaves of the building and setting fire to it. Baldwin's party were soon heard from at the rear, and they kept up a lively fusilade, aiming at the windows and doors.

No shots were returned from this quarter.

About five o'clock the sheriff received a bullet through the hat, and almost at the same instant one of his men named Beckwith was severely wounded.

In the midst of the confusion thus created, Garcia sprang from the front doorway, and ran at the top of his speed to the nearest timber directly in front of the house.

Although for nearly one hundred yards his flight was in full view of the sheriff's party, and half a dozen rifle shots were fired, not a bullet touched him, and he gained the timber unharmed.

Instant pursuit was made, but it was found that he had had a horse hitched in the timber, within two hundred yards of the house. He had reached the horse unhurt, mounted and ridden off on a trail known and travelled only by himself and his intimates, and as it was rapidly growing dark, pursuit was considered useless.

On entering the cabin it was found that Garcia's wife had been shot in the hand. It was supposed that she had assisted her husband throughout the affair, and several of the men were for arresting her and setting fire to the house.

The sheriff, however, interposed with his authority to prevent any demonstration of this kind, and the foiled party returned to Monterey, feeling rather chagrined over the failure with all their number to capture one individual, and when they had him surrounded at that.

Baldwin remained at Monterey that night, and early next morning returned to the ranch.

The fugitive Garcia, avoiding the main travelled road, and following trails with which he was familiar, moved all night, and a little after daylight halted to get his breakfast at a Mexican ranch.

Here he succeeded in exchanging his horse for a fresh one, and before night of that day he had joined Juan Soto, at the Saucilito rendezvous, as had been agreed upon.

Vasquez had already moved south with his three followers.

Deeming it useless to attempt to capture Garcia by following him into the mountains, and thinking it probable that he would leave Monterey for a time, and continue his depredations in other counties where he would not be recognized, Sheriff Keating prepared an accurate description of the robber, and sent copies of it to each sheriff and detective in the State, together with a sketch of some of his most wanton outrages. The sheriff's of San Luis Obispo, Ventura, Fresno, Tulare, Kern and Los Angeles counties were particularly requested to keep a sharp lookout for the assassin.

Garcia and Soto remained at the rendezvous only four days, barely long enough to recruit and make the necessary preparations, and then started on their southern journey, to join Vasquez and his party at San Emedio, according to the programme laid out when they parted in Monterey county.

San Emedio ranch is only one hundred and fifty or sixty miles south of New Idria Quicksilver Mines, but the fugitives were nearly a week in performing the journey, taking easy stages, in order to give their animals plenty of feed, and get them into the best possible condition for "business."

The two parties were united at last, however, and then began a round of debauchery which lasted for some ten days.

Tired and disgusted at length with this folly, the bandits began to lay plans for a systematic raid through Los Angeles county—Kern county at that time being too thinly settled to afford a profitable business for highwaymen.

Many were the plans discussed by Vasquez, Garcia, and Soto, who were the leading spirits in the enterprise, but it was a long time before they could agree. Vasquez proposed that the band move into Los Angeles under the combined leadership of Garcia and himself, and then divide, Garcia taking one division and himself the other, and, acting in concert, "clean out" the county as quickly as possible, and then escape into Sonora.

A vote being taken, however, the proposition was rejected, and Garcia was made leader of the entire party.

Vasquez was made lieutenant, and the party, by night marches, reached San Fernando Valley, near Los Angeles, without giving the alarm, and established a rendezvous in one of the numerous canons leading through the Cahuengo range of mountains to the plains of Los Angeles.

Garcia entertained the bold idea of undertaking to rob the bank and one or two of the leading mercantile house of the city, and on the second day after establishing the rendezvous, taking with him Vasquez and Soto, he entered Los Angeles to reconnoitre and post himself thoroughly on the "lay" of the town.

They first visited the quarter of Los Angeles known as Sonora, occupied exclusively by Mexicans, Indians, and half-breeds. They then separated and moved about the city, visiting saloons and stores, and making the acquaintance of people of their own nationality, and endeavoring to familiarize themselves with the streets and other topographical features of the town.

They met about four o'clock in the afternoon, by appointment, in Sonora, to compare notes. Soto and Vasquez noticed with some surprise that Garcia was half drunk—in fact, in a condition altogether unfit to appear on the streets, and they tried to dissuade him from venturing out again until he should have slept off the stupefying effects of the liberal potations he had imbibed.

There was no reason in the drunken wretch, however, and he once more staggered into the American portion of the town.

Soto and Vasquez followed at a little distance, and kept him constantly in sight, taking the opposite side of the streets through which he passed.

He entered nearly every drinking place he noticed, and was fast becoming loud and boisterous.

Suddenly, Vasquez called Soto's attention to the movements of a party of men who emerged with rapid steps from the Court House. There were five of them, and they appeared to be officers.

Crossing the streets rapidly, they entered a saloon into which Garcia had just passed, and the next instant they reappeared dragging the struggling form of the drunken bandit.

Supposing that he had been arrested merely for drunkenness, his two confederates followed to the jail, and there learned to their consternation that he had been arrested on a warrant from Monterey county, charging him with the murder of Warren Williamson and of the Indian boy John, body servant of Captain Baldwin.

Alarmed for their own safety, Vasquez and Soto made the best of their way out of the city, and hastened to rejoin the men at the rendezvous.

On Garcia's arrest being made known the party was filled with consternation, and it was finally resolved that the organization dissolve by mutual consent.

Neither Vasquez nor Soto had much faith in the honor of Garcia, and feared that in his extremity he would betray not alone themselves, but all with whom he had co-operated.

The camp was therefore abandoned next morning—Juan Soto and one of his men returning north to the old rendezvous. Vasquez chose to remain in Los Angeles county, while the balance of the desperadoes went to Kern county, where they separated, going in various directions.

On the second day after the arrest of Garcia, he was taken by the Sheriff and two of his deputies and placed on board a steamer at San Pedro, and taken north.

Two days after the steamer landed at Monterey, and Garcia was at once delivered into the hands of Sheriff Keating, who ironed him heavily, and placed him in the strongest cell in the jail.

The news that Garcia had been captured, and was then lying in Monterey jail, flew like wild-fire; and nearly all business was for the time suspended throughout the town.

The Vigilantes held an excited meeting that night, and a strong debate was held. A majority was in favor of proceeding at once to the jail, and breaking into the institution, drag the wretch from his cell and burn him alive.

Three or four of the members argued strenuously against interfering at all with the course of justice. They held that the effect of a fair trial, conviction, sentence and execution would be more lasting and beneficial to the community than vindictive and summary vengeance by an illegal mob. Others claimed, however, and with a good share of reason, that it would be utterly impossible to convict Garcia of either the murder of Captain Baldwin's servant or of Mr. Williamson. There was only the vaguest kind of circumstantial evidence in the latter case, and none at all of his complicity in the murder of the Indian boy. Of his killing Constable Hardmount even there was no positive proof.

Yet no one doubted his guilt, and he was known to be a robber and an assassin by profession. There was proof enough that he killed Joaquin Delatore, and shot Clayton and Beckwith at the time the posse surrounded his house at Tuche Rancho; but the sheriff had made no demand at that time for his surrender, and the courts would hold that the shooting was done in self-defense. So the advocates of lynching claimed that the only way to bring the murderer to justice, was to drag him from the jail and execute him without authority of judge or jury—thus summarily satisfying the demand of retributive justice, and making an example that would tend to check the enthusiasm of desperadoes throughout Monterey and the adjoining sparsely-settled counties.

These arguments finally prevailed, and when the vote was taken, it was unanimous in favor of breaking into the jail early next morning, and executing the criminal without the form of a trial.

The doomed outlaw presented a picture of the most abject terror.

From the moment of his incarceration in the Monterey jail, he knew that his fate was sealed. All his brute courage forsook him, and he yielded to feelings of overwhelming despair.

About midnight the sheriff visited his cell, and found him crouched like a wild beast in the furthest corner, evidently expecting to be dragged forth by the infuriated mob and hanged, as he knew he deserved to be.

Momentarily relieved by the appearance of the sheriff, he made an attempt to beg the official's determined interference in case an attempt was made to lynch him; but he was so unnerved by his emotions, that his tongue fairly clove to the roof of his mouth, and his appeal more nearly resembled the gibberings of an idiot, than the intelligible utterance of a sane being.

He was understood to ask for a trial—not with the hope of gaining an acquittal, but to give him time to prepare for his inevitable fate.

The sheriff's only response was an offer to send for a priest at once, adding that this was a better show than the wretch had given any of his numerous victims.

The sheriff withdrew, and half an hour later returned accompanied by a priest, whom he left alone with the criminal.

The man of God made an effort to arouse the wretched man from the demented condition his remorse and terror had reduced him to, but could elicit no response except abject pleas that the priest would make an effort to protect him from the mob.

Finally, thoroughly disgusted at his utter want of manhood, the priest withdrew, and could hardly muster sufficient feeling for the brute to make an appeal even to the sheriff to use his official authority to protect him from the mob.

The sheriff promised to guard the prisoner, if possible, against any effort to take him from the jail, but at the same time admitted that the feeling in favor of lynching was so strong even among the most respectable inhabitants of the county, that nothing he could do could prevent the Vigilantes from carrying their resolution into effect.

Shortly after daylight a mob of nearly two hundred men assembled about the jail, and though a strong guard had been detailed, with instructions to protect the prisoner at all hazards, the guards themselves were in league with the vigilantes, and the attempt to obey the sheriff's orders was a mere farce.

The guards were quickly thrust aside, the jail door broken in, and the trembling murderer ruthlessly seized and dragged from his cell, and in spite of his piteous wails and cries for mercy, the rope was adjusted, and he was swung up without granting him time even to utter a prayer to his God.

The body was allowed to hang until nearly noon, when it was cut down and delivered to Mexican acquaintances of the robber, who encoffined and buried it.

The execution was universally approved as the best course that could have been pursued to promote the welfare and safety of the community.

For nearly two years after the lynching of Garcia, Vasquez remained in Los Angeles county, finding employment as a vaquero, but committing several depredations on the highway, doing the "jobs" without assistance from others.

Major Baldwin, Pettingill, and One-eyed Jim will appear no further in this history. Baldwin, a short time subsequent to the events above narrated, returned east.

One-eyed Jim found his way once more to Arizona, while Pettingill fell in love with the girl, Margarita, married her, and settled down to the life of a ranchero.

Anita's parents sold their ranch and removed to Los Angeles county, where the girl was soon afterwards married to a respectable and wealthy American, and they still reside in that county.

CHAPTER X.

VASQUEZ DEGENERATES FROM A HIGHTONED HIGHWAYMAN, AND IS SENTENCED TO FIVE YEARS' TERM IN THE CALIFORNIA STATE PRISON FOR HORSE-STEALING—MURDER OF AN ITALIAN BUTCHER, AT ENRIQUITA, BY VASQUEZ AND HERDENANDEZ—MURDER OF OTTO LUDOVICI, AT SUNOL VALLEY—THE MURDERER MEETS HIS DEATH AT THE HANDS OF SHERIFF HARRY MORSE, OF ALAMEDA—THE CRIME, THE TIRELESS PURSUIT, AND SWIFT RETRIBUTION—JUAN SOTO TRAILED TO HIS LAIR IN THE PANOCHE MOUNTAINS, AND BROUGHT TO BAY—HE MAKES A DESPERATE RESISTANCE.

ON THE NIGHT of the 15th of July, 1857, Vasquez, in company with Juan Soto, made a descent upon the corral of one Luis Francisco, on the Santa Clara river, Los Angeles county, and stole—as described by the original complaint, now on file in the clerk's office of that county— "one mule of the value of seventy-five dollars, and nine horses of the value of forty dollars each; and all of the value of four hundred and thirty-five dollars, of the personal goods and chattels of one Luis Francisco, then and there being found, feloniously did steal, take, and carry away, against the peace and dignity of the people of the State of California, and contrary to the statute in such case made and provided."

This complaint was signed "Cameron E. Thorn, District Attorney."

The indictment was endorsed "A true bill, W. W. Childs, Foreman. Presented to the court by the foreman of the grand jury, in their presence, and ordered filed this 11th day of August, 1857.

"JOHN W. SHORE, CLERK.

"BY WM. H. SHORE, D.C.

"Witnesses: Wm. H. Peterson and Francis J. Carpenter."

Following is a record of the proceedings:

COURT OF SESSIONS,
Los Angeles Co., August 12, 1857.

The people of the State of California, vs. — Tiburcio Vasquez. Indicted for Grand Larceny.

On this day the prisoner is brought into court by the sheriff, being in custody for arraignment, E. Down, Esq., appearing for defendant, and O. E. Shore, Esq., district attorney, on the part of the State; and said defendant being asked his true name, said "Tiburcio Vasquez." Whereupon the indictment was read to him, and a copy thereof, with the endorsement thereon, given to him by the clerk, and being asked if he was ready to plead, the prisoner now pleads that he is guilty of the offence as charged in this indictment, and throws himself upon the mercy of the court.

Whereupon the court fixed Thursday, August 13, 1857, at 10 o'clock, A.M., to render judgment in the above cause.

On that date judgment was rendered as follows, to wit: "The judgment of the court is that you, Tiburcio Vasquez, be imprisoned in the State Prison of the State of California, for the full term of five years, now ensuing from this day." Whereupon the prisoner is remanded to the custody of the sheriff. Present, Hon. William G. Dryden, county judge, Russell Sackett, Esq., and William B. Osborne, Esq., associate justices.

The grand jury by whom the indictment was found, consisted of the following names: Luis Phillips, Jose Lopez, Manuel Costello, Cyrus Sanford, William Andrews, Santiago Carillo, C. Duconnor, R. D. Moore, O. Morgan, M. W. Childs, Vincente Lugo, J. Pritchard, Francisco M. Alvarado, James Mullally, Manuel Garfins, Damon Marchessault, and Jose Maria Lopez.

Vasquez was imprisoned in the California State Prison on the 26th day of August, 1857.

In regard to his prison life, Vasquez was decidedly reticent after his last capture. Following is correct translation of all he chose to say to the writer on the subject, Sheriff William R. Rowland, of Los Angeles, acting as interpreter:

"I was afterwards arrested in Los Angeles on a charge of horse-stealing committed in this county on the Santa Clara river. I was convicted, and sentenced to serve a term of five years in the State Prison. At San Quentin I was pretty roughly handled. The treatment was very rigorous. The discipline at that time was undergoing a reform."

He made no mention of his escape, which was effected on the 25th of June, 1859.

The various accounts of this exploit are so conflicting that I will here give a mere transcript from the private records as sent me by Captain James Towle, Acting Warden.

FIRST TERM

"Tiburcio Vasquez. Date of imprisonment, 26th August, 1857. Crime, grand larency. County of Los Angeles. Sentenced, five years.

Escaped June 25, 1859. Vasquez was nineteen years of age at the
time of his first arrival in this prison."

SECOND TERM

"Was brought back August 17, 1859, on a new charge of grand
larceny from Amador county, for which he was sentenced to one year.

"After serving his sentence from Amador county and the remainder
of his first term, he was discharged by expiration of sentence, August 13,
1863.

THIRD TERM

"Tiburcio Vasquez. Date of imprisonment January 18, 1867.
Crime, grand larceny, from Sonoma county. Sentenced four years.
Discharged per Act of Legislature June 4, 1870.

"During his imprisonment he escaped twice.

"On June 25th, 1859, on opening the lower prison wall gates at
4 o'clock, P.M., forty-two Mexican prisoners made a break. They were
employed in the brick yard. After passing the gate they took the gate
keeper and overseer, bound them and took them toward San Rafael.

"September 27, 1859, one month and ten days after he returned,
he with others seized the schooner *Bolinas*.

"April 2, 1861, implicated in inciting a break. Vasquez stands
well among the old prisoners. I cannot find on inquiry among them,
that he ever showed the 'white feather' here.

(Signed)   "JAMES TOWLE,
                                      "Acting Warden.
"San Quentin, Aug. 22, 1874."

Vasquez, in his statements made to his captors, claimed that his
career as a highwayman did not begin until after his return to Monterey
county from State Prison. He says:

"At the expiration of my time, I returned to Monterey county,
and resided with my mother, voting in that county. The fact of my
having been tried, convicted and sentenced to the State Prison caused
the people of the county to look upon me with suspicion. This treatment made my position peculiarly disagreeable. To escape from the
persecution of enemies, I went to a remote part of the county and went
to work on a ranch. Even there my reputation followed me, and the
shortcomings of others cast suspicion upon me, to the extent that an
attempt was made to arrest me, which I successfully resisted. No
blood was shed, and I escaped. All these facts are well known in
the county of Monterey, and can be easily proven. From this time I

commenced my career as a highwayman.

"It would be almost impossible for me to remember all the robberies I have committed. The first that comes to my recollection is that of a Jew whom I robbed as he was crossing the Soledad river, on his way to San Juan. I left him his pack and his horse, satisfying myself with his pistol and his purse.

"The affair passed off as follows: I saw the Jew approaching at a considerable distance, and stationed myself on the upper side of the wood, concealed in the brush. On the arrival of the Jew, I stepped out into the road, and the moment I confronted him he drew a pistol. I assured him he mistook my intention; that I simply wanted to buy some of his goods, and showed him some money with which to pay for them. Satisfied that I was telling the truth, he unpacked his horse to exhibit his wares, and in an unguarded moment I succeeded in taking advantage of him and disarmed him. Then I obliged him to give up his money. I then mounted my horse, and recommending the adventurous Israelite to ruminate on the mutability of human affairs, galloped away.

"I will pass over a period of ten years. In the long series of events embraced in that period I was never in the prosecution of my robberies obliged to take life.

"Some three years ago, Sheriff Henry N. Morse, of Alameda county, whose heroic adventures in my pursuit the newspapers of late have been full, desirous of capturing me, wrote to Tom McMahon, of San Juan Bautista, in Monterey county, who, through his relations with the creole (native Californian) population of that region could best serve him, to inform himself without delay in regard to my movements and whereabouts, and to notify him (Morse) with all possible dispatch.

"This coming to my ears, I determined to teach Tom a lesson, because, in his capacity as merchant, I thought he was travelling out of his way to injure me, who had always befriended him. Learning that Tom was going to Salinas to pay his taxes, I took occasion to stop him at a convenient point.

" 'How are you, Tom?' said I.

" 'Very well, friend Tiburcio,' he replied.

"I then inquired if I had ever done him any harm. He replied that I had not. I then told him what I had learned of his underhanded dealings with Morse, and that I proposed to repay him in his own way.

"Upon being called on to deliver, he handed over his coin and a fine improved Colt's revolver. I then informed him that I wanted a fine ring that ornamented his handsome hand. To this he rather objected, but on being informed that I would stand no nonsense, he made a virtue of necessity, and he and the ring parted company. I then told him that I was no assassin, I would make him a present of his cowardly life, which he was by no means loathe to accept, with permission to jog on with his fine buggy and horses."

During the period between his release from San Quentin, at the expiration of his second term, and his reincarceration from Sonoma county, Vasquez resumed his wild life, associating with Tomas Redondo, *alias* Procopio, *alias* Murieta, *alias* Red Dick, a nephew of the infamous Joaquin Murieta, and a notorious horse and cattle thief, and with Juan Soto, a more ferocious villain, Roderiguez, Faustino Lorenzano and others of the class, and committed many high-handed robberies and outrages, and innumerable lesser depredations.

Within two months after his dismissal from prison, Vasquez robbed a fish-peddler on the San Joaquin, and although closely pursued by officers, effected his escape.

Most of the time during 1864, Tiburcio and his confederates vibrated between the New Almaden, the Guadaloupe and the Enriquita Quick Silver Mines. One of the most notable of their crimes was the murder of an Italian butcher, in the latter part of that year. The butcher was found one morning in his shop at Enriquita, with a bullet hole through his head, and several knife wounds in his throat and breast. Some $400 in coin, known to have been in his possession, was missing. At the coroner's inquest, held on the body; Vasquez—the only Californian who could talk English with fluency—was employed as interpreter. The verdict was, that the "deceased came to his death from a pistol bullet, fired by some person or persons unknown."

A few days afterward, Captain J. H. Adams, sheriff of Santa Clara county, received information which led him to believe that the murder was committed by Vasquez and Faustino Lorenzano. The evidence was not sufficient to warrant an arrest, and immediately after the inquest the two scoundrels mysteriously disappeared.

Immediately after his discharge from San Quentin, June 4, 1870, Vasquez began operations on a more extensive and systematic plan than ever, joining his old associates Soto and Procopio. The counties Alameda, Santa Clara, Monterey and Fresno were chosen as their theatre of operations. Stages were robbed, farmers plundered, horses and cattle run off in rapid succession. Sheriff Harry Morse, of Ala-

meda, and Adams and Harris, of Santa Clara, made repeated attempts
to capture the depredators, but without success until the Spring of
1871.

On the evening of January 10th, of that year, as an Italian named
Otto Ludovici, who was acting as bookkeeper for Jake Scott at his
store in Sunol Valley, Alameda county, was about closing the store
for the night, a Mexican entered and purchased some liquor, and left
immediately.

In a few moments two others entered. One of them drew a pistol,
took deliberate aim at Ludovici, and fired. The ball penetrated the
left breast of the unfortunate clerk, and he sank to the floor in the
agonies of death. A bystander rushed from the apartment, and as he
was passing through the doorway a shot was fired, which passed
through one of his hands. To save himself from further attack he
fell prone to the ground and feigned death.

The ruffians, after ransacking the store and securing what coin they
could find, took their departure in a direction calculated to elude the
officers, whom they knew would, within a few hours, be on their trail
in hot pursuit.

On the following morning Sheriff Morse was informed by a telegram of the outrage, and at once instituted measures to apprehend the
murderers.

Taking with him Deputy L. C. Morehouse, of San Leandro, and
Deputy Ralph Faville, of Pleasanton, and accompanied by Sheriff
Harris, of Santa Clara county, he followed the trail of the outlaws all
through Coast Range and Inner Coast Range, but without success.

Morse and Faville then returned.

It should be born in mind that Sheriff Morse, through various
means of his own devising, makes it a point to keep pretty thoroughly
posted as to the localities of haunts frequented by desperadoes of this
character, and has, through a series of eventful years, with indefatigable industry and subtle forethought, the most minute and apparently
trivial details as to the personnel of the organized bands, and the
habits of life and individual characteristics of the members.

Hence it was that a critical inspection of the tracks and "signs,"
the evident direction from which the murderers had approached the
store, taken in connection with the manner in which the outrage had
been perpetrated, afforded him a clue to the identity of the murderers,
and established their identity in the mind of the sheriff, without a

doubt. It only remained to circumvent their almost matchless cunning, and bring them to justice.

Constant vigilance for months was at length rewarded with positive intelligence as to where the villains were hiding. One of the murderers, Juan Soto, was ascertained by Sheriff Harris to have fixed his headquarters at the old rendezvous of the gang, at the little secluded valley in the Panoche Mountains, about one hundred and thirty miles from San Leandro, and some fifty miles southeast from Gilroy, in Santa Clara county.

Sheriffs Morse and Harris, Officer Theodore C. Winchell, of San Jose, and a few reliable men, fully armed and equipped, composed the party. It was organized in two divisions, with instructions to rendezvous at the Mountain House, in Pacheco Pass.

After a brief rest at this point, a guide was procured, who led the party through a wild and desolate region to Los Banos Canon, from whence a borregero (shepherd) was induced to accompany them to a position on one of the elevations of the Panoche range of mountains, from the objective point of the sheriff's place of operations.

In the valley directly beneath, and between the party and Saucilito, were three Mexican houses, and Morse advised that the inmates of these houses be taken possession of, so as to preclude the possibility of their failing in the object of the expedition, by giving the alarm at the headquarters of the brigands.

The second guide having performed the duty required of him, prudently returned to his pastoral avocation, not wishing to draw down on himself the wrathful vengeance of the bandits by an exposure of the aid and comfort he had extended to the enemy. Here Morse again divided the party, to one section of which he gave instructions to secure the inmates of the furthest house; Harris, with three men, was to attend to the middle house. Taking with him Winchell alone, Morse made a descent upon the nearest house.

The accompanying diagram will give a sufficiently accurate idea of the scene of the unexpected meeting between the intrepid sheriff and the redoubtable brigand, and serve to illustrate the details of the desperate rencontre which ensued.

Morse and Winchell arrived at a point opposite the corral, near the southern angle of the enclosure in which the house and corral were situated, without being discovered; and there they came suddenly upon a Mexican, who was attending to some duty about the corral.

DIAGRAM OF THE SCENE.

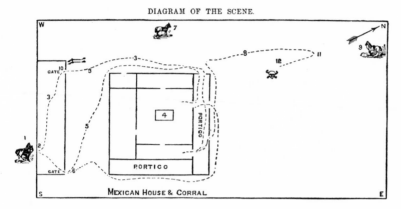

EXPLANATION.—1, Point where Morse and Winchell left their horses; 2, Where the Mexican was at work; 3, 3, 3, Their route to the house; 4, Where Soto was sitting at a table when discovered by the Sheriff; 5, Scene of the desperate encounter between Morse and the brigand; 6, Point from which Winchell fired upon the brigand as the latter turned to escape; 7, Point where Soto's first horse was fastened; 8, Soto's line of retreat toward his second horse (9); 10, Point where Harris and Morse met, after the latter had regained his Henry rifle, and from which the rifle shots were fired; 11, Point reached by the brigand when struck by the first shot; 12, Where Soto fell, killed by Morse's second shot.

Morse dismounted, secured his horse, and approaching the man, asked him for a drink of water. The Mexican at once, unsuspectingly, led the way to the house, followed closely by the sheriff who, with a lack of precaution wholly inconsistent with his habitual forethought, left his Henry rifle slung from the horn of his saddle.

Meanwhile, Winchell had dismounted, and overtaken Morse and the Mexican, the three passed around the west and north corner of the house, and stepped upon the portico together. The Mexican entered one of the middle rooms, followed by Morse, who, as he crossed the threshold, discovered three men sitting at a table; in one of whom, to his infinite surprise, he recognized the murderer of Otto Ludovici!

Instantly covering the outlaw with his revolvers, Morse ordered him to throw up his hands. Not a muscle moved in response, and not a lineament of Soto's impassive features revealed the slightest emotion, save in the deadly, indescribable regard with which he gazed full in the eye of the stern representative of the law.

The order was three times repeated without effect. With his un-occupied hand, the sheriff drew from a back pocket a pair of hand-cuffs, threw them upon the table, and ordered Winchell to place them upon Soto's wrists.

At this critical moment, a muscular Mexican Amazon sprang upon the sheriff, and seized his right arm, a desperado grasped his left, while Soto, as quick as lightning, sprang behind one of his men, and uttering a fierce imprecation, drew one of his pistols.

With a herculean effort, Morse threw aside his assailants, and dis-charged with pistol over the head of the man behind whom Soto had ensconced himself; but his aim was uncertain and the discharge merely knocked off the outlaw's hat. This "misscue" left the chances decid-edly in the brigand's favor, who would now have the first shot.

Finding the enemy closing in upon him from all sides, Morse sprang suddenly through the open doorway and gained the north corner of the portico, where he wheeled only to find himself covered by a re-volver in the hand of the now thoroughly aroused and desperate villain.

A further retreat was imperative, and was successfully effected. Passing swiftly around the western angle of the building and gaining a point about half way between it and the corral, where there was plenty of elbow room, the sheriff again wheeled and resolutely advancing upon the brigand, opened fire upon him with his revolver.

The response was instantaneous, and the contest became to the last degree exciting. Soto was a man of consummate nerve and reputed to be a "dead shot," and his failure to hit his antagonist seems astonishing. The sheriff brought all his resources of mind and muscle into action, and proved himself master of the situation.

Fortunately he had been thoroughly informed as to Soto's style of using the pistol, which was to raise it above his head, bring it suddenly down and pull the trigger the instant the weapon reached the line of sight. Availing himself of this knowledge, Morse intently watched every motion of his opponent, and by the exercise of an agility and nerve almost incredible, dodged down exactly at the right moment, and by these "tactics" successfully eluded every shot.

The necessarily rapid execution of these manoeuvres rendered it next to impossible for him to get a certain aim, and it was not until four rounds had been exchanged that a shot took effect—the ball striking Soto's revolver underneath the barrel, and wedging itself into the joint or hinge that forms the fulcrum for driving home the rammer.

It is probable that the shock for a moment paralyzed the bandit's arm, for he turned instantly and sprang toward the house. Meanwhile, Winchell had come around near the east corner of the corral with a double-barrel shot-gun, heavily loaded with buckshot, one barrel of which he now fired at the retreating desperado, but without effect.

Morse then ran for his Henry rifle at the top of his speed. Up to this time Soto had worn, from the commencement of the fight, a soldier's blue overcoat, and he now manifested his strategical talent. Running quickly around the corner of the house, he re-entered the room, threw off the coat, and compelled one of his men to put it on, secured two revolvers, and ran toward a horse hitched to a tree standing opposite and a few rods distant from the end of the building.

Sheriff Harris had heard the first shot, and spurring his horse down the slope to the scene of the combat, witnessed the fight during his approach. Reaching the corral, he threw himself from his horse, and seizing his Spencer rifle, rushed forward to the assistance of his brother officers.

Mistaking the man in the overcoat for the brigand whom he had seen fighting with Morse, he "drew a bead" upon him, but was checked by Morse, who by this time had regained his rifle, and detected the brigand's clumsy ruse at a glance.

Meanwhile, Soto's horse had become frightened at the firing, and had broken away, and Soto was making rapid strides toward a second horse, which stood hitched, ready saddled and bridled, in the north corner of the enclosure.

He had arrived at a point about one hundred and fifty yards from the officers, when he was struck in the right shoulder by a ball from Morse's Henry rifle. The wounded wretch staggered for a moment, and then turned and faced his enemies. Harris fired with his Spencer, but missed his aim; and Soto, with a revolver in each hand, his devilish eye gleaming with the appalling courage of desperation, advanced toward his assailants.

Moving forward a few paces, Morse steadily raised his rifle to his eye and fired. His aim was fatal. The rifle-ball struck the bandit in the centre of his forehead, crashing through the brain, tearing away the whole top of the skull, and laying him dead upon the ground.

On examining the body, it was found that Morse's first shot had struck the right shoulder blade and passed entirely through the right breast.

The writer recently addressed a letter to ex-Sheriff Harris, enclosing a sketch published at the time, the account being substantially as above. Following is the reply, giving a graphic description of the fight as seen by that officer:

CALAVARAS VALLEY,
Nov. 26, 1874.

DEAR SIR:—Your letter of Nov. 9th, enclosing an article clipped from the Alameda *Gazette*, descriptive of the pursuit and killing of Juan Soto, by Sheriff H. N. Morse, was received in due time.

I have carefully read the article for the first time, and must say that it is the most correct version of that expedition that I have seen in print—in fact, it is correct in every particular, save two of little or no importance. Winchell was not an officer in San Jose at that time, but was a farmer, residing on his farm about six miles east of that place. Morse did not procure my assistance in that matter; it was quite the reverse. I made up the company, and wrote Morse to accompany me, as I had information that there were parties in the Panoche Mountains that he wanted. Morse planned the attack in the Saucilito Valley, and is entitled to all and even more credit than the article in the *Gazette* gives him. I was in sight of the house, and about five hundred yards distant when the first shot was fired. Sam Winchell first rushed out of the house, then Morse, followed closely (they were not more than fifteen feet apart), by Soto, who immediately fired at Morse. I thought Morse was surely hit, for his body went almost to the ground; but, quick as a flash, he sprang erect and fired. Soto, advancing with a bound, brought his pistol down to a level and fired again, and Morse going through the same manouver as before. This was continued for three or four—I think four rounds, and I firmly believed Morse was hit every time. The shots were fired in quick succession, Soto advancing on Morse every time he fired with a leap or bound like of six or eight feet, with pistol held above his head, landing on his feet, his body erect, bringing his weapon down on a level with Morse's breast, and then firing. After firing he never moved until he had re-cocked his pistol and was ready for another shot, when, tiger like, he would spring at Morse again. Soto fired the first shot after they came out of the house and Morse returned every shot. There was about the same interval of time between each shot, Morse firing while Soto was re-cocking his pistol. Morse was retreating to his Henry Rifle, and Soto was pursuing until he received Morse's last shot, when he wavered like he was hit, and then ran into the house. What happened after this you have accurately described, except, I might add, that when he received his death shot he was advancing on Morse and myself with a five-shooter in each hand, and one in his belt. Soto was a perfect type of the desperado, over six feet high, well proportioned, and quick as a cat, with a countenance the worst I ever saw in a human face. I never shall forget how he looked in that terrible encounter, as he emerged from the house, bareheaded, with long black hair streaming in the wind, his face covered with a full beard, dressed in a soldier coat, the skirts flying in a stiff breeze from his stalwart form, and he armed with two revolvers—and his murderous action, taken altogether, completely filled my mind's eye of a real desperado.

Very respectfully,

N. R. HARRIS.

Soto was of mixed Indian and Mexican blood; stood six feet, two inches in his stockings; had straight black hair, and heavy, bushy eyebrows; was of muscular proportions, and weighed over two hundred pounds. The sinister expression of his malignant countenance gave some indication of the turbulent passions and the utterly heartless and bloodthirsty character of the man. His eyes were of that nameless hue which can only be approximately described by comparing them to those of a wild animal. His whole aspect was so ferocious as to inspire even his own people with dread.

He had committed many murders and other outrages, and was considered one of the most dangerous men in the State. He had served two terms at San Quentin. A few years since Deputy Sheriff McElroy, of Santa Clara county, attempted to arrest him at New Almaden Mines, when he fired twice at the officer, and effected his escape. Some six or seven years ago he and four others robbed the premises of Charles Garthwaite, near Pleasanton. They bound and gagged his wife, and left her in that condition, after ransacking the house for valuables. One of the party, Manuel Rojox, after having been arrested and confined in the jail at Petaluma, was taken out with his irons on by some of his friends. He was hunted down by a constable from Bogoda, whom he resisted, and from whom, after the exchange of a few shots, he escaped. Sheriff Morse succeeded in ferreting out his whereabouts, and telegraphed to the authorities at Marysville, who arrested him and lodged him in jail. He was afterwards convicted and sent to the State Prison.

After securing the horse and pistols of Soto, and leaving his inanimate form to the care of his friends, Morse and Harris pushed on with their party to the robbers' headquarters, where they captured all the Mexicans whom they found—among them the notorious cattle-thief, Gonzales, who had escaped from the authorities at Santa Cruz.

CHAPTER XI.

Vasquez's and Procopio's flight to Mexico and return—Another leaf from Vasquez's autobiography—Robbery of the stage between Gilroy and Pacheco—Sheriff Wasson captures Vasquez's outfit—Vasquez desperately wounded by Roberts—Capture of Procopio by Harry Morse—Vasquez and Chavez winter in Soladad Canon—They return and make their headquarters at Abdon Leiva's cabin, in Cantua Canon—The robbery at Firebaugh's Ferry.

A portion of the present chapter will be devoted to Vasquez's own account of certain adventures of which he seemed to be particularly proud, and which, although colored to suit his own fancy, are quite as interesting as any accounts I can get of them.

He says:

"Having resolved to rob the stage between Gilroy and Pacheco, I took position with two men in a narrow lane, making an opening in the fence. I arrested all parties coming in either direction in advance of the arrival of the stage. Taking them under some oak trees, I tied their hands behind their backs.

"Finally, when the stage approached, I saw it was covered with a multitude. However, I determined to take the chances. The coachman obeyed my order to turn and drive through the opening in the fence and halt under the oak trees.

"The passengers asked if it was life or money that I wanted. I replied that I only wanted their money. One senorita in the coach had burst into tears, and taking off her watch, and a twenty dollar piece and some small coin from her pockets, tendered them to me. I politely told her to keep them. She begged me not to injure her husband; I asked her to point out her husband, which she did, and I made him take his seat alongside of her. The balance of the party were all tied, and some four hundred dollars taken from them.

"Then telling them that I was going to bring up the balance of my party, I galloped off with my men, having realized quite as well as I had expected to.

"This adventure took place in broad daylight, and in a thickly-settled neighborhood. Doubtless, many of the party whose pockets were lightened upon that occasion, will remember the transaction.

"Four miles beyond where I left the stage coach, on the main road, I met two parties in a spring wagon, father and son, whom I stopped in order to effect a forced loan, in which I succeeded to my own satisfaction, and the great surprise of the people who were laboring in the neighboring fields.

"Five miles further on we went to a house for water, and I asked the boys who were with me whether we should go to the mountains or strike across the country to intercept the stage from Gilroy to San Juan Bautista. They decided upon the latter plan; but people who had been robbed in the morning had already alarmed the country, and as we approached Gilroy, I saw parties coming who got sufficiently near to recognize us, and open fire upon us; whereupon we found it convenient to change our course and strike for the mountains, successfully eluding our pursuers, and making good our escape.

"We then directed our course along the mountain range to those hills lying immediately around Monterey. I spent several days on a ranch, resting, amusing myself with dancing, etc., with the senoritas.

"Here I was attacked by Sheriff Tom Wasson, and a party of fifteen men, who captured eight of my horses and outfit, including my arms. I escaped, of course, on foot. I struck into the mountains and lay perdu for more than a month, during which I succeeded in renewing my mount with the best of horses, saddles, etc.

"By this time all the parties that had been following me, with the exception of that led by an American assassin named Tarpia (since, for the murder of a woman recently hung) had returned to their respective homes. I now turned my steps in the direction of the Gavilan mountains, and then passed through the large towns of Natividad, Salinas, and Watsonville to Santa Cruz, travelling only at night, inasmuch as times were very "calky."

"These events occurred two years and eight months ago.

"I remained at Santa Cruz some days unrecognized, when my presence became known to L. T. Roberts, the marshal. One night early, as I was riding through town with one of my companions, a resident of the place, Roberts emerged from a house to halt us. I was on the opposite side of my comrade, when Roberts sang out,

"Stop!"

Reining my horse back, and wheeling toward him, I sang out,

"Never!"

"Simultaneously we exchanged shots. His bullet struck me under the right arm-pit, passing out back near the spine. Mine struck him in one of the legs. My companion and myself succeeded in gaining a secure hiding-place in the mountains, where my wound—at first exceedingly painful—soon healed, and I was once more ready for business."

Shortly after the killing of Soto by Morse as detailed in the preceding chapter, Vasquez and Procopio, thinking the country was getting too hot for their safety, concluded to emigrate to Mexico. The proceeds of a couple of robberies, and $500 given Vasquez by one of his brothers, a respectable citizen of Monterey (at one time a justice of the peace), gave them the necessary funds—the $500 from the brother on the bandit's solemn promise to never return to California. Vasquez professed regret that he had brought sorrow on his relatives, who were living respectable lives, and vowed that he would never return to the State.

Within three months both Procopio and Vasquez returned to San Francisco, the former staying in the city to revel in the society of some female friends, but the latter soon striking out for the mountains. His excuse to his brother for the violation of a solemn agreement was that soon after his arrival in Mexico he was conscripted into a Mexican regiment, and was obliged to appeal to the American consul at Guaymas to effect his release; that the consul then told him that he had best leave the country at once and return to California, as he was liable to be conscripted at any time, and perhaps it would be impossible to again effect his release.

Procopio was shortly afterward captured by Sheriff Morse in a San Francisco restaurant, tried and convicted of grand larceny, and is now serving out a fourteen years term at San Quentin. Barzellas, one of the gang, was, about the same time, shot and killed by the officers in Santa Cruz. Roderiguez and another were captured, tried and convicted of robbery, and sentenced to a term of ten years. Afterward he died at the prison from drinking an excess of pure alcohol.

Vasquez now associated with him a young Mexican, in whom he had full confidence, and was as desperate as the former chief, Soto, but who exercised better judgment in emergencies, and who was faithful in carrying out the plans laid down and mutually agreed upon. This was Cleovaro Chavez, and who, since the capture of Vasquez, has himself organized a band of cut-throats, and at this time is ravaging portions of Southern California.

Chavez is about five feet, eleven inches in height, and is very muscular, weighing over two hundred pounds. His complexion is rather light for a Mexican, and he has gray eyes, short whiskers on the side of the lower jaw, small goatee, rather thin, bloodless lips, teeth regular and well preserved, a scar on one cheek, caused by a fall from a horse—a small angular cicatrix—black hair, worn rather long; short thick neck.

Vasquez, while visiting from ranch to ranch, in the mountains, enjoying himself with the senoritas and their friends, sent Chavez to San Francisco by rail, where he purchased a saddle, bridle, and a pair of revolvers, with which he returned and reported.

The two then started for King's river, with the object of robbing the stage which crosses the ferry; but it so happened that they over-slept three consecutive nights, and the vehicle passed them while they were sleeping. They concluded to abandon the enterprise and retire.

As they were crossing the plain on their way to New Idria, they saw two men approaching in the distance, carrying portmanteaux on their shoulders. They stopped and robbed the travellers of a watch, and some twenty dollars, and their penknives.

They then crossed the mountains to San Benito, stopping to await the arrival of the stage at a point about a quarter of a mile distant from the Relay House. When the stage arrived they stopped it, and compelled the passengers to get out and lie down on the ground in such a position that they could not observe their operations. Having effected the robbery, and leaving the passengers tied, they remounted and proceeded in the direction of Tres Pinos.

After travelling some three or four miles, they came upon two wagoners unhitching their teams. These men they also robbed in the same manner they had the stage passengers.

A little further on they overtook a wagon and two men, whom they also robbed.

When within two miles of Tres Pinos, they passed through an open-ing in a fence and moved in the direction of Monterey.

Having crossed the mountains and the Salinas river, they penetrated the mountains at a point fifteen or twenty miles from Monterey, and rested for some days on a ranch. Subsequently they moved eastward along the mountains towards Los Angeles, and reaching a ranch known as La Posa de Chane, they remained for twenty days among their *friends.*

Crossing the mountains to the edge of the Tulare plain, and skirting the mountains continually, passed through San Emedio, and entering Tejon Pass(took up their quarters in Soledad, where Vasquez made himself known to every one by the name of Ricardo Cantuga, there being no one in the neighborhood that knew him except one of his brothers.

He was well received, and soon gained the good will of all the rancheros living in that section, moving about openly and associating with the people. He spent several months there, and claims to have become the most popular man in the neighborhood, taking part in all the amusements of the people.

At length their funds, with which they had been quite liberal, began to get low, and Vasquez and Chavez, with a view to refilling their depleted purses, determined to return to Cantua Canon, organize a force, and renew their former exploits on their old stamping-ground.

Stopping at the ranch of Abdon Leiva, at Chilaro, they asked that worthy to suggest some place where they could perpetrate a remunerative robbery, he to accompany them on the expedition. He indicated a place not far distant, where they could steal one hundred head of cattle, and sell them in New Idria.

Vasquez replied, with a sardonic smile, that his business was not cattle-stealing, and he and Chavez abruptly rode off in a northerly direction, passing through various ranches and settlements, looking for a "job," but finding none. Parties were already looking for them, and they hid themselves away until the searchers got wearied at their ill-success, and returned to their homes.

The next move made was the raid upon Firebaugh's Ferry, on the San Joaquin river, in Fresno county. For this purpose, Vasquez returned to the house of Abdon Leiva, where he found two men who had previously co-operated with him, a Frenchman named August de Bert, and Romulo Gonzales, who agreed to go on the expedition under his leadership, making, with Leiva, five in all.

Vasquez informed the party that he had information that there was about $30,000 to be had in the place. Accordingly the gang proceeded to Firebaugh's, took possession of the place, and tied some ten or twelve men. At the same time they seized a stage which arrived, and tied the driver. Entering the house of a merchant, Vasquez found the wife in bed. Discovering the robber the woman arose and asked:

"What is the matter?"

"Nothing," replied the robber.

"Where is my husband?" cried the lady.

"He is out in the store," was the response.

"I am going out to look for him," said the woman.

Vasquez suggested that as she was in her night clothes she had better remain quiet.

She persisted in going, however, and upon finding her husband tied, she threw herself by his side, embracing him with frantic grief and many demonstrations of affection. Then raising her eyes to Vasquez, she exclaimed, with tears:

"You certainly are not sufficiently bad to take from me that watch which my husband gave me in the days of our first love?"

"No, madame," replied the robber; "I am not so very bad;" and handed her the love token. One of his men suggested that he should not return it to her, because it was a jewel of much value. [Vasquez says: "When I returned the lady her watch, which was worth about three hundred dollars, the husband said: 'This man has given us back a valuable watch. Go and get mine and give it to me.' She brought, and handed me a watch, probably worth one hundred dollars, and then got into bed, and I turned the 'captain,' as we called him, loose."]

Vasquez replied in a lofty manner that he commanded, and ordered the man to be silent. At the request of the woman the husband was untied.

The robber remarked to him as he led him to his wife's room:

"Captain, if you've got any concealed weapons here, don't use them, or you'll be the victim of my companions' fury. All that we want is money."

"Very well," was the reply; "I will obey you in everything."

Vasquez then ordered him to take the key to his safe and go with De Bert and Chavez and open it, cautioning him to see that no accident happened, as some safes were so fixed as to produce an explosion if improperly tampered with.

The contents of the safe were brought to the robber, and the men were ordered to return to their positions; then turning to the merchant, Vasquez said:

"Captain, I am very sorry to take this money. I came here upon information that Mr. Miller had made a deposit of thirty thousand dollars. And now I must bid you good night."

The robbers then galloped away, and returning to the house of Leiva in the Cantua, made that their headquarters for some time.

Vigorous efforts were made to find them, and spies were out in almost every direction for weeks, forcing them to remain perdu until the excitement subsided.

One evening Leiva visited New Idria, and while there got into a quarrel and fired upon his opponent, and shot a bystander. Efforts were made to arrest him, but he effected his escape and returned to the headquarters. Threats were made by citizens of New Idria to go out to his place and hang him, on a charge of stealing cattle, complicity in the Firebaugh affair, the wounding of this man, and other crimes and misdemeanors. These threats coming to his ears caused him considerable uneasiness; but they were never carried into effect.

Meanwhile Vasquez had established a liason with Rosaria, Leiva's wife, and he took extra pains to court the good will of the husband. She was by no means a beauty, being rather short in stature, inclined to enbonpoint, and badly pock-marked. She was vivacious in disposition, however, generous and rather romantic, and fond of adventure.

One day at Vasquez's suggestion horses were saddled and Leiva, his wife and the bandit chief rode off to New Idria. On entering the place he met three of the leading men, bitter enemies of Leiva. Vasquez directed Leiva to speak to the one who had made the attempt to arrest him, while he (Vasquez) would address a man named Arthur and a physician.

Arthur came up and shook hands with Vasquez, saying that what Leiva had done was of no consequence. The citizens of New Idria did not wish to be disturbed, and had no disposition to trouble Leiva or his friends and associates.

"That is all right," replied the robber. "I give my word to that effect."

Arthur then invited the two robbers in to drink with him, and the invitation was accepted.

Passing through German Camp, Chilian Camp, to what is called Mexican Camp, the party remained there over night, and the following night, spending the time in debauchery, and on the next morning returning to "headquarters."

On their return they found that the Frenchman, August de Bert, had left for Mexico.

Leaving Leiva and Chavez, Vasquez rode off to the ranch of Lorenzo Vasquez, and there succeeded in persuading Teodoro Moreno, his own first cousin, to join himself, Leiva, Chavez, and Gonzales, in a raid on Snyder's store, at Tres Pinos. The robbery had been discussed between Leiva and the others, and the unexpected withdrawal of De Bert had delayed operations.

Vasquez returned to Leiva's on the following day, and two days afterward Moreno joined the party, and for several days various plans were discussed, and arrangements made for the robbery.

Leiva, in spite of the assurances of Arthur and others at New Idria, that he should not be molested if he let the people of the town alone, had no faith in their promises, but thought that so soon as Vasquez and his confederates should leave him unprotected, he would be liable to attack at any moment. He was anxious to get away from that portion of the country, and therefore entered heart and soul into the scheme of robbery. He constantly expressed these fears to his confederates, and urged them to be patient until he could dispose of his property, and be ready to fly with his family as soon as the robbery should be effected.

Vasquez advised him to sell out cheap, and promised to escort him to the other side of the Colorado river.

Having succeeded in selling out the ranch, Leiva's wife and children were started on their southern journey in a wagon, and with a fine herd of stock. The family were placed in charge of a son of Joaquin Castro, and the entire party accompanied the family and stock to the San Joaquin plains, on the 23d of August, 1873, where the wagon turned south, and Vasquez, Chavez, Moreno, Gonzales, and Leiva, separated to proceed by separate routes and meet at Martinez Springs.

From thence they proceeded with Indian-like cunning, in the night, and separately, to the vicinity of Tres Pinos, arriving at a secluded spot about daylight on the 26th.

Vasquez says:

"I made it a special condition that Abdon Leiva should take command for the occasion, because it became necessary that he should go into the place in the daytime, reconnoitre, and make the necessary dispositions, and that I would make my appearance at night.

"At five o'clock of the evening of the 26th, I sent Leiva and Gonzales ahead, with orders that they should enter the town, take a few drinks and smoke a few cigars, and ascertain the inmates of Snyder's store, and they were not to do anything until my arrival.

"They started, and in a short time I sent Chavez, and about dark I followed with Moreno."

His statement, however, was not corroborated at the Moreno trial, nor that of his own, and taking into consideration his vanity, his story in regard to giving the Chilaroan command is generally regarded as exceedingly "thin."

CHAPTER XII.

THE RAID ON TRES PINOS—WANTON MASSACRE OF LEANDER DAVIDSON, GEORGE REDFORD AND BERNAL BERHURI, BY VASQUEZ AND MORENO —FLIGHT OF THE MURDERERS TO THE LOWER COUNTRY—LEIVA DISCOVERS HIS WIFE'S INFIDELITY, AND RESOLVES TO BETRAY HIS CONFEDERATES.

THE POINT selected by the maurauders for a hiding place during the day, was only about a mile and a half from Snyder's store. The bandits had, besides some provisions, a quantity of whiskey, with which to fortify their peculiar kind of courage.

At near nightfall, Vasquez announced that the time to operate had nearly arrived, and ordered the party to clean their arms. The arms were carefully attended to, and then the horses saddled and bridled.

Vasquez ordered Gonzales and Leiva to start ahead, saying that himself, Chavez and Moreno would stay back, and rob the New Idria stage. Leiva and Gonzales were to see how matters were arranged about the place, and were directed not to attempt any "business" until the arrival of the balance of the party; when they arrived they would tie up every one in the store and hotel.

Vasquez directed that any one who should resist or attempt to run off should be shot down.

Vasquez was dressed in a sack coat, with red flannel lining, white shirt, black vest, beaver pants of blue-black color, and had on Leiva's black slouch hat. Chavez had a cloak, black vest, white shirt, pants with a dark stripe down the outside seams, and Moreno's black hat. Gonzales had a light summer coat over an old coat, and had on a pair of overalls. Moreno was dressed in a gray suit, and wore a "comforter" of a variety of colors about his neck, and wore a white broad-brimmed slouch hat, with a black band. Leiva was dressed in old pants with stripes, and an old United States regulation overcoat, a flannel shirt, and a hat much like Vasquez's.

Vasquez was armed with a Henry rifle (fifteen shots), and a large navy revolver, with cartridges and a knife, a formidable weapon, which he had manufactured of reliable steel, by a friendly blacksmith. The rifle was slung muzzle downward from the horn of the saddle. The revolver was carried in a holster attached to a belt around his waist, and hung at the right side, while the knife was carried in his left breast. Chavez was armed with a double-barrel shot-gun, heavily loaded with buck-shot, and a dragoon revolver and an old revolver. Gonzales had a dragoon revolver. Moreno had the same kind of a weapon, with a white handle, and Leiva was armed with a Colt's revolver.

At dark the robbers left their hiding place together, until they reached a watering place. Vasquez led a mule he had stolen the previous day, on which to pack a portion of the plunder.

From this point Leiva and Gonzales went on ahead, according to the programme, taking the New Idria stage road to the store, while Vasquez, Chavez and Moreno remained behind.

There were ten or twelve persons in the store when Gonzales and Leiva rode up, hitched their horses in front and entered, asking for drinks. The stage had just arrived, and people were calling for their mail matter.

They drank beer twice, and then took cigars. They had been there some fifteen minutes, when Moreno came up, tied his horse, and entering the doorway drew his pistol. At the same time, Gonzales and Leiva drew their pistols, and Moreno ordered the people to lie down. Part of them had gone out with their letters and papers, and there were only six or eight remaining. Taken by surprise, those present obeyed the order, and when one raised his head or made a motion to arise, one of the scoundrels would knock him on the head with the butt of a revolver.

Handing his pistol to Leiva, Moreno proceeded to tie the hands of the unfortunate victims, and while he was doing this, Vasquez and Chavez put in an appearance, Vasquez demanding,

"Are you fellows through?"

Receiving a negative answer, Vasquez ordered Gonzales out, and Moreno and Leiva finished the tying, after which sacks were placed over the astonished prisoners' heads, and they were laid face down-ward—the "considerate" Leiva placing blankets under those who complained of the uneasy position.

Vasquez soon entered, rifle in hand, and Chavez ordered Moreno and Leiva outside.

At this juncture a Portuguese sheepherder, named Bernal Berhuri, came along, and was ordered to halt, and not obeying was shot dead by Moreno.

A teamster, named George Redford, coming up with his team, was ordered to halt. Not knowing what was up, he did not obey, and was shot dead by Vasquez.

When this occurred Leander Davidson landlord of the hotel adjoining the store, took the alarm, and attempted to close and fasten the front door, and had got it partially closed, when a shot from Vasquez's rifle entered his breast, and he fell back into the arms of his wife, expiring almost instantly.

Andrew Snyder, the storekeeper and postmaster of the place, was then taken to his house, and at his direction his wife brought out and gave to the robbers a drawer in which was their money and other valuables to the amount of over two hundred dollars.

The robbers then re-entered the store, and Vasquez took a suit of clothes, and deprived the clerk, John Utzerath, of a valuable gold watch and sleeve-buttons. Moreno packed up provisions, and the rest took various articles of clothing, a silver watch, and two saddles from the stables.

The robbers packed the mule with the provisions and the clothing, and about eight o'clock mounted, and taking with them from the stable seven valuable horses, began their flight up the San Benito creek. About fifteen miles from the store, Vasquez's horse gave out, and he mounted one of the stolen animals, and the journey was continued through night, the desperadoes arriving at the house of Lorenzo Vasquez (not a relation, though a "warm" friend of the bandit chief), between fifty and sixty miles distant from the scene of the outrage.

Tiburcio reconnoitered the premises, and finding no strangers about, ordered the balance of the party up, and they all had breakfast, and rested and fed the horses. The property taken at Snyder's was divided behind the stable. Moreno took a pair of pants, coat, and forty-five dollars and twenty-five cents, a knife and comb; Gonzales took a coat, and Vasquez sold him a vest for two dollars and fifty cents, and a watch for twenty dollars. Vasquez took the jewelry, remarking, "I am a lost man; and care not who sees it on me." Leiva took two coats, a pair of pants, and some cloth. Vasquez took a gold watch, a vest, coat, pants and hat, assigning as a reason for taking the watch that he was chief, and besides had done more than the rest in having killed two men.

Moreno then bade good-bye to his guilty comrades and rode off. Abdon Leiva, Vasquez, Chavez, and Gonzales then left the San Benito together, travelling southerly fifty miles to Buena Vista Lake, in the south-western portion of Kern county, where Gonzales left them in the direction of Bakersfield, on Kern river, Vasquez, Chavez and Leiva going on to San Emedio, where Leiva had directed Joaquin Castro and his son to await him with his wife and the horses.

After a short rest Chavez and Vasquez went on with the horses, and early next morning Joaquin Castro, receiving a share of the stolen property, took his son and returned north, while Leiva and his wife pushed on for Los Angeles by way of Tejon Pass. They joined Chavez near Fort Tejon, stayed that night at a Spanish ranch, rested next night at Stone Station, and on the following day joined Vasquez at Elizabeth Lake.

Two days after Vasquez, Chavez, Leiva and his wife and children moved on to Chico Lopez, and on the next day went to Jim Heffner's. These last two places frequently afforded a refuge for men of this class. The whole region in this portion of Los Angeles county is mountainous, difficult of access, sparsely settled, and affords numerous hiding-places for outlaws and desperadoes.

Leiva now began to sicken of the undertaking. He was not as used to deeds of violence, as his companions, and had lived a married life long enough to render the wild life, hardships, and constant peril of a hunted bandit extremely distasteful. He had held deep self-communings on the journey down, and was filled with dissatisfaction and dismal forebodings. When he thought of the imminent peril of his situation, and the insignificant sum for which he had deprived himself and children of what might have been a peaceful home, he cursed his folly, and began to cypher his best way out of the predicament he was in.

He well knew that vigorous efforts would be made to capture the party, and he reasonably concluded that if taken they would each be lynched on the spot.

The wily (perhaps conscience-stricken) Chilaroan saw but one way out of the dilemma—and that was, downright treachery to his confederates. He would give them up to the authorities, and save his own neck by turning State's evidence.

It is perhaps an axiom with scarcely an exception, that a human being so constituted as to be capable of preying on his fellows, living off society by robbery, and hesitating not to murder for the sake of plunder, cannot, in the nature of things, be true to his own comrades, when he imagines it to be to his interest or necessary to assure his own safety to betray them. There can be no "honor among thieves" further than that of sheer self-interest. A thief, robber or murderer can have no respect for his associates in crime, and few compunctions of conscience over their betrayal.

It may be that even a robber or redhanded murderer may have genuine compunction, and a desire to reform, and a willingness and determination to right the wrongs he has done to the extent of his power, but when that disposition is manifested only when the rope stares the horror-stricken wretch in the face—when he is hunted like a wild beast—and he sacrifices his associates and saves his own worthless neck by the act of penitence, we may be pardoned if we look upon the act as that of a base coward, false to his kind and faithless to every principle of honor. Sometimes justice is worked out in this way—as "God makes the evil deeds of men serve him."

I would not do injustice to a repentant criminal—even a murderer. But Leiva, by his own confession, was a voluntary robber, and claims no other motive than that of revenge in betraying his associates in crime.

He had not failed to notice the constant effort of Vasquez to be in the society of his (Leiva's) wife Rosaria, and he resolved to lay a trap to discover them in *flagrante delictu*—and then make that as an excuse for his contemplated treachery.

At or near Rock Creek, Leiva left his wife, Chavez, and Vasquez ostensibly to get some provisions, saying he would return at twelve, midnight, but made it a point to return some hours sooner than expected. He found Vasquez and his romantic Rosaria occupying the same bed, and Chavez rolled up in his blanket in a corner of the same room. The infuriated (?) husband, with a dramatic air, drew a pistol from his pocket, when Chavez whose manner of life had rendered him extremely wakeful, sprang, pantherlike, from his warm nest, and covering Leiva with his dragoon pistol, exclaimed:

"If you fire I will blow your brains out!"

Leiva weakened at once, put up his pistol, but said to Vasquez. "Be sure I will kill you if I get a chance."

And then he expressed a willingness to fight a "fair" duel, Chavez to act as second. Meanwhile, the unfortunate woman was sitting up in bed, her face covered by her hands, and weeping bitterly.

To Leiva's proposition Vasquez returned a singular and very diplomatic answer.

"No, Leiva," replied the hunted bandit, "I do not wish to add to the wrong I have already done you. I will not fight with you except compelled to. You have no right to risk depriving your children of a protector. You have a right to seek revenge if you think proper; and then I shall be justified in defending myself."

After some further conversation, an understanding was had that no hostilities should take place until they had separated. After that event, Leiva warned him he should attack him whenever and wherever they met. Next morning Leiva parted from them, leaving his wife and children at Jim Heffner's, saying that he would "shirk for himself."

Neither Vasquez nor Chavez dreamed for a moment that he had any intention of making so bold and desperate a move as giving himself up to the authorities during the state of intense excitement that prevailed throughout the whole country against them.

CHAPTER XIII.

Thrilling account of the remarkable pursuit of the Tres Pinos murderers by Sheriff Adams, of Santa Clara County— Movements of the Los Angeles party, under Sheriff W. R. Rowland—Exciting chase after Chavez along the Mesa, in Little Rock Creek Canon—Lively skirmish with Vasquez.

One of the most determined pursuits known to the criminal history of California, was now made by Captain J. H. Adams, sheriff of Santa Clara county, one of the most prompt, brave and efficient officers in the State.

The Tres Pinos raid was made on the eve of an electioneering campaign, and Captain Adams had accompanied some of the candidates to Gilroy. There is a telegraph office in the hotel where Adams stopped, and as he passed the office next morning, the operator, recognizing the officer, called him in and communicated to him the terrible news that had passed over the wires. There was a freight train due in fifteen minutes going in the direction of Hollister, and at once abandoning his electioneering schemes, he took the train and arrived in Hollister at 10 A.M.

He immediately sought some of the leading men of the place, and sought to induce them to accompany him on the pursuit of the bandits. But these people, not having lost anything by the outlaws, did not evince any particular enthusiasm on the subject.

Meanwhile, the Captain had telegraphed to Sheriff Wasson, of Monterey county, to meet him. Doctor Rankin and one or two other gentlemen came in from Tres Pinos, and advised the sheriff to get together a strong posse. At 12 o'clock, only two men had been found willing to go, and an appointment was made for some of the leading citizens to meet at 2 o'clock, P.M.

Sheriff Wasson arrived at 3 o'clock, and with his assistance, only six men were got together by 5 o'clock, and the Captain regretted that he had not gone on alone, rallied a few farmers, and started on the fresh trail. Now one whole day had been lost.

He started at once with the following force:

Captain J. H. Adams, of San Jose, commanding; Sheriff A. Wasson, of Monterey; George W. Chick, of Tres Pinos; Henry Smith, Otho Jones, Frank A. Rowds, Robert Ransfield, Frederick Beach and George M. Noble, of Hollister. Pushing rapidly to Tres Pinos, the party was then reinforced by Bolinas Smith, James W. Mills and John Shell, of San Benito. Later they were joined by Louis L. Land, of the same place.

The party started up the San Benito, the robbers then having twenty-four hours the start. The Sheriffs' posse travelled hard all night, stopping at the various ranches for some clue to the murderers, and at 4 o'clock next morning, arrived at San Benito Store, where they routed out some blacksmiths, and had their horses shod.

They were here reinforced by a volunteer, and at 7 o'clock the pursuit was resumed in the direction of Hernandez Valley, where they were rejoined by one of the party who had been detailed to make a detour around through a little valley called Bitter Water. The party now consisted of fifteen men, including the two sheriffs.

It was found that the robbers had not gone to their usual haunts in Cantua Canon. Tidings were received that the Vasquez party had stopped at Lorenzo Vasquez's place in Little Valley, but that particular friend of his noted namesake made a positive denial. They were traced to Hernandez Valley, but there the trail was lost, and the tired party rested for a few hours. Towards dark they struck a trail leading over the mountains to Cantua Canon, and although they experienced great difficulty in finding the track, at midnight reached a farmer's house in the canon which leads to Pleasant Valley, and got their suppers. The farmer informed them that Vasquez had passed there.

At that hour a fresh start was made, and as all the party were unacquainted with the country, and the darkness was intense, they made slow progress until daylight, making their way down the bushy canon as best they could.

Reaching a point a little after daylight where the valley ascends, they found a Mexican shearing sheep, and searched his cabin for stolen property, but found none.

They reached Baker's ranch, in Pleasant Valley, at 11 o'clock A.M., of the 29th of August, three days after the affair at Tres Pinos, where they halted to feed and rest horses and men. Adams' horse and four or five others would not eat. The sheriff obtained a fresh horse of a sheep-herder, and the party moved on, having got no information here except some herders had noticed tracks two miles out. These they found and followed to Carey Creek, almost opposite the northwest corner of Tulare Lake, where the track scattered out and the trail was entirely lost. After a vigorous search, however, they struck the trail of two horses at China Shoe, but it was soon lost, and after scouring the country thoroughly, and moving up the creek among deserted houses, occupied now and then by old decrepit and demented men and women, caricatures on humanity, they halted and held a council of war. From the best of their information it was thought the fugitives were thirty-six miles ahead of them.

Adams wanted Wasson to go with him to the Posa Chane, but that officer's business at home was almost imperative. Five or six of the horses could not travel any further, and fruitless efforts were made to get fresh ones at the Heiguerra and other ranches.

Adams proposed to cross the valley, and by taking the railroad and stage, get ahead of the fugitives, who were evidently heading either for Sonora, Mexico, or to some of the mountain fastnesses in Los Angeles county. Wasson concluded to return, and Adams, not familiar with the country where he was, thought it imperative to find a telegraph line by which he could communicate with officers in advance of the fugitives.

Chick was given instructions to make a vigorous effort to obtain some fresh horses, and if successful, take part of the men and follow down the west side of the lake. Adams and Wasson paid Heiguerra fifty dollars to take them across the valley by daylight to Fresno, leaving money with Chick for the party.

Adams' idea was to meet them with help from Bakersfield, in Kern county.

The two sheriffs started for Fresno at 8 P.M., not having had anything to eat since 11 o'clock in the morning. Heiguerra missed the trail and got them into a marsh at the lower end of the lake. There was no alternative but to wait for daylight, and as they could not find a dry place in the marsh, they had to get through the night with "cat naps" on their horses. At daylight they got across the slough above, and they started across the plain, but again took the wrong direction. It was excessively hot, the plain at that season of the year being a very desert, and at mid-day like a furnace. Both men and horses nearly perished. Wasson finally got into Fresno, and immediately sent back water to his brother officer.

This was on the 30th, and Wasson took a special train for home, while Adams went to Visalia, having information that four men and a herd of horses had crossed the slough in that direction. He found, however, that they were vaqueros, so one more day was lost. Adams then started for Bakersfield, where he arrived on Monday, September 1.

He immediately sought Deputy Sheriff Cross and Mr. Funk, of San Emedio, who advised him to send some men to Panama, a Spanish settlement six or eight miles south of Bakersfield, where there were some low haunts, for information.

They reported that Vasquez nor any of his party had been there. Taking Deputy Short and Mr. White, early next morning the sheriff passed through Panama, and then diverging from the stage road, they took a trail which passed through Buena Vista and Kern lakes, and led to San Emedio. On their way they met an old Mexican driving horses, and among the herd was a mule, fagged out as if hard driven for days, answering the description of Vasquez's pack mule. The old man said he had found the animal on the west side of Tulare Lake. At the same place said he had found the remains of a calf, and tracks of a band of horses with large feet which had passed along.

The three adventurers then pushed on at a rapid rate, and on the west side of the lake, finding tracks leading to San Emedio. Before reaching there they found a horse tied in some willows about a quarter of a mile from the trail, and riding to the spot they found a man lying down by the side of a brush fence.

On questioning him, he replied that he had come from Livermore in Alameda county, adding:

"You are after Vasquez, I suppose?"

"No," replied Adams; "we are only looking after stock."

The man said he had heard that the Vasquez party had passed along, and he was afraid. He did not answer the description of either Vasquez, Chavez, Moreno or Leiva, and of Gonzales the sheriff had no good description. As he had on old clothes, Adams did not think it probable that he was one of the party, but concluded to examine the contents of a sack which he had used as a pillow. A new coat, vest and a pair of pants were found, which had not been worn more than once or twice. The Mexican said it was his Sunday suit he had worn at Livermore and at New Idria mines.

It was fifteen miles back to Bakersfield, and at that time there was no jail there; and if the sheriff arrested him he had no way to take care of him without embarrassing the search after Vasquez. He was allowed to go.

Adams learned with considerable chagrin afterwards, that it was the wretch Gonzales whom he had let slip through his fingers so easily. He is still at large, and supposed to be in Mexico. He is of lighter complexion than Vasquez, about twenty-nine years of age, five feet eight or ten inches in height, has high cheek-bones, black hair, and weighs one hundred and sixty to one hundred and seventy pounds, and talks fair English.

On striking the trail on the west side of the lake, the little party felt encouraged, and pushing ahead reached San Emedio ranch at midnight, September 2d.

Funk was willing to furnish fresh horses; but the animals were in the mountains, and the sheriff could not brook the delay necessary to hunt them and bring them down. That night Vasquez and Chavez had been seen on San Emedio creek, six miles in the valley. One of them had brought two horses to a blacksmith shop two days before, and while they were being shod the man laid down and went to sleep. On the blacksmith shouting out to one of the horses, which was restive under his manipulations, the sleeper sprang to his feet terribly frightened. The horses answered the description of two of those stolen by Vasquez's gang—two large sorrel animals.

At four A.M. Adams and his men pushed ahead to Hudson's Station, about a mile from the mouth of Tejon Pass, where a stage-driver informed them that a band of horses had passed through the canon and their driver had encamped near Delno's Station.

Here Mr. White had to return to Bakersfield, to the regret of Adams, who considered him, as he expressed it, "a plucky little fellow, and a man in whose courage I had instinctive confidence." He could not stand the fatigue of the hard riding however.

Before leaving the Station the Sheriff was fortunate in getting the assistance of the deputy sheriff's brother and an elderly man named David McKenzie, both noted throughout that region for their courage and ability to undergo any amount of hard riding.

Reaching the fort, seven miles further on in the canon, where there is a telegraph office, Adams telegraphed to Sheriff Rowland, of Los Angeles, the information he had just received. Adams took a rest at the fort, receiving the hospitality of Newton Ewing, who has charge of the telegraph line. A short time before the arrival of the stage, the Short brothers and McKenzie came on, reinforced by a vaquero and hunter named Young, also one of the most intrepid men in that region, and one of the most reliable. Although minus one leg, he can ride a horse with the best, or handle a rifle or lasso.

Leaving his horse to be brought on by his little party of volunteers, Adams took the stage toward Los Angeles.

At the last station before reaching Elizabeth Lake, the captain received positive information that Vasquez got supper there the night before. Resuming his journey, he reached the lake at daylight.

While the driver was watering his horses, Adams went into Jim Heffner's, and there learned that a wagon answering the description of Leiva's had passed the day before. Being alone, the sheriff did not think it prudent to stop, and passed on to Delno's, eight miles further on, having travelled all night.

He there learned that the horses had camped two miles above, and had been driven into the mountains, but did not pass on the main road. They had gone toward Chico Lopez, where the wagon had gone. Adams expected Short and his party along about 2 o'clock that day, the 4th, but on getting this information, he procured a conveyance and met them within two miles of Heffner's, coming on one at a time, so as not to attract attention.

They at once entered the chapparal and held a council, coming to the conclusion that Vasquez was at Chico Lopez's place. The sheriff urged a forward movement at once, but Young and McKenzie thought their party not strong enough to make an attack, supposing that Vasquez had with him a strong party. Adams said that when the stage arrived Rowland would be up with assistance, and advised an attack at daylight in the morning.

At 11 o'clock the stage arrived, but Rowland was not aboard, and had sent no word. Adams could do nothing, as his party thought best not to attack, and he remained all night at Delno's Station. Next morning Young went out for information, but returned without finding the party from whom he expected to get it. However, the man accidentally came to the station shortly afterward with important information. He had seen Vasquez, who had told him he was waiting for a woman he wished to take to the lower country. The robber had also confided in him to the extent of informing him that he should pass through Cajon Pass into San Bernardino county. [Vasquez denies that he ever "gave himself away" in this manner. His movements, however, confirm the information Adams then received.]

Adams now thought the best thing to do would be to leave his party and go on to Lyons' Station (Petroliopolis). But McKenzie informed him that he knew a trail by which he could reach Cajon Pass by going only eighty miles, and the sheriff concluded to telegraph to Rowland to get a party ready, and then, letting McKenzie guide his own little band across the trail, and going on himself to Los Angeles, accompany Rowland's party into the western mouth of the Pass, and meet his party in the Cajon. Young had to return home.

Adams reached Lyons in three hours, and sent a dispatch to Rowland, receiving a reply that Rowland was on the stage and would be at Lyons in half an hour, and was asked to obtain fresh horses, but could procure none. On the arrival of the stage the driver informed him that five miles back the stage had met a Californian, and that Rowland had walked back with him to a ranch to get a horse, and that Adams might overtake him. He hastened, and was just in time to catch Rowland at Lopez Station. Rowland was much surprised to see him, and had received the same information in regard to Vasquez's intended movements, and was intending to cut him off.

The two sheriffs reached Los Angeles at half-past nine, Adams having made the trip from Delno's (85 miles) in seven hours. They found that Under-Sheriff Albert Johnston had sent six men, well armed and well mounted, already towards Cajon Pass.

The party consisted of Major H. M. Mitchell, Pete Gabriel, "Babe" Crowell, Jose Redowna, E. Sanchez, and R. Benites. They were excellent horsemen and experienced fighters, and by a forced march they entered the Pass and reached Martin's ranch, about twelve miles from San Bernardino, at seven o'clock next morning, halting for breakfast.

In the meantime, Rowland and Adams, procuring fresh horses, had overtaken the party, arriving with it at Martin's having travelled one hundred and twenty-five miles that night. Ascertaining that no man answering the description of Vasquez had passed through the canon, a portion of the posse was left on guard at Martin's. The remainder, with the sheriffs, going on to the toll-gate as an advance scout.

The information that Rowland had was that Vasquez had a band of seven men, all well mounted and armed, and that they had a number of stolen horses, had been drying stolen beef for use on their journey to Mexican territory; and that they would make their first move from Rock Creek through Cajon Pass to Agua Mauva, on the Santa Ana river.

At one o'clock on the ensuing night, an Indian was halted by one of the advance scouts, and found to be the bearer of a dispatch to the sheriff from the Short brothers and McKenzie. It announced Vasquez to be at Little Rock Creek, in camp. Notice was sent at once to Sheriff A. F. McKenney, of San Bernardino.

The men left at Martin's ranch were at once called in; the entire posse, guided by the Indian, were en route for Big Rock Creek Canon, distant by the trail leading through the coast range about 60 miles.

Reaching Little Rock Creek, twelve miles south of the point at which Vasquez was reported to be encamped, the Sheriffs' party met Deputy-Sheriff Short and his brother and McKenzie. There was very little grass for the horses, but the men obtained something to eat from a sheep-herder. The party then proceeded to La Cienega, the exact locality of Vasquez's camp not being definitely known.

At the mouth of the canon they struck the trail of a wagon and horses, and followed some six miles, when they found wagon tracks coming down, and in the discussion which ensued on the best plan to pursue, Rowland and his party and all of Adams' men, except Deputy Short, thought they ought to follow the tracks which led out of the canon towards Llano Verde and Elizabeth Lake.

Adams was not satisfied, as he could not see the tracks of horses, and he moved on up the trail with Short, and was soon satisfied that the horses had not come back.

Looking back, they saw the balance of the posse moving after the wagon tracks, towards Elizabeth Lake. Adams instantly sent Short back to inform Rowland that the horses were still up the canon, and Rowland and the party turned and hastened after Adams.

Adams, Short, and Sanchez pushed on together for some distance, until they came to the ashes of a recent camp-fire, where they halted until the balance of the party came up. There was a water-hole near by, dug in the sand, and hanging to the limbs of an adjacent tree were three quarters of a large beef, cut in pieces of various sizes. On the ground near the water-hole was the hide and head of the beef.

A discussion ensued as to what plan to adopt, a majority not being in favor of following the tracks. Rowland and Adams, however, concurred in the opinion that it was best to press on and ascertain where the trail led, and they, accompanied by Deputy Short, Major Mitchell, and Sanchez, proceeded on the trail, supposing they were followed by the balance, who, however, seem to have misunderstood the decision of the sheriffs.

The canon, commencing at the deserted camp above mentioned, is steep and rocky, crooked, and very narrow, enclosed on two sides by rugged, lofty hills, and sparsely covered with a growth of scrubby cedars, with here and there cactus patches and groups of huge sand stone and granite boulders. This mesa lay along the western side of the canon, was from fifteen to twenty feet higher than the bed of the water course, and extended for a mile and a half, with an average width of about one hundred and fifty yards. The channel of the water course averages about two hundred yards in width, and is almost continuously occupied by dense clumps of trees, principally sycamore, cottonwood, and alder, with an undergrowth of vines and bushes.

The trail was at places quite indistinct, and the men had to scatter right and left, searching for the tracks.

They had arrived at a point some three miles up the canon; Mitchell and Sanchez were exploring a side canon, Rowland, Short, and Adams were moving on, with Short some thirty steps in advance, going up a little rise. As Short reached the point of the ridge, Cleovaro Chavez, riding a large sorrel or "clay bank" horse, suddenly rode into view from behind a clump of cedars. Short instantly cried out to those behind: "Here's a man!"

Chavez took the alarm, wheeled his horse, and bending low in the saddle, dashed at full speed up the mesa.

With free use of whip and spurs the boys followed on the keen jump, firing whenever the robber's bobbing form came in view at the frequent turns. Having the freshest horse, the fugitive constantly increased the distance between himself and pursuers. The only shot gun in the party never got in range, and the firing, some eight or nine shots, was confined to the rifles—a powerful uncertain weapon, under the circumstances.

Once the robber's horse stumbled, nearly falling, but recovered, and at the upper end of the mesa Chavez spurred the animal down a steep bank, and re-entered the canon fully two hundred yards in advance of the foremost pursuer.

In the steep, rocky bed of the canon the pace was necessarily slower, although each man and horse did his level best.

The pursuers soon came to forks in the creek and some branching canons, and time was unavoidably lost in searching among many fresh tracks for the right trail.

Just after one of these provoking delays in the steep canon, and just in front of a steep bluff—a promontory running into and nearly across the canon—Mitchell, who was ahead, heard a rock rolling on a hillside. Checking his horse to see where the rock came from, he was startled by the sharp crack of a Henry rifle on the bluff in front, and a bullet whizzed past in somewhat disagreeable proximity. A light puff of smoke over the bluff caught his eye, and under it, partly behind a boulder, across which his rifle rested, lay Vasquez, in the act of firing a second shot. The horse made a quick forward movement (the spurs helped him), and bullet number two flew wilder than its predecessor, and lodged in a bank, some six feet wide of the mark.

Mitchell sought refuge behind some young saplings, but they looking inconveniently small under the circumstances, he backed his horse behind shelter of a bluff.

Adams and Rowland had dismounted and placed their animals behind the bluff, and now advancing, Adams opened a lively fire with his Henry rifle; Vasquez replying with equal energy.

Finding the distance—some two hundred yards—too great for a certain aim at the robber's head, Adams ascended the bluff behind which the horses were sheltered, to get a better position, and re-opened fire.

The firing from the promontory suddenly ceased, and Adams shouted to those below that it was time to make a rush.

Mitchell suggested that they had better go back after the rest, Rowland seconded the proposition, and Mitchell mounted, clapped spurs to his horse, and dashed down the canon.

CHAPTER XIV.

THE TREACHERY OF LEIVA AND HIS DESPERATE PLAN FOR REVENGE
ON VASQUEZ—VASQUEZ AND CHAVEZ ESCAPE—CAPTURE OF THEIR CAMP,
TWENTY-ONE HORSES AND OTHER STOLEN PROPERTY—VOLUNTARY SUR-
RENDER OF ABDON LEIVA—ARREST OF TEODORO MORENO BY LYONS AND
CHICK, SENT OUT BY ADAMS—TRAIL OF MORENO—SENT TO STATE'S
PRISON FOR LIFE—ROSARIA'S PLEASANT FICTION.

WE LEFT Abdon Leiva as he had just parted from his wife and his
confederates, Vasquez and Chavez, bent on treachery and a terrible
revenge, and determined to avoid for his own neck the threatened
halter.

Making the best possible time to Lyon's Station, he inquired for
an officer, and was introduced to W. W. Jenkins, formerly a deputy-
sheriff of Los Angeles, and to that gentleman the bandit at once surrendered, stating his reasons for leaving the band, and expressing
anxiety to render all the service he could to enable the officers to
capture Vasquez and Chavez and bring them to justice.

We return to the party at Little Rock Creek Canon. Finding
his order to charge not obeyed promptly, Adams descended from the
bluff. Hurriedly mounting, and spurring his horse up the trail to the
summit of the promontory, he found that both Chavez and Vasquez had
retreated. Passing on he found an open place, and discovered two
horses on a hill, and innumerable tracks about the place.

Rowland, Short and Sanchez there joined him, and after a brief
search found nine horses, five of them agreeing with the description
of those stolen at Tres Pinos. Mitchell and the balance of the party
soon came up, and putting out scouts as far as possible on each side,
they pushed three miles further up the canon, gathered twenty-one
horses in all, following the trail of Chavez and Vasquez to Chapparal
Mountain, where the robbers had entered the brush, into which it was
utterly useless to follow them.

Gathering the horses, they concluded to return and follow the trail
of the wagon track. On returning down the arroyo they found the
real camp and another horse ready saddled (one of the saddles from
Snyder's), a pair of pants and coat, and fresh meat hung up, coffee and
sugar and a bottle of whiskey.

They then remounted and followed the wagon track all night,
passing Barrel Springs, and at noon next day arrived at Llano Verde.
Here a teamster informed them that Leiva had stopped at his house
two days before, and had left some trunks and gone on, and that the

wife was left, and Vasquez might be with her.

The house was surrounded, entered, and thoroughly searched. It was tenanted with old men, women and children. The two trunks were found containing clothing, jewelry, etc., taken from Snyder's store. Rowland detailed Pete Gabriel, "Babe" Crowell, and Sanchez to watch the place and arrest any parties who might return to claim the property, the teamster agreeing to board them.

The balance of the party moved on all night, following the track of the wagon, passing Chico Lopez's place, and not knowing the right road, took up the right-hand valley.

The road branches near Lopez's, one fork passing to the right and the other to the left of a hill, the two roads again converging beyond the eminence.

At daylight Rowland, Adams, and Short dashed on ahead, in order to reach the lake in advance of the herd of horses, expecting to find Leiva at Heffner's. On getting in sight of the place they recognized the two horses and wagon of Leiva's, and riding up to the door they demanded if Leiva was there.

Heffner replied that he was not. He was then asked if Rosaria was there; Heffner said she was not, that a man had come in there the night before and taken her away.

It was the indefatigable Vasquez, who had crossed the mountain, taken her away in the night, and had actually passed Adams and Rowland on the back track, through their mistake in taking the wrong side of the hill.

When asked why he allowed Vasquez to take her away, Heffner replied that he thought he had no right to prevent him; that several of his band were supposed to be in the vicinity, and he was afraid of them. He said that he had taken the woman behind him on the horse, and went in the direction of Chico Lopez's.

Mitchell, Redowa, and Adams started to meet the men with the horses, exchanged for some of the best, and the band was then taken by Rowland to Delno's for feed.

Adams and his men then followed the trail of Vasquez's horse, and on getting in sight of Lopez's house, they scattered and surounded the place. The windows and doors all being open, and a number of women and girls about, but no unusual commotion visible, the pursuers were satisfied the game was not there.

The party then returned to Delno's, their horses nearly exhausted, and there found Leiva, who had been brought in by Jenkins, to whom he surrendered at Lyons' Station.

A party was organized under Johnston to pursue Vasquez and Chavez into the mountains, and Adams, nearly worn out by his incessant exertions, concluded to return to Monterey and attempt the capture of Moreno and Gonzales, who, Leiva said, had only come with Vasquez as far as Posa Chane.

Three divisions were sent out by Johnston—one to relieve Crowell and the others at the teamster's house, Llano Verde, the others to follow the trails. One of the parties went to Tehachapi Pass, in Kern county, on information which proved unreliable. The other party failed to find their way, owing to innumerable tracks made by grazing horses, but captured two additional stolen horses.

Adams reached his home in San Jose on the 11th of September, having made one of the most persistent pursuits ever made in the State. For five successive days and nights during the chase he was not out of the saddle, save to change horses, and occasionally eat a hurried meal, and on one occasion he rode one hundred and thirty miles between the hours of two o'clock P.M. and daylight the following morning.

Next morning after his return to San Jose, he went to Hollister, and proceeded with Wasson to New Idria, on information which led him to believe Gonzales and perhaps Vasquez had returned there. Deputy Sheriff Lyons and George W. Chick were sent to Bitter Water to look for Teodoro Moreno.

Adams and Wasson searched New Idria thoroughly, but missed their game. Just about daylight they learned that a "man" had left half an hour previous with a boy for the Vallecitas.

Returning to Hollister before noon, they found that Lyons and Chick had just got in with two prisoners—one of them the murderer Teodoro Moreno, and a suspected party named Anlivia.

On the 23d, Adams again got information that Gonzales was at New Idria, and taking Deputy Sheriff John Haight, of Hollister, the two officers disguised themselves thoroughly, and went to the mines, exploring all the camps, but found that he had left the night before.

From that time on, Adams made repeated attempts to capture Chavez, who occasionally returned to the vicinity of his old haunts, and a good deal of time and money were spent by the Los Angeles officer in fruitless efforts to catch Vasquez.

The most intense excitement prevailed throughout the State over the Tres Pinos affair, and the newspapers teemed with accounts of innumerable robberies attributed to Vasquez and his gang, and it was popularly believed that he actually kept a large force of armed desperadoes in the saddle. The difficulty in capturing him lay in the fact that the supposed large force he kept in the field was a myth.

It was true that at numberless Mexican haunts throughout the mountains were desperadoes, among whom he could collect a sufficient number at any time for his purposes; but after each robbery he would disperse them in different directions, seldom keeping more than one or two men with him for any length of time, and often moving quickly from one portion of the country to another alone.

The people in Southern California were especially exposed to the depredations of the desperadoes, and kept in continual alarm; and Los Angeles, where the wonderful fertility of soil, exquisite beauty of scenery, and health-giving climate was attracting the attention of Eastern capitalists, tourists and people throughout the East desirous of locating there—suffered greatly from the fact that the continued depredations of these bandits created such a general alarm as to turn the tide of travel in other directions. It is a fact well known that hundreds of people who left their business in the East and came to California for the express purpose of visiting Los Angeles and other portions of Southern California, on reaching Sacramento, and finding in the morning papers accounts of the daring operations of Vasquez, introduced with horrible head lines, and graphically written up, actually stopped short in their journey, not daring to risk their lives and property by travelling through the regions in which the bold outlaws operated—and returned to their Eastern homes, where they could rest in comparative safety.

Governor Booth issued a proclamation, offering $6,000 for the capture and conviction of Vasquez, but after the pursuit by Adams and Rowland the rascal remained quiet for nearly two months.

Moreno was placed in the jail at Salinas, and shortly afterward Leiva was brought up from Los Angeles and confined in the same prison. Both men were indicted for complicity in the Tres Pinos murders. Subsequently, Leiva, being an important witness against Moreno and against the other participators in the Tres Pinos outrage, it was not deemed a safe place at Salinas to keep him, and he was accordingly transferred to the Santa Clara jail at San Jose.

Vasquez kept the woman Rosaria in the mountains for several weeks, when, determined to emerge from his hiding-place and renew his depredations, he furnished her money to return to her friends, and also devised a fictitious story for her to make public. What the object was it is difficult to see, unless it was to relieve her of the imputation that she was voluntarily untrue to her marital vows. Everything in connection with the outlaws was eagerly seized upon by the leading papers, and as eagerly read by the people. Occasionally, of course, they were victimized by canards. The fictitious story of Leiva's wife is reproduced here as an interesting feature of the romantic affair.

Immediately after her return to Santa Clara county, she took up her adobe with a friend in San Jose, and an enterprising reporter of the Daily San Francisco *Chronicle,*—a journal known far and wide for its indefatigable enterprise in collecting and printing the news of the day—sought her out, and, accompanied by Sheriff Adams and an interpreter, interviewed the woman, and heard her remarkable story, as follows. The *Chronicle* report says:

"When questioned in reference to this affair (the quarrel between Leiva and Vasquez on her account), Mrs. Leiva strongly denied having anything to do with Vasquez of an improper nature prior to this time. * * * After Leiva had set out from Heffner's ranch, according to the woman's story, the robbers—who had been joined by others of the gang, making seven in all—started south. They suspected treachery on Leiva's part, and considered it unsafe to remain there. They had about twenty head of stolen horses with them. Mrs. Leiva was left at the ranch. They proceeded down the Rock Creek Canon—which is in San Bernardino county —until they had the skirmish with the sheriffs' party. Vasquez told her that he fired seven shots at the officers, and that Chavez was chased two miles and fired at several times. The pursuers then numbered but three men. When Vasquez fired two of them backed their horses out of sight but the third (Adams) called out to them, 'Come on, boys!' Vasquez heard the words very plainly. The robbers rode on down through the canon, leaving their band of loose horses behind, and also some of the booty secured in the raid, all of which fell into the hands of the officers. She says Vasquez came back alone to Heffner's, and then her strange story properly begins, as follows: 'About the middle of the night Vasquez came to the house. The first intimation I had that he was about was when he put his hand on my shoulder and awakened me. I was lying in bed. He had one hand on my shoulder and the other he held a pistol, which was cocked and pointed towards me. He told me to get up quick and go with him, or he would blow my brains out. I asked him what I could do with my children. He said he didn't care anything about them. I did not get up at the first time he told me to, and he came back to the bed again and said if I didn't jump out of bed he would kill me. I was afraid he would do it, and so I got up. He ordered me to get on my clothes and go with him as soon as possible. I was crying all the time I was dressing. He put me up on his horse and got up behind me, and started for the Cheviral Mountains. The next day Vasquez told me Heffner got up and let him in. We met Chavez that day in the mountains. They hid in the brush all day, and dared not go out, as they knew the officers were looking for them. We had nothing to eat that day, and not until late the following day, when Vasquez found a young calf and killed it. He brought part of the meat into camp, which we ate without even salt to put on it. All the time I was with them the only bed clothing we had was one pair of blankets and his saddle blankets. One night while we were in the mountains, Vasquez thought he heard the officers whistling to each other, and started up, saying, 'That's the officers exchanging signals.' The sound came closer and he seized his rifle. Presently, out of the bush, only a short distance from where we were lying, sprang a large California lion. It was a bright moonlight night, and it could be plainly seen. Vasquez fired quickly, and the lion fell dead with a bullet through his heart. We were eight days on the mountain, in which we had nothing to eat except meat. I was crying a good deal of the time, and Vasquez used to get very angry with me for it. My health was getting very bad on account of the exposure and ill-treatment. Vasquez then took me to a mountain on the other side of the valley, I had been pregnant for three or four months before this time, and on the 22d of September was prostrated with a miscarriage. Late on the afternoon of the same day, Vasquez and Chavez rode off and left me, sick, helpless, and alone, in the mountain. Vasquez said: 'You can get out of here the best way you can with God's help.' I started down the mountain towards the valley, and just before dark, I saw a sheep-herder's tent, to which I went. It proved to be an old American. He gave me some coffee and bread, and allowed me to stay over night. He gave me also a bed, which was the first I had lain in for nearly two weeks. It was also the first coffee and bread I had tasted in that time. In the morning he got a good breakfast for me, and then I left his tent. He could not speak Spanish, and we could not hold no conversation. I wished to find some house where I would be taken care of, as I was very sick. I travelled out into the valley as fast as I could until about one o'clock of that day, Sept. 23d, when I saw a man riding along, some distance away, and he came up to me. He proved to be a Mexican, and I told him who I was and what had happened to me. He said he would take me to a house where I would be taken care of until I got well. He put me on his horse, and about dark we arrived at his house where I was kindly taken care of during my sickness, which lasted from that time until a few days ago. When they thought me strong enough to stand the journey, the man and his wife took me to the railroad station, and paid my passage to San Jose.'"

At the November term of the District Court at Salinas, the case of Teodoro Moreno, indicted for the murder of Bernal Berhuri, came up on the 23d instant, and the entire day was consumed in the effort to obtain a jury. At eleven o'clock next day, 105 jurors having been summoned, the following jury was obtained: W. W. Lee, N. Haggerty, Rafael Pomber, N. L. Allen, E. S. House, J. Webster, B. Titus, Anson Smith, J. C. Caldwell, William Quental, and Otto Foodisch.

Messrs. P. B. Tully, of Gilroy, and R. H. Brotherton appeared for the defence, and, in the language of a report in the San Francisco *Morning Call,* these gentlemen, in the matter of selecting a jury, "out-generalled" the Prosecuting Attorney, S. F. Giel, and his coadjutor and adviser, P. K. Woodside.

The court-room was densely thronged throughout the trial. The first witness introduced by the prosecution was the "reformed" bandit, Abdon Leiva, who gave a clear and succinct account of each event in the Tres Pinos tragedy, substantially as given in this history. A rigid cross-examination failed to elicit a single lame point in his straightforward story. His story was corroborated by his wife, as far as her knowledge of the plotting of the robbery and the subsequent events.

Lorenzo Vasquez testified that he knew nothing about the plotting of the conspirators, and denied any knowledge of their having divided any of the stolen property at his place.

His wife testified that Moreno arrived after the others did, and was not present when they left some articles of jewelry, etc.

The testimony of John E. Utzerath, Snyder's clerk, Andrew Snyder, Sheriff Adams, Louis Schires, L. C. Smith, Frederick Taylor, Constable Chick, of San Benito, Edward Droux, and Mrs. Davidson closed the case for the prosecution, and confirmed circumstantially the tale of Leiva.

Manuel Larios, a brother-in-law to Tiburcio Vasquez, and Concepcion Espinosa, a woman of doubtful character, were sworn for the purpose of proving an alibi, and then the defendant, Moreno, was placed upon the stand to testify in his own behalf. Following is a synopsis of his story:

"Am twenty-nine years of age. Was born and raised in Gilroy. Have heard about the robbing of Snyder's store at Tres Pinos. That night I was stopping at Concepcion Espinosa's house, at San Carlos. I went there about sunset. I did not stay there all night, but left about two or three o'clock in the morning. Went there from Lorenzo Vasquez's house, where I arrived about half-past six in the morning. I left that early because I was sick, and I wanted to travel that distance before the sun was up, and it became hot. Tiburcio Vasquez, Chavez, Gonzales, and Abdon Leiva were also there. They were sitting down to breakfast. I left at eleven o'clock and went to Ed. Tully's house to shear sheep. For a month previous to the robbery I lived at Lorenzo Vasquez's. Left there on the Saturday previous to the robbery to go to Vallecitas to get a horse out of the band of Jose Maria Larios. I rode a horse that I was breaking for Larios. Got the horse and started back, when the horse broke away from me, and during Sunday and Monday I was trying to catch him, stopping at sheep ranches and camps to rest. I gave up the chase Tuesday, and came to Concepcion Espinosa's house that night. I was not present at a plot made at Leiva's house to rob Snyder's store. I am first cousin to Tiburcio Vasquez."

On the cross examination, conducted by P. K. Woodside, the witness was inextricably entangled in the thread of his narration about searching for the horse, and so confused that it was evident that he was dealing in fiction.

Late Thursday night, November 27th, the Jury rendered a verdict of "Guilty of murder in the second degree."

At ten o'clock next day the prisoner was brought into court. Ordering the prisoner to stand up, Judge Belden referred to the nature of the crime of which the prisoner had been accused, and after dilating upon the enormity of the offense—the murder of an innocent man, who had not even offered resistance, and who was not the party whom the robber designed to rob—the Court reviewed the testimony, which formed an unbroken chain of positive evidence against him.

The Court sentenced him to be confined in the State Prison for the term of his natural life.

The prisoner accepted the sentence with the stoical indifference which had characterized all his actions during the trial.

At 11:30 the prisoner was taken en route to San Quentin on board the cars, by Deputy-Sheriff L. P. Garrigus.

Two other indictments are pending against him, for the murder of Davidson and Redford at the same time, and if more testimony is obtained implicating him more directly, he will be brought back and again tried for his life, and probably be convicted and hung.

Since his incarceration in the State Prison the guilty wretch has lost all that stoical indifference assumed at the trial. He doubtless lives in constant dread of being retried and hung. The writer recently visited the prisoner to listen to his version of another affair. He entered the guard room with a nervous tread, gave a single furtive glance at the visitor, and then turned his glance to one of the windows, and never during the brief conversation, in which he took part only in monosyllables, did he once remove his gaze from the window.

CHAPTER XV.

Vasquez again on the highway—Daring outrage on the village of Kingston—Chavez badly wounded by J. W. Sutherland—The "Lieutenant" goes into retirement—Unsuccessful pursuit of Vasquez—He rides into Kern county, rests three days at Panama, and then disperses his gang—Preparations for the "Spring Campaign"—Chavez on his pins again.

After keeping hid away in the mountains for several weeks, until Vasquez thought that all pursuit must have been abandoned, he sent Chavez out for information, as he had never been in the meshes of the law, and could move about with little chance of recognition.

That worthy accordingly left his chief, and travelling by night, proceeded to Los Angeles, and leaving his horse and rifle at the house of George Allen *alias* "Jorge el Greigo," or "Greek George," situated on the plain near the base of the Cahuenga range of mountains, about eight miles north-east from Los Angeles, he proceeded on foot, armed only with his revolver and knife, and entered the Mexican portion of the town called Sonora.

Here he sought out a desperado named Isadore Padillo, who had formerly been tried in Tulare county for complicity in the murder of an entire Italian household, and escaped conviction through lack of sufficient evidence, and made himself known to him, inviting him to join in a new band about to be organized in which Vasquez was again to figure as chief and himself as lieutenant.

Padillo expressed himself flattered by the proposition, and readily entered into the scheme, which was to perpetrate a series of bold robberies in rapid succession, and then, if feasible, liberate Moreno from the Salinas jail before the day set for his trial.

Padillo was able to inform him that the pursuing parties sent out from Los Angeles, and, as far as newspapers could be relied upon, the parties from other points, had given up the pursuit, and they could move with comparative safety.

Chavez remained in Sonora for two days, to enable Padillo to make the necessary preparations. The two left the town one evening, Chavez on foot, and Padillo by a separate route, on horseback, and rendezvoused at Greek George's, Padillo reaching there at an early hour, and Chavez arriving about half-past nine o'clock.

Chavez had knocked down a pedestrian in the outskirts of the town and robbed him of ninety dollars in coin and a fine gold watch—an exploit which elated him greatly, but which rendered it imprudent to leave the "Greek's" for a day or two at least.

The affair produced but little excitement in the city, however, as it was attributed to some "party" unknown, who lurked in town, and none of the authorities had a suspicion that it was the work of one of Vasquez's banditti.

Paying "Greek George" liberally for his hospitality, the bandits, two days after the robbery, mounted and started for the San Francisquito Canon, reaching which about nightfall, by hard riding all night, they arrived in the vicinity of Chico Lopez's ranch soon after sunrise.

Towards evening they succeeded in reaching Vasquez without having excited any suspicion on the road, and they found the chief highly impatient at the delay Chavez had made, but encouraged at the appearance of the new recruit, and he gave Padillo a warm welcome.

Vasquez formed his plans that night, and early next morning he ordered Padillo to start out for Panama, to obtain tidings, if possible, of Gomez—a desperado of the ferocious type, who had only a short time before deliberately murdered Constable Mettler, near Tehachapi, while that officer was serving a warrant upon him. He was a fugitive from justice, but Vasquez thought he was hiding at Panama, and in case he should not be found there, Vasquez gave Padillo the name of a Mexican woman who would know of his whereabouts, and direct him where to find the murderer.

Chavez was directed to remain behind for half a day, and then taking the main road to Hudson's Station, turn toward San Emedio, go to the Posa de Chane, and there pick up all the desperadoes on whom they could rely, and come directly to the old rendezvous in the Panoche Mountains.

Vasquez did not indicate his own route to his companions, but bidding them both good-bye, and telling each to come to the rendezvous promptly as possible, whether successful in their missions or not, he left the mountain, and proceeded on his northern journey. Within a week they were all together at the appointed rendezvous. Gomez had been found and had accompanied Padillo; Chavez had picked up Blas Bicuna, while Vasquez had engaged the services of three more desperadoes, who would be soon at the rendezvous ready for a start.

The two leaders were in high spirits over their escape from the determined pursuit of Adams and the Rowland party; but not a little chagrined over the arrest of Moreno.

The probability of his turning State's evidence in case either Vasquez or Chavez should be captured before his own trial, was canvassed; but they could form no idea as to what he would do in that event. Judging from their own nature, doubtless, they came to the conclusion that he would, and they thought it would be good policy to conciliate him if possible, and Bicuna was sent to Monterey to see what chance there was to liberate him by force or stratagem, and to give him some money.

Bicuna departed on his errand, and Vasquez and the balance of the party began another round of dissipation, as a sort of training measure for their intended grand raid through the country.

Bicuna entered Salinas at night and went at once to the house of an abandoned Mexican woman whom he knew he could trust, and through her put himself in communication with the prisoner.

Moreno returned his thanks for the good offices of his friends, and for the money; but declined their offer to attempt a rescue. He assured Bicuna that the attempt would only end in failure, and in that case he would only be worse off than he already was; and in regard to Leiva, he thought that as the man had no cause for personal spite against him, he would not swear against him.

When Bicuna returned to the rendezvous and reported Moreno's views on the situation, they were heartily approved by all hands. Vasquez then tried to induce Bicuna to clandestinely visit the city of San Jose, where Leiva was confined, and through the instrumentality of some women who could manage to get access to the jail without exciting suspicion, administer poison to the traitor, through the medium of wine or some other luxury, and thus put it out of his power to do further harm than he had already done the band by the information he had furnished various officers.

Bicuna thought the matter over for a day or two, and finally confessed to Vasquez that he had too wholesome a dread of Sheriff Adams to venture on his own grounds. He would not even venture into the city, much less undertake the job of liberating Leiva from his bondage in that way.

Gomez was then approached on the subject, but gave a most emphatic "No!" to the proposition, and the bandit chief did not allude further to the subject.

The volunteers whom Vasquez had engaged soon made their appearance, and immediate attention was given to preparing for the "fall campaign."

Everything at length being in readiness, a series of robberies were committed on the highway by detachments of twos and threes in different localities, but their operations were so skillfully managed that no clue was given that rendered it certain that Vasquez was at work again, and only feeble efforts were made by the authorities in the neighborhood of the depredations to hunt up the perpetrators.

Emboldened, at length, at their continued success, a plan was finally laid to sack the little town of Kingston, about the centre of Fresno county, and near the southern boundary, and on the south bank of King's River, a stream that has its origin in the mountains in the eastern part of the county, and flowing in a south-westerly direction, nearly to the southern boundary of the county, makes a turn north, and finally empties into the San Joaquin.

It is a flourishing little town, and the bandits felt certain of making a profitable thing of sacking it. The river is spanned by a toll-bridge, owned by O. H. Bliss.

On the south side of the principal street in the main portion of the town, two stores and a hotel are clustered together, and the bridge above referred to directly fronts on these buildings, and also a stable owned by Bliss. The hotel is owned by L. Reichart, one of the stores by S. Sweet, and the other by Jacob & Einstein.

On Friday night, Dec. 26th, 1873—just five months after the terrible massacre at Tres Pinos, the little town was the scene of another of Vasquez's desperate exploits, and the whole southern country once more thrown into a fever of excitement, indignation, and speculation as to what the law-defying dare-devil would do next.

By appointment the members of the gang, numbering nine men, found their way, one by one, and by different routes, to a point about five miles north of the town, and soon after dark they approached the river and hid their horses in the thicket near the bank of the stream.

Shortly after seven o'clock they crossed the bridge on foot, and ividing, instantly took possession of the town. In less than five ninutes they had bound thirty men, and then hurriedly proceeded to ifle the safes and money-drawers, and then robbed their victims of heir watches, rings, and other valuables.

Mr. Bliss was the first person they encountered, and they compelled im to lie down, tied his hands and legs together, and took all his noney, the pitiful sum of nine dollars—business not having been very ively with Bliss that day.

Complaining that his head was hurting him, one of the party con- iderately took a blanket from a wagon near the stable, placed it under is head, and left him in that blissful position to reflect on the uncer- ainty of mundane affairs.

Another delegation halted John Potts, M. Woods, and P. Bozeman near the stable-yard, and ordered them to lie down. Bozeman and Potts silently obeyed, and were relieved of their coin, Bozeman of $180, and Potts of a small amount.

Mr. Woods fastidiously objected, on the plea that it would "soil his good clothes." He was allowed to go to the hotel and lie down there.

One man was placed on guard in front of each of the business houses, while other portions of the band entered the bar of the hotel, and Jacob & Einstein's store.

In the saloon or bar there were ten or a dozen persons, and Vasquez ordering them to lie down, they obeyed, and were immediately relieved of their watches and money.

From the proprietor of the hotel they took $400 and a watch, and from the guests various amounts.

Ed. Douglas, a plucky gentleman from Visalia, whom Vasquez and Chavez discovered in the sitting-room, peremptorily refused to lie down, when Chavez knocked him down with his revolver, and Vasquez took his money and watch.

Lance Gilroy, of Fresno, was eating his supper when these initiatory proceedings were transpiring. Blas Bicuna rudely entered the dining-room door, and Mrs. Reichart, terrified by the ominous glance of his eye, and the cocked revolver in his hand, emitted a piercing scream and fled from the apartment. Gilroy, startled by the shrill yell, sprang to his feet, and thinking it was some drunken loafer who had insulted the young lady, before Bicuna comprehended his de-

sign, the gallant Gilroy had felled the ruffian to the floor with
chair. But Gilroy's triumph was short-lived. The heavy thud
Bicuna's carcass on the floor was heard by Gomez, who was in the h—
on his way to the dining-room, and springing through the doorway,
brought the belligerent gentleman to terms, by a strong blow over t—
head with a dragoon pistol.

At the store of Jacob & Einstein the robbers experienced no di—
culty. The clerk, Ed. Ellinger, was first approached and ordered
lie down; but instead of complying, the young man sprang through t—
doorway, and flying as on the wings of the wind to Sweet's sto—
astonished the nerves of that individual by rushing up to the count—
with hair erect, and eyeballs protruding like those of a French manik—
exclaiming, in tones that froze the merchant's blood:

"The robbers have come!"

Sweet thrust his head out of the door to see, when it was instant—
seized by the "guard" and he thrown down and tied.

When Ellinger left Jacob & Co.'s store so hurriedly, the other i—
mates were tied at once, and thrown to the floor, Lewis Epstein w—
seized and the key of his safe demanded. At first he evaded compl—
ing with the unpleasant demand by pretending the clerk Ellinger h—
carried it off. Vasquez made his appearance at that instant, and telli—
him he knew he had another key, and that if he did not willingly pr—
duce it he would blow his brains out, he produced it, and the safe w—
opened and robbed. $800 in coin was taken from the safe and th—
money drawers, and a considerable amount from the pockets of th—
customers and loungers present.

Sweet's store was next attacked, but now came an unlooked-f—
change in the scene. They had taken about $60, when the cheerf—
tones of a Henry rifle interrupted the game, a second shot was hear—
the next moment and the guard fell heavily against the door, exclaimin—
in Spanish,

"I am shot!"

While the wholesale work of robbery was going on J. W. Suther—
land and James E. Flood had been informed what was in progress—
and seizing their arms arrived in haste just as the attack was made a—
Sweet's, and fired the shots which stopped the robbers, and all of ther—
made a precipitate rush for the bridge, firing right and left as they fled—
When they started J. W. Sutherland, armed with a Henry rifle, trie—
to head them off, but was not in time. Springing across the bridge—

the brave and determined man opened fire on them as they vaulted into their saddles, and one of his shots wounded Gomez slightly in the neck, and the other struck the redoubtable Chavez in the right leg, a little above the knee, inflicting a severe and intensely painful wound.

The robbers had obtained over $2,500 in hard coin, and a good deal of valuable jewelry. Vasquez, who took Reichart's watch and that of Douglass, promised to return them, but in his hurried exit from the town he had no time to make his word good.

One of the new recruits, named Monteres, afraid to make the passage of the bridge, followed the river bank down a little ways and hid. His movement was unobserved by any of the citizens.

At a Mexican house, some eight miles from the scene of the robbery, the band halted, and the wound of Chavez was dressed, as well as the scratch on Gomez's neck, and the booty divided.

Gomez volunteered to accompany the wounded "lieutenant" to a hiding-place on the Posa de Chane, while Vasquez, contrary to his usual custom, instead of dividing his force at once, kept the rest of his men together, and went in the direction of Tulare Lake.

Great excitement prevailed in Kingston, and a large crowd speedily collected, but no attempt was made to pursue the robbers until the next day. Early in the morning J. W. Sutherland, taking two volunteers with him, followed the trail of the robbers for the purpose of getting a clue to their probable destination, and about four miles from Kingston captured Monteres, who had crossed the bridge a little after midnight, and brought him into town. He confessed to being with the gang when it entered the town, and to standing guard at the hotel, but claimed that he was not a member of the organization, and did not know a single one of the bandits.

His story was that he was on his way to Kingston to buy some clothes, when he was overtaken by the robbers, who took his money and then forced him to accompany them and act the part he did. When the shooting began he ran down the river instead of across the bridge, and the band carried off his horse. He was taken to Millerton on the following Sunday by Constables Blackburn and Andy Farley, and lodged in jail. He was tried soon after, convicted, and is now serving out a fourteen year's sentence in the State Prison.

The excitement was once more at fever heat throughout Fresno, Tulare, and Kern counties, when the news of the Kingston robbery was heard. Sheriff Glascock, of Tulare, at once organized a posse of men and started out to strike the trail of the bandits; Sheriff Ashmore, of Fresno, also put scouts on their track, and measures were taken by Sheriff Coons, of Kern, who put officers on the alert to apprehend them should they pass through his territory.

On the 29th, three days after the robbery, the band was met in Tulare county, not far from Visalia, the county seat, by a citizen of the town, and he recognized one of the bandits as one of the Medina murderers, who had been tried and acquitted. The band did not disturb him, and he hastened to town with the information, and it was telegraphed all over the State. The robbers were moving westward when seen, but as there could be no calculation as to what their objective point was, no arrangements could be made to head them off.

In Bakersfield, the principal town in Kern county, and now the county seat, there was much excitement, and Vasquez and his depredations were for days the principal topic of conversation. Graphic accounts of the Kingston affair were published in the Bakersfield *Courier* and the *Southern Californian,* the local papers; and the probability of Vasquez making a raid upon the town was, at one time, considered imminent; but they are a "peculiar people" there, and there was no trepidation expressed. In fact, it was an event that would have been hailed with considerable satisfaction by a large number of the inhabitants. A respectable number of double-barrelled shot guns, Henry rifles, and Smith & Wesson's were lying about town within easy reach of men who knew how and when to use them, and who were not of the kind that would be apt to lie gently and uncomplainingly down at the command of one or two Mexican desperadoes, and yield up their coin and their manhood without a struggle.

Vasquez doubtless understood this perfectly well, and he prudently left Bakersfield out of the programme.

After his capture, however, he stated to the writer that he reached Kern River after riding here and there on the Tulare plains for a number of days after the robbery; he reached the Kern River some miles below the town, and then, waiting until nightfall, crossed the stream, halted his party, and leaving orders for them to follow, one at a time, half a mile apart, he went to Panama, the Spanish settlement before spoken of, some six miles below Bakersfield, and lay quietly resting for three days with his party—then consisting of five men.

After this rest and frolic among the Mexicans of Panama, he again separated from his band, and taking with him only **Blas Bicuna,** crossed the valley, and passing between Kern and Buena Vista Lakes, he proceeded to visit Chavez, at Posa Chane, and found his lieutenant rapidly recovering from the severe wound received at Kingston. In fact, he was nearly well. The bone had not been touched. He had suffered a great loss of blood, and the hard ride he had undergone after he received the wound had nearly "laid him out."

Soon after the Kingston affair a bill was passed by the Legislature appropriating fifteen thousand dollars, to be used by the Governor, at his discretion, in hunting down Vasquez and his gang. Rewards were offered in Monterey and one or two other counties for his apprehension, and there was a general feeling that he had had his own way long enough. He covered his tracks so well, however, during the winter, and had been so successful in the Kingston and other minor affairs, that he determined on still bolder operations when spring should open and there was plenty of grass for his horses. Temporarily dismissing Bicuna and Gomez without communicating to them his plans, he took Chavez, who had entirely recovered from his wound, and paid a visit to his friends in Soledad Canon and about Elizabeth Lake, keeping a bright lookout for spies and other enemies, and remained there, in that vicinity, for several weeks.

CHAPTER XVI.

THE EXCITEMENT THROUGHOUT SOUTHERN CALIFORNIA — THE BAKERSFIELD POSSE, UNDER DEPUTY-SHERIFF SHORT, AND THE TEHACHAPI POSSE, LED BY G. W. THOMPSON AND P. D. GREEN, SURROUND AND ATTACK LAS TUNIS—THE DARING ROBBERY AT COYOTE HOLES—VASQUEZ AND CHAVEZ ROB TWENTY MEN, AND A STAGE COACH LOADED WITH PASSENGERS.

THE OFFICERS of Kern, Los Angeles, Tulare and Fresno were continually on the alert during the winter for some clue that would lead to the arrest of Vasquez or any of his gang, and every man who had to move about much in the sparsely-settled portions of that region, constituted himself a volunteer detective; and every passing Mexican was closely scrutinized with the eye of suspicion. A singular diversity of description was current of Vasquez's size and general appearance, and he would probably have been the last man of his race in that region —if met alone and unarmed by those who were looking for him—that would have been arrested on suspicion of being Vasquez, the bandit chief, unless some one in the party actually knew him.

There were dozens of vaqueros, hunters and others who claimed to have met him, and a good many who were nearly certain they had met him, but scarcely any two of them agreed in their description of him. And the disposition of many to "draw the long bow" in telling what they knew or supposed they knew about him, greatly embarrassed the officers who were seeking information, and added to the security of the bandit, who seemed to bear a charmed life, and to be everywhere and nowhere at the same time.

There were hundreds of brave men in Kern and the adjoining counties who would face him and all the Mexican desperadoes he could rake and scrape in the whole country, or would pursue him into the mountain fastnesses and beard him in his den, if the locality of the den could only be found. There was the rub.

False information was so often given, that every rumor in regard to him was looked upon with distrust, and often attributed to Vasquez or his friends, who wished to throw dust in the eyes of their enemies.

A provoking instance of this sort of thing took place during the winter, I think in January. A dispatch from Tehachapi was received by Deputy-Sheriff Short, of Bakersfield, to the effect that an honest and reliable Mexican had brought word that Vasquez, Gomez, and others of the banditti were encamped in a narrow canon in the mountains between Tehachapi and the old Tejon Reservation. The dispatch stated that a posse would be raised at Tehachapi to blockade one entrance to the canon, and requested Short to raise a force in Bakersfield to co-operate and close in on the brigands from the opposite entrance to the canon.

There was no difficulty in raising the necessary force, and Short, with a posse of fifteen or twenty men, was soon on his way to the canon.

Meanwhile a meeting of the Tehachapi men, a class of people many of whom had "roughed it" on the plains, and some of whom had seen the hardest kind of service during the late war,—men who meant business every time, and, to use frontier vernacular, were "on the dead keen fight"—held a meeting for the purpose of organizing for the contemplated attack. They rendezvoused at the house of G. W. Thompson, the gentleman to whom the information had been given, and who had in a quiet manner notified them of what was up. They arrived at Thompson's one by one, to the number of thirty-one.

So quietly was the affair managed, that not a Mexican in the neighborhood had the slightest inkling that a movement was on foot.

After a good supper, Mr. Thompson was elected captain, and P. D. Green lieutenant. Both these men are characters worthy of more than a passing notice, known throughout the whole region as men of sterling integrity, and marked for their indomitable energy and cool, determined courage.

The party left Thompson's a little after nightfall, and about nine o'clock halted in the mouth of the canon. A detail were made to surround different houses. The particular house in which Vasquez and Gomez was supposed to be was quietly surrounded by a detail headed by Thompson and Green, and at early daylight a rush was made, and the house entered—but *they had gone!*

The two parties met half an hour later, and after exchanging mutual lamentations over their disappointment, returned to their homes.

Of course there is never any glory in a fiasco like this; but to the reflecting mind there is just as much credit due to the brave men who went out from Bakersfield and Tehachapi that night, as they would have deserved had they found Vasquez there and captured or killed him and his entire band. They went there for that purpose, were all brave, resolute men, who fully expected to have a fight with the whole band, and fully realized that the chances were that some of them would die.

Vasquez denied having been in the place at all—and I believe it is admitted by the participants in the affair that the information on which they acted was entirely false.

Although there was a large reward offered for Vasquez, Gomez was more particularly wanted by the Kern county people than the chief, on account of his cruel murder of Constable Mettler, of Tehachapi, and had he been found, the probabilities are that the county would never have been subjected to the trouble and cost of procuring him a trial and conviction.

The next notable exploit of Vasquez was the daring robbery at the Coyote Holes Station, on the stage road between Los Angeles and Owen's River, in which, with the assistance Chavez alone, he robbed twenty men at the station, and stopped the stage as it arrived, and robbed the passengers and Wells, Fargo & Co.'s treasure-box.

The affair shows with what terror and dread Vasquez was regarded, for it seems incredible that twenty able-bodied men could be found who would quietly submit to the dictation of two men, and give up their valuables. But the fact is, the muzzle of a six-shooter or Henry rifle is one of the most powerful arguments an orator of Vasquez's description can make use of; and it seems that with the assistance of a colleague with the same argument, he could sway a crowd.

On the 25th of February Vasquez and Chavez appeared on the brow of a little rise in front of the station, and suddenly opened fire with their Henry rifles.

After sending a few bullets through the roof of the building they approached the house. Posting his lieutenant, who had two Henry rifles, about fifty yards distant, where he could command the house and stables, and have a fair view of all approaches to the place, Vasquez went within twenty yards of the building and sternly called out:

"Come out, every one, or I will burn the house!"

A woman came to the door and demanded his errand.

"I am Tiburcio Vasquez," he replied. "Tell every one to come out. I will not injure them if they obey. It is the position only that I want. I am going to rob the stage when it arrives."

The woman retired, and the next moment the men came filing out, and Vasquez ordered them to fall into line, and then compelled them to sit down.

Calling them up one at a time, he "went through" them with scientific celerity. The victims were marched to a position where they could not be seen by the driver and passengers of the stage when it should arrive, again compelled to sit down in line, and calling Chavez to stand guard over them, returned to watch for the stage. As he neared the house, the thought struck him that he had not paid his compliments to the stable, and that there might be more men there.

As he approached the stable a man named W. P. Shore,—an old hunter commonly known by the sobriquet of "Texas"—made his appearance, considerably under the influence of liquor, and wanted to know "what the h-l was up." Vasquez ordered him to sit down, but the stable drainage not suiting "Texas' " ideas of an inviting spot on which to rest his haunches, he drew a revolver and fired on the bandit, much to the latter's surprise, as he was in the habit of being meekly obeyed.

Vasquez very coolly took aim at "Texas' " leg, and put a bullet through the fleshy portion of his thigh, sternly remarking,

"Next time I order, you obey!"

When the stage finally made its appearance, whirling up to the station in grand style, the bandit called to the driver to—

"Stop! Tell the passengers to come out!"

At the same time significantly tapping the barrel of his rifle. The passengers obeyed and sat down. The driver was ordered to "go ahead and unhitch," which he did, and Vasquez ordered a man to help him. In robbing the passengers, Vasquez laid his rifle on the ground a rod or two distant, and placed his pistol in his belt, taking the passengers over to him, searching their pockets and removing the valuables.

Wells and Fargo's treasure-box did not "pan-out" as he expected, most of the valuable contents being in the form of drafts and mining stocks, of which he could make no use.

One of the passengers, from which he took a pair of gloves, asked him to return them.

"How much are they worth?" inquired Vasquez.

"One dollar and a half," was the reply.

"Well," returned the robber, "here are two dollars; I will pay you for them; I need them and will keep them."

From another he had taken a spyglass, and he was asked to return that.

"No, no!" said he; "I have looked a long time for such an instrument, and have particular use for it."

He scattered about $10,000 worth of mining stock taken from the treasure-box to the four winds.

Taking six valuable horses from the stage company, and two belonging to private parties, himself and Chavez made their escape to a hiding-place near Soledad Canon.

CHAPTER XVII.

Sheriff Henry N. Morse, of Alameda county, commissioned by Governor Booth to hunt down Vasquez and his Banditti—Dick Brodden's story—"Buffalo Bill"—Exploring the Cantua—A bogus detective—One of Vasquez's telegraph operators.

Early in January, 1874, Hon. Newton Booth, Governor of the State, sent for Sheriff Morse, of Alameda, and had a long conference with that gentleman on how to effect the capture of Vasquez, and put a quietus on brigandage in the State.

Sheriff Morse — familiarly known throughout California, as "Harry Morse,"—has held the position of sheriff of the county of Alameda continuously since March 7th, 1864—eleven years—and during that period has earned the enviable distinction of being the most efficient officer in the State. When first elected sheriff the north-eastern portion of the county, around Livermore, was the rendezvous of some of the worst desperadoes in the State, and Morse made up his mind to clear them out.

As an initiatory step, he made it his first business to thoroughly study the topography of that portion of the county in which these outlaws had their hiding-places and strongholds. Leaving his office business in the hands of his under-sheriff most of the time—or whenever practicable—he was often for days at a time absent from home, scouring the hills and mountains, and making himself familiar with all the trails and with the faces and habits of the cattle-thieves and highwaymen.

He was called at first by the "Greasers," who ridiculed his bold and determined operations, the "beardless boy." But very soon they found reason to change their tune, and learned to have an almost superstitious dread of him.

Every once in a while he would, when least expected, suddenly make his appearance at one of their rendezvous, and spirit away some desperado that had been wanted for a long time; and in every case where resistance was made, he always came out victor, and more than one "Greaser" who had the temerity to stand up before him was made to bite the dust. His courage has been tested so often and under circumstances which left no room for question, that his courage and nerve have become proverbial. Combining as he does with this essential quality, those of prudence, shrewdness, and a determination that never tires, he has achieved a reputation that is not limited to this coast; and his photograph, accompanied with a description of his mental and physical characteristics, and some of his most noted achievements, may be seen at the headquarters of the principal detective centres of Europe.

He is a quiet, modest gentleman in his demeanor, fastidiously neat though plain in dress, except when on the "war-path," when he sometimes assumes disguises that render him in personal appearance more like a wandering mendicant than sheriff of one of the principal counties of the State.

A thousand anecdotes are told in regard to his adventures, some of which are as dramatic as anything in the wildest realms of romance, and some as grotesque as anything found in dime-novel literature. Here is a characteristic "yarn," in regard to the redoubtable sheriff, told by old "Dick Brodden," around the camp fire one night in the Livermore hills:

DICK BRODDEN'S STORY.

"About a year ago there was the gol darnest set of Greaser cattle thieves about these mountains ever you heard of. "Twarn't safe to turn critters into these hills, unless you stood right by 'em. These varmits could slip out in the night, throw a riata over a steer's head, and yank him down into some canon, and stick a knife into his gullet in no time. Ketch 'em at it? I guess hardly. They was too smart for that.

" 'Couldn't they watch who brought the hides in, to sell 'em?' asked one.

"Gol darn it, man, they didn't sell no hides. They knowed better'n that. They cut the hides up and braided 'em into lariats, and sold 'em in that shape.

"Wall, the thing got so common that people got kinder tired of it, and so the sheriff said he reckoned he could rake 'em in, and he sat about fixin' up his plans. These varmints were thought to have ther hidin' places in the hills back of San Leandro, and along up the Alameda creek, though whereabouts prezactly, nobody seemed to know.

"You fellars all know Morse—Sheriff Morse—I reckon? Of course you do; and if ever you go to putting your irons on anybody else's calves without their owner's being willin' you'll know him a darned sight better.

"He's known all over the State, and the Greasers in this section would rather see their grandmother's ghost, dressed in nothin' but a night-gown, than to see that sharp nose of his'n come pryin' into their fandango house. It's a sure sign some of 'em's wanted, and they generally get out of the back door without even sayin' good-night. They can't tell how to take the old fellow. Sometimes he presents himself without any disguise, and if you'd see him onct when his dander's up, you wouldn't wonder that they are scared of him. He is above low water mark, with a pair of arms and shoulders that can snake a brace of Greasers by the neck like two spring chickens. He generally has a smooth face, deep, piercing eyes, that seem as if they could look plum through a 'dobe wall.

"When Harry wants to slip up on a man, he just puts on a pair of iron-gray whiskers, and his own wife wouldn't know him. He's the bravest man on the Pacific coast, and I'll bet a horse he can dodge a bullet sixty yards every time.

"Wall, there was a party of six of us camped out on the creek bottom, about the time these fellars had been raisin' Ned. We had been out on a *rodeo,* but found that the cattle were scattered so bad that we concluded to wait for more vaqueros. One Sunday evening, about nine o'clock, as we laid around the campfire, among our blankets, all gassin' and singing', and spinnin' yarns, we heern a step up in the bushes on the hillside among the brush, which sounded like a wild varmint. Thinkin' it might be a bar, I crawled into my britches, and snatchin' a rifle, slipped out and up the hill. The rest of 'em laughed at me for gettin' up, but I knowed it was somethin'.

"As I was turnin' around a tree, peekin' up the hill, about a hundred yards from camp, somthin' bright flashed right under my nose, and gol darn my buttons if there wasn't an old gray-bearded man holdin' a pistol to my head, and with his left hand grippled hold of my rifle.

"Did I holler? Wall, scarcely. I jist dropped that gun; says I, like the gal to her lover, 'I'm yourn—take me!' And he took me. In a minute he had slung my rifle into the bushes, and I lay on my back with a pair of polished hand-cuffs on. The old gentleman politely informed me that I was one of a gang of cattle thieves, and that he wanted me to lay very quiet, while he went down and put some hand-cuffs on the rest of the crowd. He started off, but in a minute he came back and asked me several questions about the camp below, and after I told him what I had left the camp for, he just peeled off the ugliest lookin' wig and whiskers I ever saw, and gol darn my buttons if it wasn't old Morse! The minute I saw who it was, I took in the whole programmy at onct. He intended to take off my clothes, put them on, and go back and corral the other fellers. I don't know but what he would have done it if I hadn't recovered enough to mention my name.

" 'Dick Brodden!' says he, as he rolled me over, so that the moon shone full in my face. 'Why, man, what are you doin' in that crowd of Greasers?'

" 'Them's a lot of vaqueros on a *rodeo,*' says I.

"He was considerably much taken down, but he didn't say much; he first took the irons off my legs, and handed back my coat and hat, and we walked back into camp, whar the rest of the fellers were a'gittin' a little uneasy.

"He had heard of a band of thieves camped out somwhar in the canon, and had come up all alone to get a couple of 'em. I remembered seeing a camp fire further up the creek, and after taking a cup of hot coffee, we all concluded to go up with old Harry and see what it was.

"We slipped up through the brush to within a hundred yards of the camp, and found several mustangs staked on the grass. Harry looked closely at one of 'em, and then came back to where he told us to wait for him.

" 'Boys,' said he, 'I know that horse; he was stolen from San Leandro. We've got into a nest, and I wasn't mistaken, after all. Now, just stay where you are. Keep perfectly still, and don't follow me until I whistle.' And without saying another word he glided toward their camp. As he walked off with his shaggy whiskers and bushy false hair, he looked like old Rip Van Winkle. We heard a commotion among the Greasers as he approached. We heard him ask for a cup of coffee, and could hear the fellers rolling out of bed to kindle a fire.

" 'Que queres viejo?' we heard one Mexican ask.

" 'Uno tasa de cafe; tengo mucho se,' faltered the old man. Then we saw the fire blaze up, and knew the dodge was working.

"We must have waited an hour, expecting every moment to hear the signal. Suddenly a shrill, piercing whistle, followed by half-a-dozen vindictive 'carrajos!' from the Greaser captives, was heard, and we all rushed into the camp. There stood Harry Morse with a six-shooter in each hand, covering six as sneakin' lookin' Greasers as ever I ran across. They were a-cussin' and a-ragin', but not one of 'em had dared to get out of bed, for the old man had slipped all their shootin' irons away. He didn't go any further that night. Next mornin' we helped the sheriff down to San Leandro with his men, and this haul put a stop to cattle-stealin' for a while. Gol darn my dog-skin if I ever saw such a man as Harry Morse."

Precisely how matters were discussed between the Governor and the Sheriff, is of course known only to themselves, but it is understood that the Governor's proposition was for Morse to take thirty men, and move toward the lower counties, and with detachments sent right and left explore every stronghold of the bandits from Alameda county to San Bernardino, capturing or killing Vasquez and every desperado known to have co-operated with him, wherever found.

The sheriff, however, felt that a much smaller number would prove more effective, but finally consented to take eight men, and make a determined effort to capture the bandits, he to select the members of the party.

In accordance with this arrangement, the sheriff received the following as his authority from the Governor of the State:

STATE OF CALIFORNIA,
EXECUTIVE DEPARTMENT,
SACRAMENTO, CAL., JAN. 19, 1874.

H. N. MORSE, ESQ.:

Dear Sir—-The Legislature having placed five thousand dollars at the Governor's disposal, for actual costs and expenses to be incurred in the capture of Vasquez and his band, it is the desire of the Governor that you should take charge of and have full control of such persons as you may think requisite to success; keeping in view the necessity of not exceeding the appropriation. You will please communicate with this office as to your plans and probable cost.

Very respectfully,

A. HART, PRIVATE SECRETARY.

With this authority, Morse sought the co-operation of Thomas Cunningham, sheriff of San Joaquin county, to act as his lieutenant. Although a younger man than Morse, being only thirty-four years of age, he is now holding his second term of office, and has already earned most enviable distinction as a brave, energetic and efficient officer. San Joaquin county, before his election to the sheriffalty was the favorite stamping ground of escaped convicts and fugitives from other parts of the State. It is related of Morse that previous to Cunningham's election, whenever he would capture a criminal in Alameda, or in one of the lower counties, he would sarcastically remark: "Why the devil didn't you go to San Joaquin; you would be safe enough there?" It is no longer the case, as he has driven the thieves and scoundrels from that region by his untiring vigilance and his executive ability. He is also an agreeable man, with nothing ferocious in his features to indicate the courage and nerve he is known to possess. He is a rollicking, jovial man, full of dry humor, fond of his joke—and a most agreeable companion on an expedition of this character—the life of the camp. He readily consented to accompanying the expedition, and assisted Morse in laying out a programme of operations. The balance of the party was made up as follows:

Harry Thomas, deputy-sheriff of Fresno county, a young man of sterling character, noted for his energy and courage, and who is accredited with having done more towards delivering Fresno county from the depredations of criminals than any sheriff the county has ever had. He is a strict temperance man, and his principles of every kind are strict.

Ambrose Calderwood, formerly sheriff of Santa Cruz county—1864-65—now residing in Oakland, Alameda county. A gentleman familiar with the dangers and hardships of trailing desperadoes, and who distinguished himself while sheriff as a most efficient officer. He once had a desperate hand-to-hand encounter in a dark room with a desperate outlaw named Lorenzano, whom he over-powered and secured after he had shot him in the shoulder, himself receiving a knife wound in the arm.

Ralph Faville, of Pleasanton, Alameda county, for many years a deputy under Sheriff Morse, and noted for his success in hunting cattle thieves and desperadoes.

George B. Morse, a son of the sheriff. Although only eighteen years of age, is noted for his superior horsemanship, and is an excellent shot.

A. B. Henderson, now news editor of the leading San Francisco daily, the *Chronicle*. He is better known among journalists as "Boyd Henderson." Some two years ago his letters to the New York *Herald*, detailing his experience among the "Lowery Outlaws" in North Carolina, among whom he spent ten days, attracted much attention. Boyd Henderson was the first newspaper correspondent who succeeded in passing through the Spanish lines, and "interviewing" the insurgents of Cuba. He returned from his trip through Southern California thoroughly endorsed by the sheriff—the only fault that officers found with him being his enormous appetite.

Ramon Romero, of San Leandro, a Mexican, was attached to the expedition, on account of his knowledge of the country. He is an accomplished horseman, and could from the saddle throw a lasso or pick up a pin from the ground with equal ease. He proved very useful as a forager on the expedition.

A. J. McDavid, of Sunol. A veteran hunter and a splendid rifle shot. McDavid was employed to drive the wagon, and when the rest of the party were absent he remained as guard.

These parties were seen, and their consent obtained, and the 12th of March fixed upon for the movement. An earlier date could not safely be chosen, on account of the winter rains rendering many of the streams impassable, and it was also necessary to wait until the grass was well up and feed for the horses could be relied upon.

Meanwhile every preparation had been made. Horses had been furnished from the camp of Miller & Lee, and had been sent to Firebaugh's Ferry a week prior to the day fixed upon for making a start. McDavid and Geo. B. Morse arrived at Firebaugh's with the baggage wagon and provisions on the evening of the 11th.

On Thursday, March 12th, at 4 P.M., Morse and Calderwood were joined at the Central Pacific Depot by Henderson; at San Leandro by Ramon Romero.

At Lathrop the party expected to find Sheriff Cunningham, who was to join them there and take the Southern Pacific train for Berenda. On reaching there, however, to Morse's intense disappointment, he looked in vain among the passengers waiting about the depot for the familiar features of his promised lieutenant. He finally concluded to telegraph, to learn what was the matter, and going to the window of the telegraph office, took a blank, and indited the following:

LATHROP, March 12, 1874.

T. CUNNINGHAM, Sheriff, Stockton.

Party here. What's up?

MORSE.

"Nothing!" said a deep, gruff voice in the sheriff's ear. Turning angrily he beheld a tall, uncouth figure, with shocking red hair and whiskers to match, staring impudently over his shoulder at the dispatch. The indignant sheriff was about to send the boor spinning across the room, when he suddenly recognized the familiar twinkle of "Tom's" eye. The uncouth figure was that of Sheriff Cunningham, so disguised that his own mother would not have known him.

In retaliation for the joke, Morse christened him lieutenant "Buffalo Bill," an appellation that clung to him like a poor man's plaster during the adventurous trip.

Both Chavez and Vasquez had numerous friends among the Mexicans in and about Stockton, the county seat of San Joaquin, and Cunningham was constantly watched, and he determined that he would leave the city unrecognized. His ruse was thoroughly successful.

On reaching Berenda the party left the railroad, and reached Firebaugh's Ferry about noon on the 13th, and there found Thomas, Faville, George Morse, and McDavid, which made the party of adventurers complete. On the following day they crossed a barren plain, with no water for men or animals until they reached Panoche creek at the foot of the inner coast range, at 1 P.M., a distance of 24 miles, and there selected for a camping place a little canon out of sight of the Cantua road.

Sunday and Monday, 15th and 16th, were occupied in exploring the Cantua, the party working in twos, except Romero, who was sent by a wide detour to "interview" Mexicans. He remained all night at a house where Vasquez usually stopped, and his errand was not suspected. He learned that Vasquez had not been there for several weeks, but was expected in a few days.

On the following day the party moved south, passing the Posa de Chane, and camped on the western bank of the Pulvederas. They passed the domicile of a white man, who showed them a "late paper"— date, February 22d! Nearest post-office, fifty miles.

On Wednesday the wagon was taken into a canon, where, it was thought, it would be thoroughly concealed, and Morse and Cunningham rode to the house of one Culp, and dismounted. Morse himself was about as thoroughly disguised as Cunningham. While the two officers were standing and chattering together Cunningham cracking his usual jokes, they were considerably astonished at the sudden apparition of a tall, rakish young American, rather nobbily dressed, and with a "gallus look" generally, sauntering toward them at a leisurely, self-assured gait, looking as though pretty well satisfied with himself and the world generally. A diamond pin glittered on his snowy shirt-front, his five dollar felt hat set jauntily on four hairs, and a half-consumed real Havana pointed like a telescope toward his left eye. Halting before the officers, withdrawing the cigar-stub from beneath his delicate mustache, and leering at Morse with a grin which was a cross between the simper of a drygoods clerk and the smile of a San Francisco hoodlum, he remarked:

"I know what you fellers is on."

Morse was considerably taken back, and replied with some warmth: "Oh! What do you mean? We ain't *on* anything."

"Oh, it's too thin—too thin!" adding, with his under lip thrust out, á la butcher boy, "I'm on it meself!" at the same time pulling aside the lapel of his coat and exhibiting a pair of hand-cuffs peeping out of the inside pocket.

Morse eyed him from head to foot curiously for a moment, and then turned away with a look of intense disgust, leaving Cunningham to "josh" with the singular apparition if he chose.

Cunningham soon left him and rode with Morse to the camp where the wagon was, Morse riding on a little distance, and finally moving up the side of the canon to a point from which he could get a good view of the valley beneath.

About a hour afterward Morse was surprised to see Cunningham and Ramon, mounted, and streaking it like mad across the plain below. He hastened to the wagon, where he learned from George that the "exquisite" above referred to, had the cheek, a few minutes after he left, to saunter into camp, and that, after looking about for a few moments, had ridden off.

Soon after he left, Cunningham's suspicions were aroused by his actions and appearance, and he ordered Calderwood, Thomas, and Ramon to mount and accompany him in pursuit.

It turned out that Cunningham's party came in sight of him three or four miles from camp, when he, perceiving them, turned, and rode off on another trail. Cunningham and Ramon rode across a canon, and, by a detour, cut him off, and coming on to him suddenly, Cunningham rode alongside and clapping a pistol to his left ear, remarked:

"Throw up your hands!"

"That's me!" was the unperturbed reply. The reins fell to the horse's neck and the jeweled hands went up as if the "gallus" figure were an automaton, and the muzzle of Tom's pistol had set it going.

He was deprived of two revolvers and a bowie, and a pair of hand-cuffs, and brought to camp. He was there searched, and in his pockets were found a large silver watch, a small diamond ring (with the name of "John Robb" engraved on each), a memorandum book, a number of papers, and a sealed letter with a U.S. stamp upon the envelope, and addressed, "Alexander D. Redwood, Lock Box No. 7, Gilroy." The letter was opened with the prisoner's consent, and was found to contain, among other things, the following:

"There is a party here in search of Vasquez; they have a four-horse wagon and a Greaser to interpret for them. They are the biggest set of fools I ever saw, for Vasquez is a hundred miles from here."

This letter, signed "40," Robb said, was to David Watson, Gilroy. He said he was searching for Chavez, whom he had wounded a short time before, and whose knife he had taken. He also exhibited a photograph, which he said was that of Chavez, but which Harry Thomas recognized as that of Ciatanna Garcia, whom he (Thomas) killed in 1872. Morse and Cunningham went to Culp's and found there a soldier's blue overcoat and another knife belonging to Robb.

Morse overcame his disgust sufficiently to sleep with Robb that night.

CHAPTER XVIII.

BOYD HENDERSON INTERVIEWS MARIANNA MURIETA, RELICT OF THE LATE JOAQUIN MURIETA, THE "MARAUDER OF THE MINES"—WHAT JOAQUIN'S WIDOW THINKS OF VASQUEZ—EXPLORING THE JACALITAS FOR TRACES OF THE BANDITS—A HIDING PLACE FOR STOLEN HORSES—ARREST OF NICHOLAS RUIZ—THE START FOR TEJON CANON.

ABOUT ten o'clock on the following morning Morse, Cunningham, Henderson, and George left camp to visit Marianna, the widow of the famous Joaquin Murieta, the "Marauder of the Mines," previously sending Ramon off to the Jacalitas in search of information.

At Kell's house, some five miles from camp, a pleasant-looking but dirty little woman (who recognized Cunningham) directed the trail-hunters to Jones', two miles further on. The woman stated that Robb had been there a few days before and had inquired for a man who had been shot in the hip.

There being no one at home at Jones', the party hunted the barn for eggs, and then rode on over a country every square mile of which contained half a dozen good hiding places for robbers. On their route they discerned a curiously constructed house, built in, on, and against rocks which overhung a little creek.

Twelve miles from Jones', and eighteen from camp, they found the famous Marianna, in a sheepherder's tent, on Kettleman's Plains. She is now forty-three years of age, and not ill-looking. One drink of whiskey set her talking volubly (in Spanish), and a second filled her with animation. She says that Joaquin was but nineteen years of age when he was killed by Billy Henderson (now owner of a ranch near Los Angeles), of Harry Love's party; that he had fair complexion, light hair, and blue eyes. Once when she left him to unite her fortunes with those of Charlie Baker, Joaquin followed her, burnt Baker's camp, shot her in the arm, cut her across the breasts and face, and left her for dead. A well-defined scar reaches from her left ear to her nose.

She stated that on the 1st of January Chavez was here with a bad wound in his right leg, which was black and horribly swollen. He was accompanied by a tall, dark man (supposed by Morse to be Manuel Lopez), [This must, probably, have been Gomez, whom Vasquez detailed to accompany Chavez, after the Kingston raid, Dec. 26.] who had been shot in the neck, and whose clothes were covered with dried blood stains—injuries undoubtedly received at Kingston, at the hands of J. W. Sutherland. She stated further that Vasquez had recently shaved his face, was supplied with a red wig and mustache, and blackens his lower eyelids so that no one would recognize him except by his left eye, which is apparently sunken. She drew comparisons between Joaquin and Vasquez, to the disadvantage of the latter, whom she considered but a petty thief, and despite her infidelity to, and wounds at the hands of, her husband, she takes great pride in being called "Joaquin's widow."

Henderson says:

"Despite her loose mode of life, her present fondness for *aguadiente*, and a scar extending across her face, from nose to ear, she is not by any means a homely or repulsive-looking woman. Her lips still retain their fine curves, and her teeth are a marvel of preservation. It required no very strong draughts on the imagination to believe that 'twenty years ago' she possessed a figure which was a model of grace, and that then, arrayed in the brilliant-hued garments her husband admired, with her magnificent eyes, either sparkling at the daring deeds of her protector, or looking with defiance at his hunters; she was the woman of rare beauty and witchery who could maintain her supremacy in the robber's ardent affections, even after his discovery of her infidelity to himself. Then, too, more in harmony with her appearance, was her soft, musical name.

"Scarcely less than her tongue do her eyes, head and gracefully-shrugged shoulders assist to convey her ideas, while, under the exciting influence of her stories, her swinging arms, and her small feet stamping the earth, give strong emphasis to her assertions. All her life she has been associated with cattle thieves, highway robbers and murderers. Personally and well acquainted with all the later bandits—Vasquez, Chavez, *et id genus omne*—and being a woman of apparently keen observation, she tells some stories of surpassing interest, the subjects of all her tales being like those described in 'Sir Peter's lament,' when

'He told them of men who cared not a d—n,
    For the law or the new police,
And had very few scruples for killing a lamb
    If they fancied they wanted the fleece.'

And she differs somewhat in her version of the death of Joaquin from the accepted one. She says, Joaquin, flying before the hot pursuit of Harry Love, determined to unearth his buried treasure and escape to Mexico. This treasure was concealed near the Tres Piedras, a favorite haunt of the robber, the spot where 'Three-Fingered Jack' was killed, and now commonly known as 'The Joaquin Rocks.'

"Arriving with five of his men at a spot on the Cantua, opposite the house in which Marianna had lived while true to her husband, and which has been later that occupied by Abdon Leiva, a favorite haunt of the Vasquez gang, he stopped at the creek to bathe with cold water the chafed backs of his horses, and here Harry Love's party dashed in, and Joaquin met his death. Marianna claims that the head was not removed, but that the mutilated body is buried under a tree on the banks of the Cantua. In the place described by her, I found a small oak with a rude cross cut in its bark on the side furthest from the road. The head which has been on exhibition in a San Francisco museum, she says, is that of Pedro Venda, an Indian." [While at Los Angeles, recently, I was introduced to W. T. Henderson, who was a member of Love's party, and who killed Joaquin. He is highly respected in Los Angeles county, where he owns and works a ranch, and his word can't be doubted. He saw the head severed from Joaquin's body, and was one of its exhibitors before it was sold to the museum. Joaquin was well known to him. In fact the boy was at his house often, before he began his career of crime.]

From this time on until the 8th of April was spent in exploring the Jacalitas, and in fact every hole and corner in Diablo and Santa Lucia range of mountains infested by brigands, and horse and cattle thieves. In the valley of the Jacalitas, and all through the foothills, were score of horses, mostly captured mustangs, and many American horses. Nine-tenths of them and ninety-nine one hundreth of all those of the horned cattle were stolen from other parts of the State—this being the great centre for hiding stolen horses and cattle. The Jacalitas runs through an extremely rocky and mountainous country, and in its course makes frequent acute angles. Its waters are of crystal clearness. It has no particular outlet, but (like all streams in this section) gradually sinks from the sight. The houses are hovels, the sides made of sticks stuck perpendicularly in the ground, and these bound together with smaller ones, the whole plastered over with mud. The roofs are formed of branches covered with earth. We saw one house of braided "tulles" brought from Tulare Lake, eighteen miles distant.

The party was harrassed greatly by false information, which kept them hurrying hither and thither day after day, with scarcely an opportunity for the rest absolutely necessary to keep up their vitality.

On the 21st Ramon arrested Nicholas Ruiz, who was suspected of having had a hand in the Kingston robbery. At night he was handcuffed to a wagon wheel after being furnished two pairs of blankets. Robb, who was still retained in durance odd, offered to stand guard over the new prisoner, but his services were politely declined. This genius puzzled the party as completely as the main problem they were working so hard to solve. There was no place in Nevada, California or Utah with which he was not thoroughly familiar. He was very gay and apparently free from care.

The Mexicans in this vicinity laughed at the efforts of the sheriffs to do anything. Most of them are robbers, and would take life any time for $5, if they got the opportunity. Many of these wretches fled to the mountains, taking their horses with them, being afraid of arrest.

On the 23d the wife of the prisoner Ruiz visited the camp, and there being no proof on which to hold him he was discharged. The gay and festive Robb—self-constituted detective and "bandit-sharp"—was released, though all thought him a robber.

It was subsequently ascertained that this estimate was correct. He was an escapee from the Santa Cruz jail; and subsequent developments proved conclusively that he was operating with the Vasquez gang, and one of a large number throughout the country who were in league— Vasquez being the figure-head and trusted leader.

When arrested he was on his way with the letter to the next "telegraph" station, and within a week the movements of Morse's party would have been made known to Vasquez, and there would have been a change in the entire programme. The detention of this individual, and of all other suspicious characters whom Morse thought likely to divine his errand and send information to the outlaw, left Vasquez in entire ignorance of the movement; and he never heard of the move until after his last robbery near Los Angeles.

On the 27th the party began crossing the covert, and a little after noon began to descend the west side of the mountain, and on the following day struck the plains of Salinas, about four o'clock P.M., reaching the San Antonio post office at eight o'clock, where they heard of Robb again. He rode a good horse, and never carried any blankets; always had "good stopping places," and plenty of money.

Calderwood and Faville were sent off on a scout that morning in the direction of Jolon. A drunken Irishman from that place met the balance of the party, and informed them that he had met two detectives on the road, "one with a defective eye and one with a red nose" (describing Calderwood and Faville), and added, "they are the darndest fools of detectives I iver saw."

On the 30th, six miles from Jolon, the party passed the old mission of San Antonio, and there heard information that Chavez, Refuffio, and Manuel Lopez were at a point fourteen miles distant that morning.

Acting on this information, Morse decided to go after them, and make a determined effort to capture them.

He crossed the Coast Range with his party, over difficult and dangerous trails, finding snow on the mountain tops, and day after day exploring the canons and mountain trails, searching cabins and hiding places, but without accomplishing the object of their mission.

They had, however, accumulated a fund of information for future use, and were by no means discouraged, but turned back to the lower coast range, and on Wednesday, April 8th, started from the Alamo Solo south over Kettleman's Plains, on their way towards Fort Tejon and the Elizabeth Lake country, satisfied that Vasquez was in Los Angeles county. The party had now been in the saddle twenty-seven days, during which they had thoroughly explored the difficult, and in many places almost inaccessible, wilderness in which Vasquez and his gang had their most secure hiding-places. During these twenty-seven days they had travelled over one thousand miles, making an average of over thirty-seven miles each day.

CHAPTER XIX.

VASQUEZ AGAIN IN THE SADDLE—THE LAST "CAMPAIGN" OF THE BANDIT CHIEF—ROBBERY OF ALEXANDER REPETTO, NEAR LOS ANGELES —BILLY ROWLAND ON THE ROBBERS' TRAIL—DARING ROBBERY OF CHARLEY MILES, JOHN OSBORNE AND JOHN RHOADES, WITHIN SIGHT OF THE SHERIFF'S PARTY.

MEANWHILE Vasquez and Chavez had remained quietly in their retreat near Soladad, in blissful ignorance of the fact that Morse and his party were scouring every hole and corner of the country, looking for them, and having thoroughly wearied of their seclusion, made ready for a renewal of their operations on a more daring scale than ever. It is the aim of the writer to give the facts in this narrative without indulging in any perversion of the truth for the sake of effect. It is evident to any one that in the life of one who only semi-occasionally came to the surface, and then sank into temporary oblivion, shunning the sight of the world and plodding in dark, something must be left to conjecture.

This much is certain, however, that during the winter of 1873-4, Vasquez and his coadjutors planned an extensive raid through the country, such as would eclipse anything in the operations of banditti in modern times. The definite or rather ultimate plan or objective point of the scheme has been buried in temporary oblivion by Vasquez's discomfiture at the outset of operations, and the whole matter may never see the light except through his voluntary confession. But this much is certain.

He had his eye upon a point considerably removed from his usual "stamping ground," where a successful robbery would put him in possession of the means to arm and equip one hundred and fifty or two hundred men. With that force, divided into three divisions and acting in concert, in accordance with his plans, and under his orders—a series of bold movements, including the sacking of the principal towns in Southern California—were contemplated. What he intended to do in case of success is problematical. He says he intended to leave the State. Doubtless he would have found it advisable to do so. This scheme, visionary and impracticable as it was—considering the worthless material he had to depend upon to constitute his force—was, without doubt, in contemplation, the leading spirits being Vasquez, Chavez, Gomez, Manuel Lopez, and Isidore Padillo.

As an initiatory step Vasquez, with Chavez and two or three others were to perpetrate, in quick succession, one or more robberies in Los Angeles, and with the proceeds purchase arms and equipments for the contemplated grand raid in the spring.

About the last of March Vasquez, Chavez, Padillo, Lebrado Corona, and another man, whose name is unknown to the authorities, took up their headquarters at the house of Greek George, on the La Brea Rancho, about eight miles from the city of Los Angeles, in a northeasterly direction. The house was situated in the plain, about sixty or seventy rods from the base of a range of high hills, running nearly east and west, and over which, through the canons, were several trails leading to the San Fernando Valley.

The spot was most excellently chosen. Close to the house, on the south side, was a monte, with plenty of good water, and within a few rods, along the monte, a willow thicket, which afforded an excellent concealment for horses or men. Surrounding the house on the three other sides, was a dense thicket of mustard, growing to the height of from five to seven feet. A wagon track ran parallel with the course of the mountain, about six or eight rods distant from the house. Few but Mexicans had occasion to travel it, and seldom had any one any errand at the house who would have any occasion to mistrust that the quiet homely adobe building was the headquarters of the desperadoes whose exploits were causing such consternation throughout the State.

The bandits took their meals in the kitchen of the house, but slept at night in their blankets among the tall mustard plants, with the exception of the chief, who had a bed in the building, which he usually occupied, although he occasionally crossed to San Fernando Valley, where there were several houses at which he was welcome.

Corona was only about twenty years of age, and had never accompanied Vasquez on any of his expeditions; but the robber had managed to get control of him, and the young fellow was so won by the romantic bearing and vivacious conversation of the bandit chief, that he was eager to make his first essay in the life of crime which Vasquez had pictured as such a glorious one. It was almost a repetition of the course taken by Garcia with Vasquez, when the latter was a stripling, and eager to enter a life full of adventure.

Corona could be sent to Los Angeles for news, and elsewhere through the country, or be safely employed as a spy or scout in whatever portion of the country the band might choose to move, with little danger of apprehension, and he was regarded as a valuable acquisition. He was accordingly directed to mount his horse and move about here and there among his Mexican acquaintances, and endeavor to find out what ranches in the vicinity were in funds, and where a profitable haul could be made.

After several days scouting here and there he returned with the cheerful intelligence that one Alexander Repetto, an Italian, who owned and lived on a ranch some six miles south-east from Los Angeles, had lately made some sales of wool, etc., and Vasquez resolved to rob him.

It will be necessary, in order to give an intelligible idea of the boldness of the robbery, and enable the reader to thoroughly appreciate the plan of the escape and the determined nature of the pursuit, to explain the topography of the country in the vicinity of Los Angeles. Soledad Canon lies about the centre of the county, in the San Gabriel

range of mountains, and runs nearly east and west, opening upon the
Mojave Desert in the east, and giving an outlet to the Soledad Creek
into the Santa Clara River, which flows through Ventura county to the
sea. Several spurs or ribs extend from the backbone of the main
range from points to the north-east of Los Angeles, running in a general
southwesterly direction, and between them lie wild and gloomy canons,
notably the Big and Little Tejunga, lying between grand and rugged
ridges known by the name given them by the Indians, as the Tejunga
Mountains—bold, precipitous, bare of timber except occasional patches
of spruce on some of the sides, and the usual willows, alders, and sycamores along the stream at the bottom of the deep gorges and canons,
and the chapparal on the mountain sides.

To the west from the termination of these spurs, from a point
nearly north of the city, enclosed on the north by the main range and
on the south by the "Sierra Santa Monica" Mountains, lies the San
Fernando Valley. The Los Angeles River runs east near the base
of this range (which, towards its eastern extremity, gradually descends
into a lower range south and east of the city, terminating abruptly
there), and winds around the base toward the south.

The old San Gabriel Mission lies about seven miles from the city,
a little south of east, and El Monte lies two miles southeast from the
mission.

An erratic stream called the Arroyo Seco has its raise in the Tejunga range, and finding its tortuous way through a dismal canon,
dashing madly down precipices, passes south for five or six miles in
a deep gulch, separated by a range of high hills from the Los Angeles
Valley, turns abruptly west around their southern base and empties
into the river directly opposite the city.

Between this gulch through which the stream passes, and a bold,
precipitous spur of the San Gabriel range, which sits south some two
miles in width, bare of trees except a small portion some two miles
down from the spur of the mountain, and here are some thrifty live oaks.

A tract of several thousand acres of this magnificent natural garden
has been purchased by an association of capitalists, most of them from
Indianapolis, Ind., under the name of the Los Angeles Orange Grove
Association, and the whole is being laid out in vineyards, olive, walnut,
peach, and orange orchards. A large reservoir has been constructed,
and some artesian wells put down, to ensure against the contingency of
a dry season at any time.

Standing at the lower or southern end of this noble plain, and looking north upon the wall of perpendicular rock which rises for hundreds
of feet, and to the left (as you stand) of the Arroyo Seco Canon, you
see what looks like an exactly straight line running from the base of
the mountain diagonally upward and to the right until it is lost to view
in the dark shadows of the canon.   It is in reality a narrow, steep trail,
called Moore's Trail, after the name of Captain Moore, who constructed
it, intending to put a road across the Tejunga Mountains into the Big
Tejunga Canon; and thence across the mountains to the Soledad.   All
difficulties were overcome, and the trail constructed for a distance of
some nine miles, until a point was reached, within sight of the Tejunga.
The trail terminates abruptly on a high ridge, looking down a flat
descending toward the Tejunga, sloping from the brows of the semicirc-
ular collection of knobs, spars, and ridges which enclose it on three
sides.   The flat itself is seamed with precipitous gulches, and ribbed
with ridges running between them, and the whole is covered with manzanita chapparal of such vigorous and lusty growth, and so densely
crowded, that a full grown grizzly bear could scarcely force his way
through it.   The descent from the lower edge of this flat to the bottom
of the canon was abrupt and precipitous.

In forming his plan for the robbery of Repetto—knowing that from
the vicinity of the ranch to the city, immediate pursuit was inevitable—
Vasquez selected Moore's trail as a line of retreat to the Soledad
rendezvous—not dreaming that Morse and his party were rapidly
approaching their stronghold in a manner that would blockade every
avenue of escape.   He engaged the services of a Mexican guide who
professed to know the route—to pilot horses and party across the
mountains to the Big Tejunga, from whence he knew the route well
enough himself, having more than once had occasion to travel it.

Making his way from Greek George's house, through an adjacent
trail through the hills, he crossed the San Fernando Valley, and crossing the railroad about two miles south of the San Fernando depot, he
proceeded to a point where the Verduga and Tejunga Canons open
side by side into a broad level plain, broken on one side by a rocky
gulch, through which the Tejunga creek flows, and where there are
but two houses—"Sutton's ranch"—and proceeding up the Verduga
Canon, encamped at its intersection with the Orange Grove Association's land, in a secluded spot in the bottom of the Arroyo Seco, breaking
camp next morning (April 12, 1874) in time to reach Repetto's place

soon after daylight. Dismounting near the ranch, and leaving three of his men hidden behind a fence in the rear of the house, he took Corona with him, and inquired for Repetto. When the Italian made his appearance, the two men claimed to be sheep-shearers, looking for a job. They were informed that the proprietor of the ranch had no work for them, but they entered into conversation, when Repetto's suspicions were excited by noticing the fact that Vasquez's smooth hands did not present the appearance of having been used to the business of shearing sheep, or of other manual labor, and intimated as much in his remarks.

The robber very promptly acknowledged the soft impeachment, and smilingly stepped to the door and gave a preconcerted signal. The next moment Signor Repetto found himself in the power of the terrible Vasquez and four of his merciless myrmidons.

Vasquez had no need to tell him the nature of his unpleasant errand —the magic of the name and the ominous Henry rifles and six-shooters told the story.

The bandit, however, made the customary demand.

Repetto assured him that eighty dollars in coin was every cent there was about the premises.

The indignant robber told the Italian bluntly that he lied, and compelled him to produce his books and accounts. The eighty dollars were promptly seized, and the tell-tale books produced, and a critical examination of the same showed the wily robber that even if Repetto's story was true literally, that he had no money in the house, yet there was a very respectable amount deposited to his credit in Temple & Workman's Bank, of Los Angeles.

Vasquez's consummate assurance was equal to the emergency, and he coolly gave the Italian his choice, to sign an order or check on the bank for $800, or be hanged to a limb of one of the ornamental trees in front of his residence; at the same time expressing great regret at the situation which imposed upon him the necessity of using harsh measures, and of robbing him at all. He said that he only wanted to make a "loan" of the amount, to enable him to carry out a scheme he had in view, and that he would very shortly return it. But smilingly assured Signor Repetto that the loan *must* be forthcoming immediately.

Repetto, showing no disposition to obey, was taken out into the yard and tied to the bole of an olive tree until he came to his senses and cried "peccavi." Upon his release he entered the house and signed the required document, and handing it to his nephew, who was present and witnessed all the proceedings, told him to mount and ride to the city, get the check cashed, and return with the money as quickly as possible, without giving the alarm. Vasquez followed the young man into the yard and gave him some additional instructions, to the effect that he must be cool and not show any agitation when presenting the check; just lay the check down in the ordinary manner, and not give, by his manner, the slightest cause for suspicion.

"Remember," said the robber, "your uncle's life is at stake as well as your own. If you dare to betray me I will kill your uncle, escape from any force the sheriff may send after me, and I will make it my next business to kill you. You cannot hide from me, for I have men all over the country, and can get hold of you at any time. If you go, get the money, and bring it in all right neither you nor your uncle will be harmed, and the money will soon be returned—but beware how you betray me, either by design or any foolish nervousness. Adios!"

The young man made the best possible time to Los Angeles.

As soon as he had gone, Vasquez, who had discovered a telescope lying on a side-table, took a good view of the approaches from every direction through the instrument, and then handing it to Corona, stationed him outside the house, with instructions to keep a sharp lookout and to give instant alarm if any horsemen came in sight, and then the others busied themselves cooking breakfast.

The nephew crossed the bridge, and entered Los Angeles at an ordinary pace, after "loping" the animal nearly all the way from Repetto's, and did his level best to carry out Vasquez's instructions to the letter—for he verily believed that not only his own but his uncle's life hung on a very slender thread.

He was not equal to the emergency, however, for on presenting the check, his emotion was so great as to excite instant suspicion that something was wrong.

The cashier examined the check narrowly, to see if the signature was genuine, and finding it all right, was at an utter loss to understand the young gentleman's emotion.

Questions failing to elicit any satisfactory solution, the cashier communicated at once with the president of the bank, Mr. Temple, who sent for the sheriff, and then had the young man invited into the president's apartment.

Mr. Temple spoke kindly to him, said he hoped there was nothing wrong, and inquired as to the health of his uncle. Thus cornered, the young man fairly broke down, and burst into tears.

Sheriff Rowland soon after made his appearance, and joined with Mr. Temple in endeavoring to soothe the young man's agitation—assuring him that if he had done anything out of the way in a moment of temptation, that he was in good hands, and that if he made a clean breast of his transgressions they would protect him.

He then told his story, greatly to the astonishment of Mr. Temple and the sheriff.

Having made the disclosure, however, the young man insisted on the check being cashed.

The sheriff lost no time in organizing a force for the capture, sending at once a courier post haste to El Monte for a party to co-operate with one from Los Angeles, which was got together as quickly as possible.

The young man was delayed at the bank until he could be restrained no longer, when Mr. Temple gave him five hundred dollars in gold, and with that he remounted, and gallopped away to Repetto's.

Billy Rowland's hastily organized force was not long in following, but kept about a mile in the rear, so as not to give the alarm prematurely. On reaching the place, the young man threw himself from his horse and rushing into the house, flung the bag of coin upon the table.

Almost at the same instant Padillo, who had relieved Corona as sentinel, saw a party of armed horsemen emerging from a ravine in some low hills, and instantly gave the alarm.

Without waiting to count the coin, Vasquez shouted the order "To horse!" and rushing from the house, vaulted into their saddles, and dashed off at the top of their speed, heading toward the Orange Grove Association's land on the Arroyo Seco.

Vasquez, as usual on such occasions, had an extra horse along, so that in the events of a long ride he could change off, and beat his pursuers.

All the party were well mounted, while the sheriff in the emergency had no opportunity to select his mount, but had to take such animals as he could get at a moment's notice at the livery stables in the city. A few of them were fast for a short distance, but of no account on a long, fatiguing chase.

Finding that his party could distance the pursuers, Vasquez prudently slackened his gait, and only rode fast enough to keep beyond range of rifle shots, occasionally flying ahead as he came in sight of houses where there was a possibility some fresh horseman might join in the pursuit.

In crossing the Orange Grove Association's land, the bandits met a wagon containing Charley Miles, Superintendent of the Los Angeles Water Company, John Osborne, expressman, and John Rhoades, who were returning from a visit to the reservoir, then in course of construction, and the fugitive bandit resolved to rob the party under the sheriff's very nose.

Spurring his animals to the top of their speed for a few hundred yards, to increase the distance from the pursuing party, he halted, and as the wagon approached, Vasquez, directing his men to surround it, sang out to Miles,

"Stop, and hand me that watch and your money!"

Miles, thinking it all a joke, took it in good part, laughed, and making some indifferent reply, waited to hear what the real errand of the horseman was.

The next moment, however, he felt the muzzle of a Henry rifle fooling around his left ear, and at once became serious, and began to draw the watch from his pocket.

"Hurry up!" shouted the impatient bandit. "Don't you see those d——d s—s of b——s coming yonder? I'm Vasquez, and they're after me!"

Miles handed over his two hundred and fifty dollar watch with considerable alacrity; Osborne handed over a seventy dollar watch, and Rhoades handed over what money he had with him—only a few dollars, however.

The foremost of the sheriff's party, Rowland himself, Harris and Sanchez, were by this time getting in unpleasant proximity, and the robbers again put spurs to their horses, and continued their flight, and, closely followed by the pursuing party, at length crossed the deep bed of the arroyo, at the head of the Verduga Canon, and gave the signal agreed upon—the firing of volleys from their rifles—for the guide to make his appearance.

That individual, however, failed to respond. It was too late at this crisis to think of changing his plans, and Vasquez ordered his party forward, greatly disappointed in the unexpected failure of his guide, blaming himself for his folly in not previously exploring the trail before trusting himself and party upon it, and with not a few forebodings as to the result.

CHAPTER XX.

Arrival of Harry Morse and party at Elizabeth Lake—Their vigorous search through the San Gabriel Range—Vasquez's perilous position in the Tejunga Mountains—Vigorous pursuit by General Baldwin—The bandits' appalling descent into the "Apollyon's Gulch"—Narrow escape of Chavez—The flight to San Fernando after abandoning the horses—Morse, Rowland, and Cunningham co-operate—Major Mitchell on the trail—Sam Bryant's leap for life.

We left Sheriff Morse and his company, at the close of the eighteenth chapter, at the Alamo Solo, in Kern county, en route for Los Angeles county, by way of Tejon Pass, April 9th. After a fatiguing ride of three days, passing San Emedio on the 11th, they reached Hudson's Station, near the head of Tejon Canon, at 2 P.M. on Sunday, the 12th. Here they found a welcome from the courteous and gentlemanly proprietor of the station, William B. Rose, where they got the first "square" meal they had had for many days, and which they were just in a condition to appreciate. McDavid did not arrive with the wagon until nightfall, having missed his way. Rose furnished the party with late papers (down to the 11th), and facilities for writing.

A terrific sand-storm had desolated the whole neighborhood here the previous Fall, stripping vegetation from the hills and plain, or covering it with sand. Stages were compelled to stop running for three days; no fires could be built at the station, and things generally were turned upside down.

The party left Hudson's (now called Bose's) Station next morning early, and started for Fort Tejon, situated in a wide flat in the canon. The fort consisted of about a dozen or more substantial adobe buildings, with officers' quarters, barracks, etc., beautifully located in the flat among large spreading live oaks, the buildings surrounding a fine parade ground. The buildings were originally erected by the United States Government as a garrison for troops in charge of the Tejon Indian Reservation. The last soldiers were removed in 1864, and soon after the buildings were purchased by General Beal, ex-Indian Agent, with several hundred acres of land—the entire reservation. Useless millions of the people's money have been squandered at this spot.

They left the fort early next morning for a thorough search of the Elizabeth Lake country, Soledad, and in fact the whole mountainous country between the fort, Mojave Desert and San Fernando Valley.

On Wednesday, the 15th, the memorable day of the Repetto robbery, Morse, acting on information received of a responsible party living at the Llano Verde, took his party to Rocky Creek Canon, and camped that night on the mesa, along which Adams' and party had pursued Chavez one day in September of the previous year, and where the exciting skirmish took place with Vasquez, in which Adams made his lone charge into the enemy's camp.

Meanwhile, a resident of Llano Verde had been employed to explore the mountains in the vicinity of Elizabeth Lake and Llano Verde, for traces of the bandits, or their hiding-place.

Returning from a fruitless search of the Rocky Creek region, the party made preparations for exploring the country in the direction of Tehachapi.

On their way towards Fort Tejon, they stopped at noon at Cow Spring Station, on the 17th, and there heard of the Repetto robbery, which took place two days before, and that Billy Rowland, with fifteen men, was in hot pursuit in the direction of Soledad. The news was brought from Delno's, where a dispatch to that effect had been received the previous night.

Morse and Cunningham, of course, at once decided to turn back, and head off the fugitives or join in the pursuit with the Los Angeles party, and immediately sent Faville to Delno's Station with a dispatch to Los Angeles, to learn the exact situation.

On the same day an extra stage was met, containing as passengers Hon. Leland Stanford, President of the Central Pacific Railroad Company, on his way from Los Angeles, with a party of eight men. The same party were on a visit to the Orange Grove Association's grounds on the day of the robbery, and narrowly escaped being favored with Vasquez's polite attentions. From this time until the 1st of May, Morse's party scouted the mountains and canons and guarded the trails from the San Fernando Valley to Elizabeth Lake, moving rapidly from point to point, in the endeavor to co-operate with the different parties sent out from Los Angeles.

When Vasquez and his men entered upon Morse's trail, Sam Byrant, Mitchell, Harris and Tom Vincent continued the pursuit under the

leadership of General Baldwin, deputy-sheriff, while Sheriff Rowland
with the balance of the pursuing party, returned to Los Angeles. The
sheriff was well mounted, but the rest of the men were mounted on
"hacks" that were already played out, and Rowland determined to send
out men properly mounted to reinforce those still on the trail.

The trail was a very narrow, difficult path, winding around the
angles and turns of the precipitous gorge, where, in many places, a
single misstep would have sent man or horse whirling down upon the
boulders in the bed of the arroyo, hundreds of feet below.

The fugitives were compelled to dismount and lead their animals
along the steep and narrow trail; but the pursuers gained no advantage
as they were obliged to resort to the same expedient, and both parties
made but slow progress.

Reaching the forks of the Arroyo Seco, some three miles from the
mouth of the canon, the trail led up the branch canon, down which ran
the west or right fork (as the water runs) of the stream, Chavez proposed a halt. A rest for a few moments was indeed imperative, and
Vasquez interposed no objection.

The bloodthirsty lieutenant then warmly advocated moving further
on the trail until a suitable spot was found, and for the party to lay
in ambush.

The chief ordered a forward movement, and continued on until the
darkness rendered their further progress unsafe, if not impossible.
They found a small patch of wild grass in an opening, where they
picketed their horses, and dividing some bread and meat they had
prudently brought from Repetto's, camped by the side of the trail for
the night. The pursuers had stopped a mile below them, also prevented by the darkness from proceeding further.

At early daylight the bandits hurried forward, the chief refusing
to listen to the proposition of Chavez to ambush the pursuing party.
He said that what they had already done had sufficiently inflamed
the people against them to insure to a moral certainty the lynching
of any one on the spot, that should by accident fall into the hands of
any party not a sheriff's posse, and that if they should ambush Rowland or any of his men, or those of any sheriff's party, they would have
half the people of the State hunting them.

The pursuers had not come within sight of them since they entered
upon the trail, and they began to feel a sense of security, when a terrible fear seized them, and nerved them to use their utmost endeavors

to get into the Tejunga without the loss of a moment's time; and that was that it might, and probably would, occur to Rowland to send a party by way of Sutton's ranch to the mouths of the Little and Big Tejunga Canons, to cut them off. To add to their peril, that was a movement that could easily be made at night, as most of the way was by old, well defined trails and wagon roads across the plains. This fear lent renewed energies to the fugitives, and accelerated their flight.

Their hearts were at last gladdened by the fact, apparent from the contour of the surrounding peaks and ridges, that they had nearly arrived at the highest point, and that they must, within a few rods, begin to descend the northern slope of the mountain towards the Big Tejunga.

They were doomed to a most unlooked for, fearful, and disastrous disappointment as they came to the summit of the ridge.

The trail ended abruptly!

On getting the narrow trail constructed to this point, the surveyors had decided the continuance of the scheme of putting a road through to Soledad was either impracticable or would not repay the enormous outlay of money and labor necessary to its construction, and it had been suddenly abandoned.

Before the astonished bandits, only a mile and a half distant, lay their haven, the grand old canon; but between them and the refuge was many a "great gulf fixed."

They looked to the right and to the left, but before them, sweeping in a steep slope down to the brink of the great canon, and extending on each hand to the wall of mountains which enclosed the "flat" spoken of in our introductory description, were acres and acres of dense man-zanita chapparal—traversed by gulches so narrow that they looked to be but a few yards wide, yet were so deep that the tops of tall spruce and fir trees rose but a few feet above their sides—so closely entwined that it did not seem possible that either horse or man could be forced through it.

And how to get down into the canon, even if they could force their animals through the brush?

It was a fearful situation. An armed party, thirsting for their blood and for the price set upon their heads, pressing hotly on their rear—no food—no water, unless they could find a stream at the bottom of some of the gulches—no guide—nothing but desperation. It might take them two days to find their way into the canon. In the meantime, the Tejunga, or the trails to Soledad, would be alive with myrmidons of the law, lying in wait.

There was no alternative, however. They *must* force their way through that formidable thicket of manzanita. Vasquez ordered Padillo to turn back a short distance on the trail and keep a sharp look out for the pursuing party. Then turning back himself a few yards, he directed Chavez to open the way from the trail by a ridge that ran at right angles with its general course, and strike out.

Dismounting, the burly robber, who is a giant in strength, twisted and broke the branches and pushed his way foot by foot into the cruel wall of vegetation, leading his unwilling horse after him, and Vasquez, Corona, and the nameless robber, forcing their horses into the trail thus made, slowly followed.

At the first convenient ridge or narrow spine they turned to the left again, and were now joined by Padillo. After three hours of painful toil they had accomplished a distance that placed them but little more than beyond rifle shot of the end of Moore's trail. As far as a fight in that ground was concerned, a conflict would be in their favor; for they could hold their own against considerable odds. They could even abandon their horses, and glide into some one of the gulches, and, remaining concealed, baffle pursuit for days, perhaps weeks.

But how could they live? There were few or no birds there; no deer, no quail—and as for bears, they are never easily found or obtained even when there are plenty of tracks, and they had seen no bear sign as yet, although they knew that it was probable, almost certain, that they must ascend from the Tejunga to the heads of some of the gulches.

They slowly and painfully worked their way through the chapparal, foot by foot,—wherever the ground admitted separating and multiplying the number of trails to baffle the pursuing party as much as possible.

As the sun rose high in the heavens the heat became stifling, and both men and horses were suffering the tortures of thirst.

At three o'clock the pursuing party came in sight on the ridge— or at least one man could be seen by the fugitives, and they knew that if they were themselves sighted in return, it would save the pursuers the trouble of looking for the trail, and that they would push ahead with all possible speed. They were on an extremely narrow ridge, still at least half a mile from the canon, well concealed from the pursuers by the high bushes in which they had taken shelter.

To their left, immediately below them, ran a narrow, deep gulch, and Padillo was directed to examine as to the practicability of getting the horses into it. He returned, after nearly half an hour's examination of the neighborhood, and reported that the sides of the gulf were so steep that it would be almost impossible to get the animals down it, but he thought with care the feat might be accomplished; that once in the bottom of the gulch he thought they could find their way down into the canon.

All mounted, and Chavez taking the lead, all followed down to the brink of the perilous descent. It was barely possible, as Padillo had reported, that by taking a diagonal course toward the head of the stream, the horses might make the descent. Without dismounting, Chavez spurred his unwilling horse past the bushes to the bare side of the steep gulch, and began the perilous descent, followed closely by Vasquez and the other three, who, however, chose to lead their animals.

He had descended safely for some fifty feet, and had reached a rocky precipice when he was compelled to force his horse upon a space of flat rock where his path would not be more than from six to eight inches in width. In his impatience he drove the spurs into the horse's flanks so violently that the animal gave a sudden spring, missed its footing, and with a snort of terror slipped from the edge of the precipice, and striking from crag to crag, fell a mangled lifeless mass at the bottom of the gulch, a hundred feet below. Chavez had been on his guard, and the moment the horse made the spring and he saw the danger was imminent he threw himself from the saddle, attempted to land on the narrow strip of rock, and did so, but could not keep his balance; but in the moment of falling into the frightful abyss his quick eye caught sight of a jagged rock jutting out into the chasm a few feet further on and twenty feet below; and gathering all his energies he made the daring leap and landed safely, and from there made his way, from point to point, to the bottom of the gulch where lay his dead horse.

Vasquez and his men were nearly an hour in making the descent, but finally arrived at the bottom without accident, where they found Chavez, who greeted them with the unwelcome information that they were caught in a trap from which it would be utterly impossible to extricate the horses, and a difficult task to get out themselves.

The fact was that about five rods below where the carcass of the horse lay, the little stream which ran down the gulch fell over a precipice eighteen or twenty feet down. It was simply impossible to get the horses past the obstacle, as the gorge at the brink of the precipice was not much wider than the stream, and its sides were a perpendicular wall of rock. Even if they could have got past the falls, the stream below was choked by fallen trees, rocks, etc., so that they would have found it impossible to get their animals through without the aid of an axe and pick to make a passable trail.

It was fast getting dark in the gloomy canon, and the robbers, clambering up the opposite side of the gorge from the point where they had descended into it, and getting past the falls, descended again, and after toiling for half an hour down the bed of the stream, at length to their infinite relief, they found themselves in the Tejunga Canon, and about four miles from its mouth.

There were hiding places in the canon above the point at which they had entered it—retreats where they would be absolutely secure, but the question of subsistence was now imperative, and they had no alternative but to seek the nearest habitations of their friends.

Turning down the canon, the discomfited bandits silently wended their way past Sutton's ranch and followed the trail to the mouth of the Little Tejunga, where they obtained some supper at a Mexican house, which they were in a condition to thoroughly appreciate. Tired and almost exhausted as he was, Vasquez resolved to continue his flight.

Chavez, Padillo, and the two others sought a hiding-place in the mountain side, within a short distance from the house, making arrangements with the Mexican who owned the place to supply them with provisions; while Vasquez, borrowing a horse of the man whose hospitality he and his men were receiving, proceeded to San Fernando Valley, where he halted at the house of a prominent Mexican, who, for some reason best known to the two, was always ready to afford him a refuge. The next day he crossed a trail to the house of Greek George, and at night sent back the horse, and a message to Chavez and his companions to join him, one at a time, cautioning them to move only at night, and exercise the utmost vigilance.

Later, on the night of the 17th, General Baldwin and party returned to the city, having searched through the chapparal and in the gulches, following the trails here and there in the flat, until thoroughly satisfied that the bandits had made their escape to the San Fernando Valley, and believing they had probably gone thence in the direction of Soledad. They had not succeeded in tracing the trail to the gulch where the horses were so effectually checked.

Scouting parties were sent out in various directions, and on the 20th Morse and Cunningham, leaving their party in camp near Lyon's Station, took the stage for Los Angeles (after having first sent scouts by different routes through the Placeritas), to confer with Rowland. After an interview with the Los Angeles sheriff, it was determined to thoroughly search all through the Tejunga and surrounding region, and then to decide what course to pursue.

They returned to their party on the 21st, and on the 22d received a dispatch from ex-Sheriff Burns, of Los Angeles, that Vasquez had been seen at San Fernando the day before, and that Rowland had started out with a posse, at 11 P.M. of the 21st, in pursuit.

Cunningham, with one division of the party, started through from the Placeritas by the old Indian trail, toward San Fernando, while Morse took one man by another trail from Lyons' Station.

Reaching the San Fernando Plain, Cunningham and his party joined Rowland and his men, and together they rode to Lopez's Station, in the San Fernando Pass, where they found Morse, who had come across by the other trail.

After a consultation it was decided to search all through the Placeritas—searching the mountains both from the San Fernando Valley and Placeritas sides, and the parties separated.

Meanwhile, on the 20th, Major Mitchell, believing that by following Morse's trail where the tracks of the retreating robbers had been abandoned by General Baldwin and party, some clue might be obtained as to the direction the fugitives had taken, made up a party, consisting of Sam Bryant, Tom Vincent, and others, and entering on the trail on the Arroyo Seco, followed it to its termination on the ridge, and then, guided by the broken branches of the chapparal, worked their way through the dense manzanita with a patient energy and determination more surprising than the desperation that had taken the bandits through the same labyrinth, and after almost super-human exertions, at last had the satisfaction of finding the spot where the bandits had made their descent into the gulch.

The abandoned animals, half famished in their dismal prison house of rock, heard the voices of the trail hunters on the cliffs above, and their anxious neighing, sounding as from the bowels of the earth— echoing and re-echoing through the mountain gorges, thrilled the brave little party with the hope that they had at last discovered the hiding-place of the fugitive bandits.

Believing that "what man has done man can do," they instantly prepared for the descent.

Taking the lead, Sam Bryant rode his horse to the verge of the steep treacherous side of the gulch at a point a little below where Chavez had started, and began the diagonal descent, followed by the balance of the party. He had descended about one-third of the way when the earth gave way under the horse; the animal made a desperate effort to regain its feet, but without avail—and flying downward with the rushing avalanche of loose rocks and earth, fell lifeless to the bottom of the gulch. The brave and agile Texan, familiar from boyhood with scenes of peril and danger, never lost his presence of mind for a moment, but lifting his feet from the stirrups, and quick as lightning placing them on the animal's back, sprang away out into the frightful chasm, and alighting in the branches of a tree top, which towered upwards from the bottom of the gulch nearly or quite one hundred feet. It was an appalling, desperate leap, but the brave man landed safely, and made his descent down the body of the tree, where he was soon joined by his companions, who led their horses down the perilous slope without accident. It being found impossible to extricate either their own horses or those of the bandits without making a trail up the opposite bank, one of the party was dispatched to Sutton's for the necessary tools, and the trail dug. On the 21st they were got out with the loss of only one more horse, which slipped from the trail into the gulch, below the falls. The boys named the locality "Apollyon Gulch."

CHAPTER XXI.

"Old Tex."—Morse's party scouting in the Placeritas—An accomplished professional liar—Major Mitchell and party explore the Tejunga for traces of the Bandits—Crawling through the chapparal on hands and knees—A starlight rider across the San Fernando Plains—Sutton's ranch—Verduga Canon—Floral park of fifteen thousand acres—Phillipi's Bee Ranch—The ride to San Gabriel Canon.

On the 24th, Morse's party, which had been scouting in two divisions, were united and proceeded to the mouth of the Little Tejunga, where Rowland had agreed to meet them. After waiting some two hours, however, and the Los Angeles party not arriving, they proceeded up the canon, having for a guide Henry Kagel. After searching for tracks for five or six miles, and finding no trace, they returned, and at

Fruta's house found Major Mitchell, with five men, just in from a scout.

The two parties soon separated, Mitchell returning to Los Angeles, and the Morse party going to Lyons' Station, which they reached at 4 P.M. They received here false information, to the effect that Vasquez and three of his gang had slept near there the night before.

On the following morning they rode over the trail to Soledad Canon, and thence to Moore's Canon. They were informed that at a house four miles up the canon, Vasquez, badly injured by a fall from his horse, had certainly been the night before. Removing their superfluous baggage, and leaving Faville in charge of it, the party started at 2:30 P.M. up the long and winding canon.

On sighting the house, they advanced at a rapid gallop and dashed up and surrounded the house. They found there an Irishman known to Morse, and a well known character of Southern California—"Old Tex."—a famous hunter. Returning to the mouth of the canon, they packed their baggage on the horses again, and going up the Soledad Canon; camped for the night at Soledad Station, on the Cerro Gordo wagon route, where they found that their last night's informant was an accomplished professional liar.

Leaving Soledad on the 26th, they took the trail over the mountains to Llano Verde. On the next day they reached Fort Tejon, en route for home.

Determined to make every possible exertion to get some clue to the mysterious hiding-place of the bandits, Rowland organized another expedition, thoroughly armed and equipped, and placed it under the command of Major H. M. Mitchell, with directions to explore the Tejunga Canon for a distance of twenty or thirty miles from its mouth, and in case a trail or clue to the escaped robbers was found to follow it even if it led to Mexico or Greenland. The party was made up as follows:

Major H. M. Mitchell, in charge; B. S.—or "Budd"—Bryant, constable, of El Monte; Sam Bryant, constable, of Los Angeles; Tom Vincent, of Los Angeles; and George A. Beers, of Alameda county. Mitchell had seen hard service in the cavalry during the late war, and as a deputy-sheriff had been most indefatigable in the pursuit of the Vasquez gang, from the date of the Tres Pinos robberies, whenever there was a clue as to their movements. The Bryants had also been on several expeditions after the bandits. They were Texans, having

crossed from the Lone Star State years ago, undergoing the hardships
and perils of the trip overland through Texas, and their record in Los
Angeles is that of men to whom fear is unknown. Tom Vincent is a
prospector, familiar with the mountains, an excellent marksman, good
fighter, and keen on the scent of a trail. Last, and least of the party,
was the writer, who had been in Southern California for nearly a year,
moving here and there in search of information that might aid in effecting the capture. He had been invited nearly a year before to accompany the Morse expedition, but that move having been delayed, he
"went it alone" until after the Repetto affair.

Morse being supposed still to be scouting in the Placeritas, with
headquarters at Lyons' Station, I started from Los Angeles at 10
o'clock P.M., on Sunday night, April 26th, with instructions from
Sheriff Rowland to meet and communicate with that party. Reaching
Lyons' Station at early daylight, after a star-light ride across the San
Fernando Plains, I returned as far as Lopez's, where several of the
wagons employed in bringing bullion from the Cerro Gordo Mines
were encamped, and "interviewed" one of the teamsters whom I knew;
but he had seen nothing of Morse or his men, and returning to Lyons'
Station, the obliging telegraph operator, Mr. Haines, kindly loaned
me a fresh horse; and turning the mustang I had ridden for nearly fifty
miles without rest, into a luxuriant pasture, I mounted Haines' tough
little roan, and followed a trail over the mountains to the San Fernando
Valley, which I reached without meeting any trace of the Morse party,
and rode across a stretch of plain to the depot, where I telegraphed to
Los Angeles for instructions, receiving in reply, the following telegram
from Albert J. Johnston, under-sheriff:

"Inquire for Sutton's Ranch, mouth Tejunga. Mitchell will be
there this evening.   A. J. JOHNSTON."

The depot had just been completed, and neither the operator, nor
any one about the locality—all being new-comers—could give me the
slightest information as to where the "Tejunga" was; but having a
tolerably correct idea of its general direction from the city, I struck
out across the plain, taking a bee-line for a depression in the mountains
about due east from the depot, and had the good luck to strike the
ranch without difficulty a little before nightfall.

My only credentials to admission to the hospitality of the old
Texan was the dispatch from Mr. Johnston, armed with which, I

ascended from a wide gully through which I had been following a tortuous trail, running through gravel beds and winding and twisting like a serpent among huge boulders torn from their mountain beds and hurled into the plain by the heavy floods to which the Tejunga and other mountain streams in this part of the country are subject during the winter season—and asked permission to picket my horse, and camp for the night. As soon as my errand was known, I was welcomed to the ranch, and the little roan was speedily refreshing himself in an adjacent pasturage. Supper was soon laid, and having ridden something over seventy miles, the bounteous repast of venison, home-made bread, and butter of the best quality, honey of a flavor such as no other locality produces, with hot coffee and other luxuries, was most thoroughly appreciated.

The family consists of the old gentleman and his wife, John, the youngest son, a fine young man of eighteen or twenty, "Abe" (married, and occupying a house near by), and two young ladies—a daughter and step-daughter—about sixteen years of age each, whose modest grace and beauty would adorn a palace. Although only twenty miles from the leading city of Southern California, the ranch—seems as far removed from the busy marts of commerce as though there was no human habitation within a thousand miles. Grizzly bears from the adjacent mountains pay nocturnal visits to the ranch, scenting the luscious contents of the beehives from afar. They never get nearer, however, than to cause a commotion among the cattle, when the clamor of the dogs rousts out the old gentleman—still active, although over seventy —and his sons, who, armed with their Henry rifles, glide here and there among the oaks, trying to get a shot at the varmits"—reminding one who views the romantic scene by moonlight, of "La Longue Carrabine," alias "Hawk-eye," alias "Path-finder," and his coadjutors, of Cooper. Although living in this solitude, annoyed by the predatory attacks of grizzlies and California lions, and exposed to the mercy of Mexican desperadoes, the family presents a picture of quiet contentment and peace to be found in too few households.

About nine o'clock Sam Bryant and Vincent arrived at the ranch with the intelligence that Mitchell and Budd Bryant had started with them, but that Mitchell had to return to get a shoe fastened on one of his horse's feet, and that Budd had returned with him. They would be on in the morning early.

Nine o'clock next morning we mounted, and, accompanied by Abe and John Sutton, whose services proved invaluable from their knowledge of the mountain trails, we left the ranch and proceeded to a little bee ranch, just at the mouth of the Big Tejunga Canon, kept by an enterprising and highly intelligent, well-educated German, named Phillipi. It is about one and a half miles distant from Sutton's where we halted to await the arrival of Major Mitchell and Budd Bryant.

While awaiting the arrival of those gentlemen I will give the reader a description of this bee ranch, which will, I think, be read with interest by Eastern readers, to whom some of its features will doubtless be novel. At or near the mouth of almost every little ravine, or small canon, opening from the southern slope of the Tejunga Mountains, and, in fact, all along the southern base of the San Gabriel range to the mouth of the San Gabriel Canon—wherever a supply of water can be depended on—may be found a bee ranch, and the proprietors, although living lives of solitude, are making money, with a slight outlay of labor and capital, a good deal faster than any other set of men with moderate means, I know of. A brief description of the principal features of this little ranch of Phillipi's will give a good idea of them all.

He lives in a small house or cabin, sufficiently large to accommodate himself and one other man with room in which to work, and in the rear is an enclosure surrounded by a stockade, to prevent the ravages of grizzlies, whose appetite for honey is simply ravenous; in fact, honey is one of the principal articles of diet of the grizzly in this region, and in the caves and crevices of the Tejunga Mountains are tons of this nectar, and it is the great problem of Los Angeles county grizzlies how to get at these grand repositories of sweetness.

Phillipi has over two hundred hives, and underneath each row of hives a cool stream of water runs constantly during the hot season, supplied from a spring in the adjacent mountains. The hives are square, unpainted wooden boxes, closed on top by a cover which can be lifted off at any moment, and the condition of the interior of the hive seen at a glance. Light frames of wood, made of thin pieces about an inch and a quarter square are set down into the hive side by side, just far enough apart for the bees to go between them, and these are held by resting the top pieces (each end of which projects a little for the purpose) upon cleats upon opposite sides of the hive close to the top. When one of these frames is found to be filled, it is lifted out and taken to the house. Here is a cylinder of zinc, say two and a half feet in diameter, and of about the same depth. This shaft runs through the centre, with arms provided with appliances to hold one of these frames in an upright position each side of the shaft, and standing out from it like wings.

The form filled with honey, just from the hive, is placed over a large shallow pan, and Phillipi (the boys of our party called him the "Bee-sharp") takes a thin, extremely sharp knife, and dexterously removes in a few seconds the thin layer of wax with which the honey makers have sealed up the mouths of the cells on one side of the frame. The frame is then set upright in one of the arms of the shaft in the cylinder described, and by the turning of a crank made to revolve rapidly in the direction opposite the side of the comb on which the mouths of the cells have been opened. Within a very few seconds all the honey has been thrown from the comb by centrifugal force, and the frame is lifted out, and the same operation repeated with the other side. The honey thus obtained is of the utmost clearness, and absolutely free from every impurity. The frame of the empty comb is replaced in the hive, and all the busy bees now have to do is to mend any portion of the comb that may have been unavoidably mutilated in the operation, and then go to work and fill it up again with honey, seal the mouths of the cells, and it is once more ready for Mr. Phillipi's manipulations. Thus the bees are relieved from the great labor of building a new comb when the hive is robbed, and can devote all their time to the honey—making a business of collecting and depositing honey for their owner. There are none of the climatic difficulties to overcome here that the apiarist has to contend against in the East, and the honey season is three times as long.

In June of last year, the last time I saw this industrious German, whom the bees are fast making a rich man, he informed me that he had already that season taken to Los Angeles and shipped to San Francisco and the East over three tons of honey thus obtained.

Bee culture is getting to be a very important industry in Southern California.

While waiting for the arrival of Mitchell and Bryant the time was thus utilized in posting ourselves on bee matters, and just as we were getting impatient, Deputy-Sheriff Sanchez rode in from Los Angeles, with orders from Rowland for us to turn about; and instead of going up the Tejunga Canon, take to the south of the Tejunga Mountains through the Verduga Canon, across the Arroyo Seco, and passing through the lands of the Orange Grove Association, skirt the base of the mountains to San Gabriel Canon, forty-five miles distant, in the direction of San Bernardino county.

We instantly mounted, and turning back half a mile towards Sutton's filed south into the Verduga, and hastened towards the point indicated. The reason for this move was that some one had sent word to the sheriff that four or five mounted men, armed with rifles, had been seen entering the San Gabriel Canon. Our course through the Verduga lay near the southern side, most of the way skirting the base of the hills. The "canon" merits a description. As stated in a preceding chapter, it is a plain nine miles long by from one to three miles in breadth, sloping from the upper or northern side to the base of the hills on the south. With the exception of some extensive cleared fields sowed with grain near the centre and in the widest portion, it is covered with a thick growth of a variety of flowering shrubs, and when we passed through it, and for months afterward, it seemed one vast field of bloom. It was to me the most charming sight I ever beheld. The grand mountains towering up to the sky on one hand, the undulating, wooded hills on the other, and walled in between them, blooming from base to base, was this magnificant flower garden of Nature's own arranging—a vast floral park of over 15,000 acres. When we first entered, we passed through acres of cactus of a hundred different varieties, many of which were in bloom. This grand floral paradise was the home of countless birds of a thousand varieties, and as we rode along on our sanguinary errand, we were greeted with a succession of concerts as charming to the senses as any that art and nature combined have ever produced.

Descending into the gulch called the Arroyo Seco, after the name of the stream which passes through it, we halted to rest our horses underneath some sycamores, near where Vasquez and his party encamped the night before his disastrous exploit at Repetto's, and then ascending the eastern side, crossed the barren plain at the head of the lands of the Orange Grove Association, and then made our way, sometimes without a trail, through low chapparal, and part of the way over a magnificent road winding along magnificent live oaks, in the rear of the vineyards, olive and orange orchards of Major-General Stoneman, Colonel McKeman, and others, and a little before nightfall were joined by Major Mitchell and Budd Bryant, and all spent the night at Thompson's ranch, at the mouth of the San Gabriel Canon—our destination.

We learned, not much to our disappointment, as we had anticipated this result, that the information on which we had been sent down here, was wholly false. However, our horses had a plentiful supply of grain, and we were most hospitably entertained by Mr. Thompson and his interesting family, and next morning we retraced our steps over the same route, and stopped at Phillipi's for dinner at two o'clock P.M.

We then remounted, and followed a rather blind trail up the Tejunga Canon some four miles, and went into camp on a little flat, where there was plenty of feed for the horses, close by the mouth of the gorge down which the bandits had escaped, after abandoning their horses. All along the sandy trail by which we reached the spot were grizzly bear tracks of the largest size, and tracks of California lions were abundant.

Next morning we proceeded up the Tejunga, moving slowly along, scanning the ground on every side and carefully looking out for tracks but finding but old mule tracks and the tracks of wild animals.

Much of the scenery in the Tejunga is grand, and even sublime—worth a trip across the continent to see. The grand and soul-inspiring views were rendered still more enjoyable by the pure, life-giving atmosphere of this mountain region. In the two or three days I spent there, notwithstanding the excessive fatigue of going over a three or four mile trail over spurs of the mountain nearly two thousand feet above the bed of the canon—to get around the falls of the Tejunga—I felt as though I had grown five years younger, and obtained a new lease of life.

We tried hard, towards night, to find a cabin which Phillipi had assured us, was hidden away in a little side canon, some twenty miles up, but had to go into camp just before dark, where there was some grass, and appease our ravenous appetites with a supper of jerked beef.

Early next morning we found the cabin in a little nook in the mountain about a mile and a half further on and up. It was tenantless, but we managed to open the door, and inside found plenty of barley for our jaded horses, and bacon, flour, tea, coffee, condensed milk, sugar, molasses,—in fact, all that we desired to build us up for further exertions.

The cabin was built by two young men from Anaheim, named McChesney and McDowell, in association with some others whose names I have forgotten. It is over twenty miles from any other habitation, and the two young men named spent most of the summer season here, mining for gold. They have got some rich paying claims. This whole range of mountains abounds in mineral wealth, and will soon be as noted a mining locality as there is on the Pacific coast. I visited the spot again some days after, when McChesney and McDowell were at "home," and in prospecting around, found a ledge of rich ore, and brought away several specimens.

After the meal Mitchell left us to ascend a mountain and prospect for a way to get through to Soledad. He came back in about two hours and reported that it would not do to undertake to get through. He thought the route impracticable; so we remounted and returned to the spot where we encamped the first night, opposite where the bandits had descended into the canon—convinced now for a certainty that they had gone towards San Fernando, and were not in the mountains. Budd Bryant and the two Sutton boys were here obliged to leave, their duties at home demanding their attention. I accompanied Mitchell, Sam Bryant, and Vincent up the gulch to where the robbers had made their descent into "Apollyon's Gulch," and where Sam Bryant saved his life by his daring leap from his horse's back into the branches of a tree.

It seemed scarcely possible that a horse could be made to go where these horses had made the descent. The desperate escape of Vasquez and his followers, and the daring pursuit of the brave party who followed his trail down the precipice one hundred and fifty feet into this dismal gorge, is alike one of the most marvellous exploits in the whole life of the notorious bandit whose principal deeds I have here recorded, and an exhibition of determined pluck and daring on the part of the pursuers, not excelled by any one of the numerous parties which at different times attempted his capture, except, perhaps, the brave and determined charge of Captain Adams at Little Rock Creek Canon.

Returning from our visit of inspection of "Apollyon's Gulch," we took supper at Phillipi's; we bade the hospitable German good-bye, and, about nightfall, started for Los Angeles—reaching the city about half-past nine P.M.

Mitchell almost immediately organized another trip to the San Jose range of mountains, in the southern portion of the county. In fact, several scouts were sent in various directions, but without accomplishing anything towards effecting the capture. Vasquez was playing it exceedingly fine.

CHAPTER XXII.

MORSE RETURNS FROM FORT TEJON WITH IMPORTANT INFORMATION —"A SELL!"—CLOSE OF THE MORSE EXPEDITION—BOOTH'S PROCLAMATION—ROWLAND'S PARTY STEAL A MARCH ON VASQUEZ AND HIS RECRUIT, CORONA—THE FORWARD MOVEMENT ON GREEK GEORGE'S HOUSE—A NEW WAY TO CHARGE THE ENEMY.

WE LEFT HARRY MORSE and his party at Fort Tejon, April 26th, on their way home from their southern expedition.

On the 27th, he received information of the highest importance, which led him to believe that Vasquez was not only in Los Angeles county, and not far from that city, but that the exact house in which he was hiding would be pointed out to him—for a "consideration." There seemed to be no doubt as to the genuineness of this information. The question now was, how to avail himself of it and effect the capture. He felt that if he were sheriff of Los Angeles county, he would not like to have an officer from a distant county come and effect the capture of Vasquez—about whom such a hue and cry had been raised—under his very nose; and he also thought it would be difficult if not impossible to move his whole party, now that its presence in the county was known to everybody. He therefore determined to leave his men at Tejon, return at once to Los Angeles, lay his information before Rowland, and if it proved correct, to take Cunningham, one other man (not of his own party, who could be relied upon), and with Rowland—making a party of only four—make a descent upon the rendezvous of the bandits.

Morse took the stage for Los Angeles on the evening of the 27th, accompanied by Henderson. He went to the office of the Los Angeles Real Estate Agency, and informed Sheriff Rowland, through H. C. Wiley, of the firm of Wiley & Berry, 43 and 45 Temple Block, of his presence, asking him to meet him there.

Rowland soon responded, and Morse laid before him the information which he had received—that Vasquez's guide could be found at a certain ranch near the city, and that he was "open to negotiations."

Morse then made the proposition to Rowland that they should together lay a plan to effect the capture.

Rowland received the information and Morse's proposition with a quiet smile, and assured the Alameda county sheriff that his information was "a sell." He said he knew the party well, met him almost every day, and was confident he knew nothing about Vasquez.

Morse was greatly disappointed, but having become tolerably used to disappointment by this time, he indulged in no tears, but took the stage and rejoined his command, reaching Fort Tejon at nine A.M., on Thursday, April 30th, and at 11 o'clock the party broke camp and started for the New Idria Mines, by the way of Templone Ranch, and on May 12th, after having re-searched much of the ground explored on the trip down, the party arrived at Barta's, in San Joaquin county, and this hunt for Vasquez was ended.

The party had been sixty-one days on the scout, having searched hundreds of miles of territory—the roughest, most mountainous, and, in some cases, the most dreary and dangerous in California—and had during the time travelled 2700 miles—a daily average of over forty-five miles.

As the party had been fitted out by the Governor at the expense of the State, in pursuance of an Act of the Legislature, the failure was felt by its members much more keenly than if it had been a mere private enterprise. The hunt would not have been given up at this juncture, but that the private affairs of nearly every man in the party demanded their attention.

After disorganizing, an appointment was made by some of the members of the party to meet at the residence of the sheriff on the 17th to reorganize for another expedition.

On the 8th of May, 1874, Governor Booth issued the following proclamation:

STATE OF CALIFORNIA,
EXECUTIVE DEPARTMENT,
SACRAMENTO, MAY 8, 1874.

WHEREAS, on August 26, A.D., 1873, near the town of Hollister, in this State, several murders were perpetrated by one Tiburcio Vasquez, and by men associated with him, and supposed to be under his control; and, notwithstanding a proclamation offering a large reward for the apprehension of the murderers, they are still at large, and are engaged in violating the laws and committing crimes in the southern part of the State; Now, therefore, revoking the proclamation of $2,000 or $3,000 reward issued January 24th, 1874, by the authority in me vested, and in pursuance of a special law enacted for the purpose of arresting and punishing the said criminals; I, Newton Booth, Governor of the State of California, do hereby offer a reward of $8,000 for the arrest of the

said Tiburcio Vasquez, payable on his being delivered alive to the sheriff
of the county of Monterey; and I do further proclaim that if during
an attempt to arrest him he shall make such resistance as to endanger
the persons or lives of whosoever may arrest him, and shall in consequence thereof be killed, I offer a reward of $6,000, payable upon
proof of his death and the circumstances attending it, to the man or
men who may have killed him.   Only one of the above rewards will be
paid.   If Tiburcio Vasquez shall be necessarily killed the said sum of
$6,000 will be paid; if he be arrested, and delivered to the sheriff of
Monterey county alive, the said sum of $8,000 will be paid.

NEWTON BOOTH, Governor.

While the tone of this proclamation increased the anxiety of those
who had made such vigorous efforts to effect the capture of the re-
nowned bandit, it could hardly increase their efforts, for they were already doing all they could do, but without doubt the issue of that
proclamation virtually cooked Tiburcio's goose.   Subsequent events
warrant the belief that the information brought one hundred and ten
miles from Fort Tejon to Los Angeles, April 27th, by Henry Morse
to Billy Rowland was correct, notwithstanding the opinion of the latter
at the time to the contrary, and that the increased reward led to negotiations with Rowland by the same parties, which led to his betrayal into
our hands.   Be that as it may, it would be manifestly improper to
publish the real facts of the betrayal even if the writer had them at his
command, and it only remains for me to describe the modus operandi
attending the capture, and to relate subsequent events.

The rendezvous of Vasquez and his men being revealed, the
question was how to capture him with the least possible trouble and
loss of life.   On the evening of May 13th a ranchero named D. K.
Smith, who had been employed by Rowland to reconnoitre the premises
of "Greek George," to learn as nearly as possible the exact number
the capturing party would have contend with, returned with the information that there were five of them.   He had obtained this information
by driving to the place, and stopping to ask the way to a neighboring
ranch—pretending that he was making contracts with families to cut
their wheat.

On receiving this information, Rowland, who had already decided
on the make-up of his party, sent word to the following persons to
assemble quietly at eight o'clock P.M., at the law office of Major H. M.
Mitchell, in Temple Block: Albert J. Johnston, under sheriff; H.

M. Mitchell, special deputy; Emil Harris, detective; F. Hartley, chief
of police of Los Angeles; Sam Bryant, constable; W. E. Rogers, of
Los Angeles; Geo. A. Beers, of Alameda county, a correspondent of
the San Francisco *Chronicle;* and D. K. Smith, farmer—eight men in
all.

These people having met with the sheriff at the place designated,
a council was held as to the best plan of procedure—Sheriff Rowland
frankly saying that he would rather the robbers should escape than
have any of the party killed; he wanted, if possible, to capture the
entire gang alive.

It was a fact known to all of us that the sheriff, Mitchell, Bryant,
in fact, all who were known to belong to the sheriff's "outfit," were
continually shadowed by spies; that an eye was kept upon the gun
shop where our arms were, as well as a constant espionage upon the
transactions of the various livery stables and corrals throughout the
city, so that it was next to impossible for any of the party to move
without the fact reaching Vasquez immediately by way of the "grapevine" telegraph.

Rowland was especially watched, and it was out of the question
for him to accompany the party, for his absence from town would be
instantly known and the hunted bandits be put upon their guard.

The house of "Greek George" is in shape like an inverted and re-
versed L, and the situation is shown with sufficient accuracy by the
diagram on the following page.

The following programme was finally adopted. The arms, consisting of Henry rifles, revolvers, double-barrelled shotguns, and bowie
knives, were to be boxed up and placed on a dray and conveyed by a
round-about way to Jones' corral, in the outskirts of the city. The
horses should be gradually taken there from the different stables, at
different times, and by different routes during the night, by employees
of the corral. The members of the expedition were also to reach the
corral, going singly, at different hours and by different routes—every
man to be on hand at two o'clock A.M., on the 13th. To prevent any
unpleasant interruption it was arranged that if any persons called at
the corral to procure horses, they should not be admitted, the excuse
being that "all the horses were out;" and if any one wanted to stable
an animal, the "corral was full—no empty stalls."

One after another the conspirators glided like shadows through the
streets, and at two o'clock the mysterious conclave had assembled.

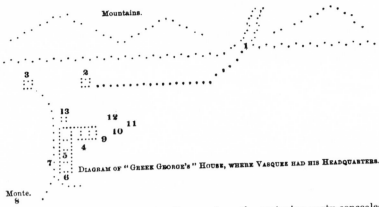

DIAGRAM OF " GREEK GEORGE'S " HOUSE, WHERE VASQUEZ HAD HIS HEADQUARTERS.

EXPLANATION.—1, Nicholas Canon, where the capturing party concealed themselves during the night of May 13th, and from which they emerged on the afternoon of the 14th. 2, Where the wagon halted and the party got out. 3, Where Vasquez's horse was picketed. 4, "Greek George's" house. 5, Room where Vasquez was eating his dinner. 6, Room from which he sprang when surprised. 7. Where he was stopped by Beers, and where he surrendered. 8. Hartley's position. 9, 10, 11, 12, Positions of Johnston, Bryant, Rogers, and Harris, on approaching the inner angle of the house, and where Vasquez was discovered through the open door. 13, Position of Beers, guarding north and west sides of the house, and from which he shot Vasquez as the latter came up the path to get his horse.

Selecting their arms—each man having indicated his preference—they mounted, and emerging from the corral slowly and silently, wended their way out of the city, and crossing the plains in a northerly direction, entered Nicholas Canon from the La Brea ranch, about a mile and a quarter east of "Greek George's" house, and proceeded far enough up the canon to effectually conceal themselves from view.

At early daylight, Mitchell and Johnston left the party, and going up a side canon, rose the mountain, and moved along its crest for over a mile, and then crawling on their bellies to a point from which they could get a good view of the premises of "Greek George," they watched the place until nearly noon.

A dense fog came across the valley from the sea, twenty miles distant, and settling along the base of the mountain, so obscured the view, that the field-glasses brought by Major Mitchell proved of very little account, and it was after ten o'clock, before it was dissipated sufficiently to give them a fair view of the rendezvous. They were greatly puzzled at seeing two men about the place dressed exactly as the bandit chief had been described to them. Yet they could not both be Vasquez, and at that distance it was simply impossible to tell which was which.

About noon one of them took a white horse, which was picketed at the edge of a mustard patch which surrounded the house, and led him to the monte, [See Chapter XIX. for description of the house and surroundings.] and watered him in the stream there, and then re-picketed him. A few moments later his counterpart rode off on another white horse across the valley.

Meanwhile, the little party lying under the shade in the canon were trying to possess their souls in patience, but it was hard work. So many failures had been made that this sort of thing was growing monotonous, and the suspense distasteful.

Here we were, lying idle in a canon, only a mile from the headquarters of the bandits, whom we had ridden hundreds of miles to find, and—doing nothing. To mount and emerge from our hiding-place and dash upon the robbers and attempt to effect a capture in broad daylight, was simply to undertake an impossibility. An armed party would not get a dozen yards into the plain before it would be seen from the house, when the bandits would mount and away on horses fleeter than those on which we were mounted, and the result would be another fiasco. We could trail them to the mountains and then lose them altogether.

But "fortune favors the brave." About ten o'clock, as we lay around upon the grass, under the shade of the oaks, in every attitude, our rifles by our sides, waiting with what patience we could for the return of Mitchell and Johnston, an empty box wagon, drawn by a team of four horses, and containing two Mexicans, came up the canon after wood. The Mexicans were doubtless considerably astonished at finding the unusually silent and deserted canon alive with men horribly "heeled" with six-shooters, Henry rifles, double-barrel shot-guns and bowie knives, and their astonishment was by no means diminished when the tall form of Sam Bryant arose from its recumbent position, and towering aloft, advanced like a Fate to the wagon and signalled the driver to stop. The command was obeyed, and for some minutes not a word was offered by Sam in explanation. The Mexicans looked at each other and at us, but said not a word. At last Sam kindly informed them that no harm was intended, and all that was required was for them to remain quiet until they had permission to proceed.

They sat on the spring seat over the forward part of the box for two mortal hours, in precisely the same attitude they were in when first halted, saying not a word to each other or to us.

At length Johnston and Mitchell reappeared, and preparations were made for business. The wagon was turned around and we mounted our horses and rode to near the mouth of the canon, where Mitchell had a little bee ranch, attended to by his partners, and here we stopped, dismounted and consulted.

Mitchell thought that the person he had seen riding in the direction of Los Angeles was probably Vasquez, while his counterpart remaining at the house was Chavez, and that the others were doubtless concealed in the willows at the monte a few rods distance from the house.

The arrangement between him and Johnston was that he would take one man, D. K. Smith, and making a detour through a branch canon, leave the mountains below the house and pursue the man who had ridden off, while the balance of the party with Johnston should surround the house and capture the inmates. Necessity is the mother of invention. The problem of how to reach the house was cleverly solved by utilizing the wagon and its driver as well.

Mitchell and Smith started on their mission. Leaving our horses picketed near the bee ranch, the remaining six of us—Johnston, Rogers, Bryant, Hartley, Harris, and myself—packed ourselves into the wagon so closely that no portion of our bodies or limbs was exposed above the edge of the box, and our hearts arose about as far above zero as they had been a few moments before depressed below.

Johnston then requested Bryant, the only one of the party who could speak Spanish fluently, to direct the Mexican to drive directly to the house of "Greek George," and to inform them that if they did not obey, or if they made the slightest signal that would indicate to the robbers that there was anything the matter with his wagon box, or did anything whatever to thwart the object of the ruse, we would riddle both himself and his companion with bullets. It is needless to say that the Mexicans were perfectly obedient.

It was one of the most ludicrous positions I ever found myself in. Here we were, six able-bodied heroes, after galloping madly over the plains and through the mountain gorges for weeks, thirsting—fairly famishing—for a little blood; hunting high and low, and looking day and night, some of us for months, for a hand-to-hand conflict with the terrible Vasquez—our "lives in our hands," as a local paper remarked;

and now, instead of the dashing charge we had looked forward to, when we should ride thundering into the enemy's camp to smite right and left, here we were, packed together like sardines in a box, the merciless noonday sun fairly scorching us with its intense heat and blinding us with its fierce glare, jolted over the rough road, "going it blind," as it were—thrusting ourselves into the den of lions, and trusting to our prowess and "luck" to "get away" with the "trick."

Vasquez, poor unfortunate bandit, who thought himself so secure, yet had already been betrayed by worse men than himself, saw the fatal wagon coming, but he knew the horses—knew the man driving, and his companion, and knew the wagon, and of course could not dream that the narrow box contained a whole sheriff's posse; and so, after scanning the plain in every direction, he quietly laid aside his weapons, and with his newest recruit, Lebrado Corona, entered the kitchen and sat down to his dinner.

When the wagon had arrived opposite, and some four or five rods distant from the south side of the house, and close to where Vasquez's white horse was feeding, the team was stopped and we sprang to the ground. We had no orders, and it was for every man to use his own judgment, acting according to circumstances. Bending low, we approached the mustard thicket. Hartley rapidly skirted it around to the right towards the willows. The rest of the party entered the mustard thicket, moving towards the house, Sam Bryant and myself being the first to reach the domicile. We struck the northwest corner, and there halted and looked around. Johnston, Harris, and Rogers were close at hand, but strung out to the left, closing in towards the east end of the adobe wing of the building.

Bryant asked me to hold that position, watching the two windows in the north side of the house and a window on the west, and a path running along the west side of the house to where the white horse was picketed, saying that if I would not he would. I saw the importance of the position at a glance, and consented, when Bryant moved to the left and around the east end of the building with Johnston and the others.

Looking cautiously across the court, they discovered through an open door two men eating their dinner. With stealthy, cat-like tread they crossed the court, and would have caught Vasquez and Corona as they sat, for their backs were to the door, but the wife of "Greek George" happened to catch sight of them, and instantly gave the alarm, at the same instant trying to slam the door shut.

All sprang forward, and Harris shoved the door open with the muzzle of his double-barrel shot-gun in time to see the form of Vasquez flying through an opening about eighteen inches square, in the south end, and instantly fired, but in his haste he missed the flying bandit by about six feet—as shown by the bullet marks in the wall on examining the place afterward. With a presence of mind which stamps young Corona as endowed with at least one essential quality for becoming an accomplished bandit, on the first appearance of the pursuers at the door he snatched up a little child that was prattling at his side, and held the little innocent as a shield before him.

At the sound of Harris' shot I stepped into the path leading along the west side of the house, and the next instant the agile form of Vasquez came flying around the corner towards me, and I fired. He threw up both hands, at the same instant crying out, "No shoot! no shoot!" and Hartley gave him a charge of buck-shot from his double-barrel gun. Johnston and the others closing in upon him immediately, he was led around the east end of the building.

Finding that no more bandits made their appearance, I passed around and found Vasquez and Corona standing side by side against the east end of the building, with the balance of our party standing around watching them, and on the alert for any of the gang that might put in their appearance at the eleventh hour.

CHAPTER XXIII.

CAPTURE OF THE BANDIT CHIEF AT LAST—WONDERFUL NERVE OF THE WOUNDED ROBBER—HIS ADMIRATION FOR THE STRATEGY OF HIS ENEMIES —THE TRIP TO SAN FRANCISCO AND SALINAS—VASQUEZ REMOVED TO SANTA CLARA FOR SAFE KEEPING.

THE SCENE was so ludicrously in contrast with my anticipations of the result of a collision with Vasquez and his terrible bandits, that although the chief now stood before us a bleeding captive, the crimson tide of life flowing from a half a dozen bullet holes,—and for ought he or we knew had received his death wound—there was somehow a lack of the dramatic excitement and horror usually attendant upon scenes of blood and carnage. I thought I could detect an incipient smile (rather sickly and feeble, though, I must confess) upon the bandit's countenance as though astonishment and admiration at the cunning ruse by which we had stolen a march upon him worthy of a General in the field, so completely took possession of him that he had no thought of himself.

I laid my rifle one side, and approaching addressed him kindly, asking him if he was badly hurt.

"Well," he replied, with an indescribable shrug of the shoulders, "me gone in!"

"Oh, I guess not," I replied. "Come around here in the shade, and let me examine your wounds. Perhaps I can help you."

He expressed his thanks, and knitting his brow as though to repress any audible expression of pain, or to choke down the emotions which must have racked his soul at finding himself so suddenly in the hands of the representatives of the law—and with the doom of almost certain death on the scaffold before him, even if he survived his wounds—he leaned on my right shoulder, with the captive Corona supporting him on the other side, and walked with our help around to the shade of a porch on the south side of the wing of the building. Corona brought a sheep skin and placed it upon the ground, and we laid the wounded man upon it.

The woman of the house having no old linen, I entered a bed-room and tore some long strips from the sheets of the bed. The room proved to be that which had been occupied by Vasquez. The bed, only wide enough for a single person, stood against the south-west corner of the little room. Behind it, with the muzzle thrust downward, and the breech within easy reach of a recumbent occupant, was a Henry rifle of the newest and most improved pattern. By the bedside, near the head of the bed, there was a dagger sticking upright in the floor.

I went at once to the wounded man and began dressing his wounds. My shot had struck the shoulder, while the buck-shot from Hartley's double-barrel gun had struck him in half a dozen places, making painful flesh wounds in the left arm, left forearm and the shoulder-blade, but none of the balls had penetrated the vitals. Whatever may be thought of this man's courage, he certainly, on that occasion, at least, exhibited astonishing self-possession and command of nerve. There was not the slightest tremor in his voice, and his heart beat steadily and calmly.

He admitted his identity as soon as I began dressing his wounds, saying, with a bitter smile, and the characteristic shrug of the shoulders and elevation of the eyebrows:

"Well, well! Me Vasquez! Me gone in now! It's all my fault. I don't blame you, boys. Me guilty man, I know. You all brave boys, and it's my fault"—meaning, as I understood him at the time, to allude to the wounds he had received, which he would have avoided by not trying to escape.

Harris, who evidently had not heard him confess to his identity, now approached, gun in hand, and looking down at him, remarked, with an ominous shake of the head:

"It's no use, Tiburcio; it's no use. I know you too well! I've been after you for two years."

The bandit looked up for a moment, with an inquiring look, but made no reply.

I had found a very neat pocket memorandum book under his pillow, which I now handed him, at the same time assuring him that as near as I could judge his wounds were not fatal, but would soon heal; that no vital spots were touched, and no bones broken—a fact of which by this time he was probably self-conscious.

Thus encouraged, he became more voluble, and even indulged in a little pertinent sarcasm. He repeated two or three times the expression, looking me intently in the face, "You good man, kind man," and then lifting his eyebrows, and accompanying the remark with a shrug of the shoulders and a most expressive wink of the left eye.

"You dress my wounds and nurse me careful, you boys get $8,000! If you let me die, you only get six. You get $2,000 for being kind!" and then he indulged in something like a chuckle.

I was already afflicted with a little inward chagrin at having fired so hastily on a man unarmed and wholly at our mercy; and this *ungrateful* thrust annoyed me, and I turned the facetious bandit over to the delicate care and attention of Greek George's wife, who proceeded to apply the bandages which I had rolled up in shape for use.

During this conversation, which had been listened to attentively by the balance of the party, Under-Sheriff Johnston occasionally chipping in and addressing words of cheer to the wounded man, and giving directions, I noticed that Corona was apparently lost sight of. The embryo bandit had not failed to notice the same thing, and appeared inclined to profit by it; for every time I casually glanced in his direction I found him further off. He was slowly and almost imperceptibly edging towards the south end of the building, doubtless intending, when he should get near enough to render the attempt safe, to dodge around the corner, make for Vasquez's horse, and mount and ride away.

Taking a rope from the top of a little shed, I called him towards me, and, with the permission of Johnston, tied his wrists together, and anchored him to one of the posts of the portico. I then went and brought in the horse, a splendid white animal, full of life and beauty. It proved to be a stolen animal, however, and of course was subsequently turned over to its owner.

Vasquez wore next to his heart, suspended by a green silk ribbon from his neck, a "charm" worked in green silk, containing something which he seemed deeply solicitous in regard to, and begged me not to remove it. The request was respected of course.

A thorough search of the house revealed a small arsenal, consisting of three or four rifles, several revolvers, several hundred rounds of ammunition, and some fine saddles, lariats, and other traps, which were taken possession of.

In one of Vasquez's vests, which Hartley raked out from in under a bed, was found the fine gold watch of which Charley Miles was robbed when he met the robbers in their flight on the day of the Repetto robbery.

A little boy and girl of tender years made their appearance from the house during the dressing of the wounds.

The look of mute wonder which stole across their childish features as they gazed from one to another of the armed men standing sternly around, suddenly gave place to an expression of the intense pity that involuntarily welled up in their little sinless hearts at sight of the blood flowing from the prostrate bandit's wounds, and they broke out in frantic wails and agonizing expressions of grief; and they looked up at us, wringing their little hands and gazing from one face to another, as though looking for signs of pity there, and appealing for mercy for a suffering fellow creature.

All spoke kindly and tried to soothe the terrified children, and assured them that all was being done that could be done; and Vasquez himself spoke in sprightly, reassuring words to his little friends, and the woman coaxed them into the house where they could no longer see the blood and the wounds.

The effect of this diversion was remarkable. "One touch of nature makes the whole world kin!" There was a gradual thawing out of the frozen sternness of the captors; Vasquez was spoken to more kindly by all of us, who now seemed to realize that the capture having been effected, he was to be treated as a human being, and regarded, as far as we were concerned, as innocent until the law had established his guilt. There was nothing maudlin or ridiculous in the manifestation of this feeling. Simply, all spoke kindly and acted generously towards the man, doing any little thing for his comfort that the promptings of humanity, aroused into action by its spontaneous exhibition in the conduct of the children, suggested. Johnston went to a neighboring ranch and procured a spring wagon and a pair of mules, and drove over; a mattress was placed in the vehicle and the wounded man was carefully lifted upon it. The guns and other captured property were placed in the wagon beside him, and Corona was released from his bonds and permitted to ride with him to attend to his wants.

Johnston took the lines, and we all left the place, guarding the wagon, in the direction of the canon. Half a mile out on the road we were overtaken by Major Mitchell and Smith, who had returned with the man whom they had followed (but who proved to be an innocent person), and leaving them to guard the wagon, Johnston driving, we proceeded to the canon, mounted our horses, and soon overtook the cavalcade, and assisted in convoying the wagon with its rare freight into the city.

As the cavalcade entered the town and it began to be rumored about that Vasquez had been captured, the whole city was thrown into a state of excitement, and by the time we arrived in front of the jail, a crowd of several hundred had assembled, which was constantly increased by fresh arrivals; but, to the credit of the Los Angeles people, not the slightest manifestation of a disposition was made to enforce lynch law, or in any way to interfere with the due course of the law.

The prisoners were incarcerated in the jail, and the wounds of Vasquez promptly attended to. The bullets were extracted by Dr. Wise, and the wounds bandaged by Dr. Widney, the jail physician.

For days there was a constant stream of visitors anxious to see and converse with the captive bandit, and they were accommodated by the courteous sheriff as far as lay in his power, and to every one who called on him, Vasquez was polite, and conversed freely in regard to his career, making no attempt to deny the numerous robberies he had planned and executed; but always asserting that he had never in the whole course of his career found it necessary to kill. He had always, he said, strictly forbidden his men to taking human life or to insult or violate women.

Among the visitors were a great many ladies, many of them belonging to the higher circles of society. Occasionally a lady visitor would present the bandit with a bouquet. Some of the newspapers in other portions of the State hearing of this, animadverted in the harshest terms, and characterized the conduct of the people, especially that of the women, as "toadying to villainy" and "lionizing Vasquez."

These comments were very unjust, although, perhaps, natural enough on the part of those who heard exaggerated accounts of what took place. During the height of the excitement I spent a good deal of my time in the cell with the captive, listening to his narrative of his adventures, and I am prepared to say that I saw no disposition on the part of the people to "lionize" the man. The visits were a manifestation only of the most natural desire to see and converse with a man who had become so notorious, and of whose personal appearance and characteristics there existed so many different descriptions.

Vasquez had offers of gratuitous legal assistance from several quarters, and he was treated by the sheriff and his assistants with kindness, all his wants and necessities being promptly supplied, and his wounds rapidly healed, and his good health seemed hardly to have been impaired by his rough experience on the day of his capture. Guards were placed in the jail yard every night until his departure.

On the 22d, the physician announced that the captive was sufficiently recovered to stand the trip north, and preparations were made for his removal to Monterey county.

On the same day the *Evening Express* contained the following, and which was copied into the *Star* and the *Herald* on the following morning. It was doubtless a "paroxysmal" emanation from the maudlin brain of some enthusiastic embryo lawyer, who wanted a finger in the pie:

To THE PUBLIC:—Wounded, a prisoner, and in the shadow of approaching death, or a more to be dreaded incarceration, an unfortunate and sinful man appeals to the charitable among men, of whatever nation, to contribute to a fund to enable him to place his case fairly before the world and the jury to sit in judgment upon him, hereby asserting his innocence of the higher crimes imputed to him, and his ability to establish the fact at a fair and impartial trial.

TIBURCIO VASQUEZ.

In Jail at Los Angeles, May 22, 1874.

On the 23d the prisoner was taken from the Los Angeles jail privately in a hack, about 4 o'clock P.M., securely ironed and handcuffed to Under-Sheriff Johnston, and conveyed to the cars to connect with the

Steamer Senator, and conveyed to San Francisco, with Mitchell and Rogers as escort, Sheriff Rowland being in charge.

At San Francisco the bandit was interviewed by a cohort of newspaper reporters and privileged visitors, and he talked freely with everybody. Sheriff Morse paid a visit to the captive in whose pursuit he had spent much time and patience, and in the interview Vasquez most emphatically denied the report that had appeared in a newspaper as one of his numerous statements, that he had full knowledge of Morse's movements, and had been around his camps nights, and admitted that the first knowledge he had of the Morse party was through the newspapers after the Repetto robbery.

On the 27th Vasquez was taken from San Francisco by Sheriff J. B. Smith, of Monterey county, and Sheriff Adams, of Santa Clara, to Salinas, Monterey county, and lodged in the jail. All along the route the people were frantic to get sight of the prisoner, but no attempt was made by his friends to effect a rescue, or by his enemies to lynch him.

As a specimen of the newspaper comments of the hour, the following by the sarcastic editor of the *Mercury,* published at San Jose, is perhaps a fair selection:

"The eminent cut-throat has come and gone. He passed through on the 11:30 train in custody of Sheriff Smith's posse. * * * Perhaps there was not one present but felt that the prisoner was going to certain and merited doom under the law of the land; yet had he by any possibility jumped from that car and escaped, some of them would have cheered him as they would a bad dog set loose with a tin pan tied to his tail. All of which is consistent with the inconsistency of human nature. As long as Vasquez, the vulgar, ordinary, cowardly highway assassin and robber, was at large, the cry was, 'Down with him!' but he is no sooner brought down than an exceedingly vulgar sentiment discloses itself, commiserating the robber on account of his insignificant wounds, and 'Oh! poor-fellow'-ing him for a sort of 'bloody, bold, and resolute' hero of delightful romance. This sentiment will begin to dissipate towards Tres Pinos, where the feeling against the outlaw is intense; and the San Francisco papers affect to know that an attempt to lynch him is not among the improbabilities, by the exasperated friends of the victims of his atrocities."

The widely different descriptions of Vasquez's personal appearance at this time, by the various newspaper reporters who interviewed him, would constitute, if collected together, a literary curiosity decidedly amusing. The following by a reporter of the *Post,* the leading evening journal of the coast, is an exceptionally excellent pen-portrait, conscientiously, intelligently, and most accurately drawn:

"There is nothing particularly ferocious in the appearance of the famous outlaw, and every day in the week there are three times as forbidding-looking fellows, in the police docks, charged with petit larceny and assault and battery. He is about the medium height, with a wiry, compact, yet slight figure, and does not, probably, weigh more than one hundred and forty-five pounds. His face, once seen, is never forgotten. It is that of a man self-possessed, cool, quiet, and determined, and indicates the stealth of the panther rather than the ferocity of the tiger. In every lineament of his pale, saffron face there is a will strongly marked; and one is impressed with his ability to organize and plan; but there seems to be some requisite wanting in the execution. The features are quite regular, forehead high and retreating, and head well shaped. His eye is a light gray and deep-set (the left upper eyelid drooping, giving the eye the appearance of being defective), and when speaking of matters that interest him, his whole face lights up with animation and his eye fairly sparkles. The expression of dogged resolution fades away into smiles, and in listening to his peculiarly soft voice one almost forgets the brutal robber and murderer, whose revolting crimes have so shocked the whole State, and made his name a terror in the southern country."

Monterey county had been divided, meanwhile, by an act of the Legislature, and Tres Pinos, the scene of the robbery and murder for which Vasquez had been indicted, was included in the newly-created county of San Benito.

He was closely guarded at Salinas; but in a short time, the jail being considered unsafe, the prisoner was transferred to the care of Sheriff Adams for safe-keeping, and placed in the jail at San Jose, the county seat of Santa Clara county.

On his first arraignment in San Benito, a change of venue to Santa Clara was obtained, and the case set for the January term of the District Court of Santa Clara county, at San Jose.

Corona was tried at Los Angeles in July, on an indictment charging him with complicity in the Repetto robbery, convicted and sentenced to seven years imprisonment at San Quentin.

CHAPTER XXIV.

THE TRIAL OF VASQUEZ AT SAN JOSE—THE JURY FIND HIM GUILTY
OF MURDER IN THE FIRST DEGREE, AND AFFIX THE DEATH PENALTY—
JUDGE BELDEN'S CHARGE, ETC.

ON the 5th of January, 1875, Tiburcio Vasquez was arraigned in
the Third District Court at San Jose, before Judge Belden, on an
indictment charging him with the murder of Leander Davidson, at Tres
Pinos, Monterey county (now San Benito), August 26th, 1873.

P. B. Tully, Esq., appeared for the defendant, and moved for a
continuance of the case; when the case was called, Mr. Tully arose, and
stated that ex-Judge Darwin of San Francisco, had withdrawn from
the case without warning, and he was left alone to do the work. That
at a late hour Monday night, Darwin had expressed dissatisfaction with
some act of the defendant, and announced his determination of throwing
up the case, but after some talk had consented to remain, and with that
understanding the attorneys had parted. Consequently, he (Tully)
was very much surprised to learn, just before court opened, that Mr.
Darwin had gone back on the arrangement of the previous evening,
and had withdrawn as counsel. Mr. Darwin had had exclusive control
of the subpoenas and other papers in the case. This, he thought, was
good cause for a continuance for ten days at least. He was not prepared to conduct the case without time to procure assistant counsel and
to prepare his defence.

Judge Belden thought that the excuse was one that could be urged
every time the case was called for trial. The case had been set for
that day, four months ago, after several continuances for various reasons. Moreover, Mr. Tully was a resident in the same county where
the alleged crime was committed, and would naturally be considered to
know fully as much about the circumstances as Mr. Darwin, who resided in San Francisco. Mr. Tully, too had, by himself, conducted
the defence of Teodoro Moreno, tried a year ago for complicity in the
crime charged against Vasquez. All these things tended to show that
Mr. Tully was fully equal to the present emergency, and he would
therefore over-rule the motion for continuance.

The regular panel was then called, and Messrs. Collins and Moultrie
were employed to assist in the defence. The panel was exhausted
and five jurors obtained up to noon, when the court adjourned after
ordering a special venue for fifty additional jurors, returnable at two
o'clock, P.M.

The following persons were duly enpanelled to hear the case: Tyler Brundage, Frank Hamilton, L. Bomberger, Noah Parr, M. Tobin, George C. Fitzgerald, J. M. Moorehead, G. W. Reynolds, S. T. Woodson, M. Lublines, C. S. Towle, and Hugh O'Rouke; and the court adjourned.

The court met on Wednesday, 6th instant, pursuant to adjournment. The galleries were filled with ladies representing the elite and respectability of the city.

There was a large representation of San Jose and San Francisco reporters present. One of them in his report remarked: "Vasquez seemed pleased at the sight of the large crowd in the Court room, but his glances were generally unblushingly bestowed upon the ladies in the gallery.

N. C. Briggs, the District Attorney of San Benito county, made a brief statement of the facts which the prosecution intended to prove, viz: That in August, 1873, a conspiracy was formed by Vasquez, Chavez, Moreno, Gonzales and Leiva to rob Snyder's store at Tres Pinos, 12 miles south of Hollister. The locality was described to the jury, and the plan of the robbery, with the antecedent and subsequent facts connected with the crime. He claimed that Vasquez killed Redford and Davidson.

J. H. Scull was sworn as interpreter.

The first witness called for the State was the traitor, Leiva. His evidence was substantially the same with that which he had given on the trial of Moreno—with the addition of positively fixing the killing of Redford and Davidson on Vasquez, questions which were not asked him on the former trial.

Rosaria Leiva, Capt. J. H. Adams, sheriff of Santa Clara, Andrew Snyder, John Utzerath, his clerk, L. C. Smith, D. F. M. Phail, Louis Scherrer, E. S. Burton, John Haley, Mrs. Snyder, and Mrs. Lizzie Moore were respectively examined on behalf of the State, their testimony substantiating the indictment, and the circumstances as related in the history herein contained.

The only witnesses called for the defense were Joaquin Castro, Captain Adams, and the prisoner in his own behalf.

Vasquez testified as follows:

"I was at Leiva's place in the Cantua on the 24th of August, 1873; he told me, in the presence of Chavez, that he wanted to please me in this robbing expedition, and he wanted to know our opinion about it as to whether we would assent to it or not; the agreement was to rob and not to kill. Gonzales and Moreno were brought in and induced to join; an agreement was made that no blood should be shed, and no women violated; we arrived on the top of the hill, in the same place spoken of by Leiva as the place where we stopped the day preceding the robbery, on the 26th; Leiva said he would go ahead with his pistol concealed in his breast, and that Gonzales would follow—that the rest should stay behind about one hour, hiding."

He then describes his movements up to the time of the murders, against which he claims to have remonstrated—which he solemnly denied having had any hand in, saying: "I did not kill any human being on that occasion; I am innocent of killing any one since I was born; I did not kill any one at Tres Pinos; there was no necessity."

Sheriff Adams was called by the defence and testified that Leiva had never stated to him that he saw Vasquez shoot Davidson; he said Vasquez shot two persons; don't recollect that he made the statement that he saw Vasquez shoot through the door; had several conversations with him in which he pretended to disclose all the facts. The defence here rested.

On Saturday, the 8th instant, the attendance was large. Vasquez's sister, Senora Larrios, of Vallecitas, occupied a seat in the gallery, from which she could plainly see her brother. Her little daughter accompanied her.

N. C. Briggs made the opening argument for the prosecution. He made an eloquent and feeling exhortation, and his argument was able and comprehensive.

In the afternoon the court room was densely crowded, and Vasquez seemed elated at the sight of so many faces. Besides the sheriff and his deputies, the following officers were in attendance: Sheriff Rowland, of Los Angeles; Deputy-Sheriff Hinman, of Gilroy; Constable John E. Haight, of Santa Clara; Constable E. E. Burke, of Mountain View; and Constable Van Buren, of Mayfield.

W. H. Collins closed the case for the defence. He confined himself almost wholly to an appeal to the mercy of the jury, on whom rested the responsibility of affixing the death penalty in case they found him guilty, or of consigning him to a prison for life. It was a most eloquent and pathetic appeal.

Attorney-General Love then closed the case on behalf of the State, arguing and submitting the case on the theory that the defendant was guilty of murder in the first degree, or guilty of nothing. He wanted no compromise verdict. The cause of public justice would suffer rather than gain by it, and the people would be disgusted with it. He said: "You, the jury, as a part of this government, are intrusted with the administration of a portion of its laws. Unless the law is vindicated, all the great rights and benefits of humanity become impossible, and life itself an empty vanity. 'He who is merciful to the bad is cruel to the good.' All that the State asks is justice. If you believe he is wrongfully accused, for God's sake let him go. But if you believe he is guilty, punish him, so that others may be deterred from following his example." [Applause among the spectators.] In going over the testimony, he said it was conclusively shown that "the little man with the black cloak" was Vasquez, and that Vasquez was the man who shot Davidson.

Following is the charge of Judge Belden to the jury.

CHARGE TO THE JURY

"*Gentlemen of the Jury:* The defendant, Tiburcio Vasquez, is indicted by the grand jury of the county of Monterey for the crime of murder, alleged to have been committed in what was then the county of Monterey, on or about the 25th day of August, 1873, in the felonious killing of one Leander Davidson.

"The theory upon which this indictment is prosecuted is that the defendant, Vasquez, was engaged with others in a felonious robbery of one Snyder, at a place called Tres Pinos; and that while so engaged, and in the furtherance of the robbery in which all were associated, the deceased was shot by Vasquez or by some of the party there associated with him in the robbery.

"As this is the single theory upon which the prosecution relies for a conviction, I shall confine myself to such definitions and suggestions as may be applicable to this view of the case.

"Murder is defined by our statutes to be the unlawful killing of a human being with malice aforethought. Such malice may be expressed or implied. It is expressed when there is manifested a deliberate intention unlawfully to take the life of a fellow creature. It is implied when no considerable provocation appears, or when the circumstances of the killing show an abandoned and malignant heart.

"All murder which is perpetrated by means of lying in wait, torture, or by any other kind of wilful, deliberate and premeditated killing, or which is committed in the perpetration or attempt to perpetrate arson, rape, robbery, burglary, or mayhem is murder in the first degree, and all other kinds of murder are murder in the second degree.

"Robbery is the 'felonious taking of personal property, in the possession of another, from his person or immediate presence, and against his will by means of force or fear.'

"Testimony has been introduced before you tending to show that the defendant, Vasquez, and others were engaged in the robbery of one Snyder at Tres Pinos, and that while so engaged, and in furtherance of the common purpose of Vasquez and his associates to accomplish this robbery, the deceased was slain by the defendant or some of the parties with whom he was then engaged in the robbery.

"Upon this point I instruct you that, if from the evidence you believe the defendant, Vasquez, with others, associated with and confederated themselves to commit the robbery, that, in pursuance of such association and agreement they proceeded to the store of Snyder at Tres Pinos, and actually engaged in the commission of such robbery, as before concerted, that in carrying out and consummating the same, and in furtherance of successfully accomplishing the same,—of overcoming resistance, preventing interference, avoiding detection, or facilitating their escape—any of the parties thus engaged in the robbery feloniously killed the deceased; such killing is, upon the part of all who were then associated in, and perpetrating, such robbery, murder in the first degree, whoever of the party may have fired the fatal shot, or given the mortal blow.

"That it is not necessary for the prosecution to show that the defendant fired the fatal shot, or by whom it was fired. It is sufficient if it was fired by one of the members of the party there associated together for, and actually engaged in robbery, and that it was fired in furtherance of the common purpose to commit this robbery, that in such a case all of the persons thus associated in the robbery, are equally accountable for the homicide, and all thus associating and acting, are guilty of murder in the first degree.

"It is no defence to a party associated with others in the perpetration of a robbery, that he did not propose or intend to take life in its perpetration, or that he forbade his associates to kill, or that he disapproved or regretted that any person was thus slain by his associates. If the homicide in question was committed by one of his associates engaged in the robbery in furtherance of their common purpose to rob, he is as accountable as though his own hand had intentionally given the fatal blow, and is guilty of murder in the first degree. * * * A conviction cannot be had on the testimony of an accomplice unless such accomplice is corraborated by such other evidences as would in itself, and without the aid of the testimony of the accomplice, tend to convict the defendant of the commission of the offence.

"Should your verdict be a conviction of murder in the first degree, it is your privilege to determine, and in your verdict to find that the punishment to be inflicted shall be either death or imprisonment for life in the State's Prison."

The jury then retired.

It was rumored that in case the jury failed to bring in a verdict awarding the death penalty, an attempt would be made to seize Vasquez in open court, and hurry him off to some convenient spot, where the services of Judge Lynch would be invoked. During the entire session of this last day of the trial Vasquez's sister occupied her accustomed seat in the southern corner of the gallery. While Attorney-General Love was delivering his impassioned speech to the jury, in which he urged and implored them to bring in a verdict which the hangman could consummate, she sat with bowed head, and rocked to and fro, her child clutched convulsively to her bosom.

At seven P.M. the court met. Long before this hour the auditorium and gallery were filled to overflowing. Nine-tenths of the occupants of the gallery were ladies. At three minutes past eight o'clock the jury came into court. Conversation instantly ceased, and when they took their seats a preternatural silence rested over the place. The order was given to bring in the prisoner, and a moment after Vasquez walked into the room, accompanied by the officers.

His face wore a deadly pallor, and he glanced nervously from right to left as if expecting to see the frightful gibbet, with all its ghastly belongings.

As he took his seat, several of the officers spoke to him, but though looking directly at them, he failed to show that he either saw or heard them.

The names of the jury having been called by the Court, the judge said:

"Gentlemen of the Jury, have you agreed upon your verdict?"

G. W. Reynolds (Foreman)—We have (handing a slip of paper to the judge, who looked at it earnestly for a quarter of a minute, and handed it to the clerk).

The Court—Mr. Clerk, read the verdict.

Mr. Pomeroy, the clerk, stood up, and amidst breathless silence, read as follows:

"We, the jury, find the defendant guilty of murder in the first degree, and assign the death penalty.

"GEO. W. REYNOLDS, FOREMAN."

There was no applause on the part of the spectators, though the announcement of the verdict gave general satisfaction.

Some of the ladies in the gallery were considerably affected, and brought their handkerchiefs into play.

Mr. Collins excepted to the form of the verdict, and announced the intention of the defence to prepare and submit a bill of exceptions on motion for a new trial, and asked that sentence be postponed to allow time for this action.

The Court, with the consent of District Attorney Briggs, set Saturday, January 23d, at ten A.M., as the time for passing sentence.

CHAPTER XXV.

VASQUEZ'S SENTENCE—HIS IMPERTURBABLE DEMEANOR—EFFORTS OF COUNSEL TO OBTAIN A NEW TRIAL—ADVERSE DECISION OF THE SUPREME COURT—EFFORTS TO INDUCE GOVERNOR PACHECO TO GRANT A RESPITE—THREATS OF CLEOVARO CHAVEZ—THE GOVERNOR WILL NOT INTERCEDE—THE LAST HOPE GONE—PREPARATIONS FOR THE EXECUTION—VASQUEZ'S EXHORTATION TO HIS OLD ASSOCIATES—AN ADDRESS TO FATHER AND MOTHER—PATHETIC FAREWELL TO HIS BROTHER AND SISTER—THE DOOMED BANDIT INSPECTS HIS COFFIN—THE LAST NIGHT ON EARTH—THE TERRIBLE ORDEAL OF THE DEATH PENALTY.

ON Saturday, Jan. 23d,—two weeks from the date of the rendering of the verdict—Judge Belden formally pronounced sentence, and ordered the execution to take place in the jail-yard at San Jose, on Friday, March 15th, 1875. The sentence was unqualified in its condemnation of the culprit's unjustifiable career; but the imperturbable bandit calmly listened to the soothing remarks of the judge, without a sign of emotion, and it is only fair to say, without the slightest exhibition of bravado. It was evident that he was either possessed of an inhuman or unnatural heart, so that he had no care even for himself, or had the most absolute control of his nerves.

I have witnessed the conduct of many criminals undergoing sentence of death, some of whom were undoubtedly entitled to be called "brave" men; but in every case except that of Vasquez, the effort to appear firm and collected was apparent in the rigidity of the features of the condemned, and in every attitude. This man's self-possession was supreme.

Following is the text of the sentence:

"Vasquez, stand up! The ruling of this court denying the motion for a new trial made in your behalf, leaves to me but a single duty, that of pronouncing the judgment which the law prescribes for the offence of which you stand convicted. I deem it, however, befitting this place and this occasion that something more than the mere formal words of the sentence should be spoken. This life you have led, your wretched career, soon to be ended, is full of admonition to those who give heed to the transgressor. It points to a life of crime, of violence, and outlawry, with its fit ending in a death of shame. Well may those who are following in the footsteps of your earlier years, take warning from your fate, and turn, while they may, from the path that leads to certain destruction. The motive of your life, as shown by the criminal records of the State, disclosed by your associates, and told by yourself, is one unbroken record of lawlessness and outrage; and you entered upon manhood a convicted felon in the Penitentiary of the State. The sharp admonition of this early punishment was wholly lost upon you, and when restored to liberty you adopted the life of a robber, and entered upon a career of outrage, pillage and murder, with neither limit nor interruption, until the strong hand of the law reached forth and grappled you. For years, in this section of the State plagued by your presence, outrages known to be yours, crimes self-aroused, made your name the synonym for all that was wicked and infamous; and the broadest charity can scarce hope that even the much we know is all that is to be known. What hidden crimes, what secret deeds of violence, unseen and unrecognized by men, may stain your hands and burden your conscience, yourself can alone know. This was your accepted career—that of a robber—the deeds of your every day life, when the crime for which you are now called to answer was committed. The story of the deed has been again and again repeated—told by the witness of that blood-stained tragedy, by your accomplice, who confronted you, and by yourself proven and confessed. It appears that you planned the robbery of the store at Tres Pinos, and with a band of kindred spirits, armed and prepared for murder as well as for pillage, you attacked the place you proposed plundering. Your number, your preparation, and the completeness of your surprise, made resistance hopeless, and it was not even attempted; and without bloodshed and opposition you might have secured your booty and made your escape. This did not content you. The men you slew were not those whose goods you coveted; two of them were strangers and wayfarers that an unhappy chance threw in your cruel way. They possessed nothing you could desire; they made no obstacle to your purpose. Helpless, unarmed, and unresisting, you slew them in the mere wantonness of butchery, and with the corpses at your feet you gathered the paltry spoils of your four-fold crime and fled to the mountains. Aided by the situation of the country, you eluded for a time the officers who were in your pursuit, and at last seemed to have fancied that your offences were forgotten and your safety assured. Unfortunate man! Vain delusion! The blood of your murdered victims cried unceasingly for vengeance, and there could be for your crimes no forgetfulness, for you no refuge. Justice might be for a time delayed—she would not be baffled. The State, whose laws you set at defiance, whose citizens you had ruthlessly murdered, aroused herself for retributive justice. The commonwealth, with all her resources of men and treasure, was upon your track with tireless purpose and exhaustless means. She followed you in all your wanderings, and made of your vicious associates her most efficient instruments. In every camp that gave you shelter her officers bartered for your surrender. In the confederates you trusted, she found the man ready to betray you. From such a pursuit there could be no escape, and you are here—here with the record of your lawless life well nigh ended, without one act of generosity or deed of even courage to relieve its utter depravity. The appeals you have made to your countrymen for aid in your present distress have met a response becoming them and befitting you. Shocked at your atrocities, they have neither aided you to escape the punishment merited, nor pretended the sympathy you have sought to invoke. They have left you to answer alone at the bar of justice. With the memory of your victims before you, and the dark shadow of an approaching doom about you, indulge no illusive hope that the fate can be averted or long delayed. Every appeal that zeal could suggest or eloquence urge was pressed upon your jury in the hope that they might be persuaded to leave for you the pitiful boon of life; but the jury heard of the story of your crimes from yourself; they accepted the responsibility of adjudging the penalty merited, and in their deliberations they determined, and in their verdict declared you unworthy to live. Of that verdict there can be but one opinion—that of an unqualified approval. Upon this verdict the law declares the judgment, and speaking through the court, awards the doom—a penalty commensurate with the crimes of which you stand convicted, and therein merited by the three-fold murder that stains your hands. The judgment is—death. That you be taken hence, and securely kept by the sheriff of Santa Clara county, until Friday, the 19th day of March, 1875. That upon that day, between the hours of 9 o'clock in the morning, and four in the afternoon, you be by him hanged by the neck until you are dead. And may the Lord have mercy on your soul."

After delivery of the terrible but well-deserved sentence, Vasquez was guarded with increased vigilance, Sheriff Adams perfecting arrangements that rendered it impossible for the prisoner to escape, either by strategy or by the forcible assistance of his outside friends. His attorneys had done all that great legal ability and eloquence could do to obtain a verdict that would secure a sentence of imprisonment for life, and, having failed in that, now lost no time in filing in the Supreme Court a transcript of the proceedings and objections to the rulings of the court in the trial of the case. The perfecting of the appeal under Section 1,243 of the Amendments to the Penal Code of the State of California stays the execution of the judgment pending the consideration of the matter by the tribunal of last resort. Vasquez and his friends had strong hopes that the Supreme Court would grant him a new trial; or at least obtain a new lease of life by the failure of the court to arrive at a decision before the day appointed for his execution.

Shortly after the promulgation of the sentence, the following letter (in Spanish) was dropped in Wells, Fargo & Co.'s express letter box, at Hollister, San Benito county:

NOTICE TO THE TOWN OF HOLLISTER.

Captain Cleovaro Chavez to the Inhabitants of Hollister:

Know you, that in regard to the acts committed by the captain of my company, I say that, finding myself guilty of those acts, I flew to Mexico; but having been informed while there that Vasquez was under sentence of death, I have returned as far as this place with the aim of disclosing the falseness of the evidence sworn against him, and in case Vasquez should be hanged, to quickly mete out a recompense. Because, do not believe that I am in want of resources and lack of sufficient valor to take him, or meet death in the attempt. I wish first to see the result. For this reason I let you know that if Vasquez is hung by his enemies, who, through fear, have turned against him, I will show you I know how to avenge the death of my captain. I do not exact of you to set him free, but do not want him hung, because he was not bloody. I can prove under oath that in time gone by Tom McMahon (a leading citizen of Hollister) will remember that Vasquez and his company saved his life. It was I subsequently who was at the head of the affair at Tres Pinos, in which the murders were committed. Mr. Vasquez certainly was our captain; but on account of Abdon I neglected the orders that Vasquez had imposed upon us. If this is not sufficient, or if by this means Vasquez does not get his sentence appealed, then you will have to suffer as in the times of Joaquin Murieta— the just with the unjust alike will be reached by my revenge. Let him be punished according to law, then you will never more hear of me in this country or in this State—neither of me or of my company.

If he has mitigation given him, let it be published in the papers. Nothing more.

CLEOVARO CHAVEZ & Co.

It was thought by many that this threatening letter was a fraud, and emanated from some wag; but it was generally thought to be a genuine threat, and caused a good deal of anxiety among residents of San Benito county and of Los Angeles county.

Meanwhile the conduct of the doomed bandit in his prison was unexceptionable, and he was visited by hundreds every week, many of his visitors being ladies and gentlemen of the highest respectability, who called not to "lionize" the outlaw, but to gratify a natural desire to see and converse with the man or monster about whom so much had been said and written.

To all who called upon him he was affable and polite, and always ready to converse freely. Rev. Father Serda, of St. Patrick's Church, his spirtual adviser, visited him frequently, endeavoring to direct his thoughts into the proper channel. It is said by those of his attendants who were most with him in his last days, that Vasquez had not the slightest belief in a future state of existence, but tacitly followed the usual routine of the confessional, and obeyed the forms of the Catholic Church, out of a desire to alleviate as far as possible the affliction of his brothers and sisters.

Meanwhile Chavez began to carry out his threats, and resumed operations in Kern county. About the 10th of February he made his appearance, accompanied with several armed men, at Scoby's store, on the south fork of Kern river. They captured five horses, a large amount of store goods, and $800 in coin. Sheriff Bowers telegraphed to the sheriff of Los Angeles county that the bandits were shaping their course that way, and preparations were made to effect their capture; but the wily leader avoided Los Angeles county, doubled on his track, and eluded his pursuers.

Governor Pacheco offered an additional reward of $2,000 for Chavez's capture, and constant efforts have been made to effect his capture; but, up to the present writing, without success, and he is now operating in the mountainous region of Inyo county.

On the 10th of March Vasquez was interviewed by Mr. Foote, of the San Jose *Patriot,* who refers to Vasquez "cheerful, in conversation as usual, and in appearance looking as well as at any time during his confinement. He smiled and asked how many days he had yet to live, and stated that published reports about his expecting executive clemency were unfounded. He said: 'I have the natural feeling of a person in my position. I understand the matter thoroughly. I feel that I have to die a violent death; but it is natural, you know, to hope that something may happen to defer the matter. If it does not, I have made no petition, and leave all to my attorneys. I shall do as others have done who could not help themselves.' "

On the 12th of March the Supreme Court announced its decision adverse to the application of Vasquez's counsel, and Sheriff Adams began to make preparations for the final ordeal, securing the gallows upon which Charles Mortimer, the notorious murderer and robber, and Cotta, and Estrada were hanged at Sacramento.

About the same time some of the prominent citizens of Los Angeles, including Sheriff Rowland, Judge Sepulveda, and others, telegraphed to the Governor, representing that, in their opinion, the execution of Vasquez would endanger the lives of innocent persons, and advising that the execution be at least deferred for a time.

Governor Pacheco very firmly replied that he had carefully and conscientiously examined into the merits of the case, and could find no good reason for the exercise of executive clemency; that the quality of mercy was not sound that prolonged life while there was no ground for hope; and declined to interfere.

On finding his last hope gone, Vasquez expressed his determination to die as became "a man and a Californian."

On the night of the 17th Sheriff Adams, Under-Sheriff Winchell, and the writer, spent several hours with the condemned man, to give him an opportunity to put on record any confession or last words he might wish to say. He was cheerful and ready to converse as ever, and went through the details of his capture with apparently as great a relish as though he was not himself the unfortunate victim of the episode—commenting rather sarcastically on some features of the affair, and asserting that, when he threw up his hands, after being shot, he exclaimed (being unarmed): "Shoot, you cowards! shoot!"

The affair at Rock Creek, in which Captain Adams charged upon his position and captured his horses, he discussed and compared notes with the Sheriff, their united version agreeing with the description in the preceding chapters. He denied in toto Leiva's story of finding him in bed with his wife and attempting to kill him on the spot, and being only prevented by the interposition of Chavez.

On being informed that Abdon Leiva, on whose testimony mainly he had been convicted, he expressed a desire to see him, he replied: "I do not wish to see him. Why should I? What good would it do me or him? He would only embrace the opportunity to insult me, and I do not wish to be annoyed. I am ready to see everybody else, and shall die like a man; and wish to avoid any unnecessary annoyance."

He remarked with a good deal of earnestness: "I like if there is ever a petition circulated for the pardon of Teodoro Moreno, indicted for complicity in the Tres Pinos murders, or for a commutation of his sentence, which is for life, that you would not only sign it, but that you would also urge others to do so. I assure you that he is innocent of murder. He is well known as a hard working, good man. The only crimes I ever knew him to commit were with me at Firebaugh's Ferry and Tres Pinos. I assert as a dying man, that the man found dead near the door of Snyder's store, was killed by Abdon Leiva. The two others were killed by Gonzales, now supposed to be in Mexico."

One of the party, desirous of obtaining some expression of the bandit's belief in regard to a future state of existence, remarked:

"I believe implicitly in a future state of existence—in the immortality of the soul. What is your belief on that point?"

The condemned man replied:

"The sages and wise men say so; but for my part I don't know."

He added:

"I hope your belief is correct, for in that case I shall see my old sweethearts together on Friday."

In reply to a question of Sheriff Adams, he denied having been in the habit of getting drunk after his robberies. If he had he would have been caught. On the contrary it had been his habit to keep guard while his men enjoyed themselves with liquor and women.

It was then suggested to him that as we were alone and undisturbed, perhaps if he had any last words to say to the public, his former associates, or his relations, to incorporate in the account of his life now written with the exception of the final chapter, now would be a more favorable time than on the morrow, when he would be overwhelmed with visitors.

He immediately answered, looking upward as though in deep thought, "To the fathers and mothers of children." He then dictated in Spanish the following, substantially as it appears here, with the exception of the concluding touching portion, which was partly dictated to him by Mr. Collins on the following day, when the document was brought to him for his final approval and signature:

"To the Fathers and Mothers of Children: Standing upon the portals of the unknown and unknowable world, and looking back upon the life of this, as I have seen, I would urge upon you to make it your greatest aim here to so train, instruct, and govern the young to whom you have given life, that they be kept aloof as far as is in the nature of things possible, from the degrading companionship of the immoral and vicious. The general welfare of society depends upon the strict performance on your part of this duty. The state of society in the next generation depends upon the manner in which the children of the present are instructed and trained.

"I wish the children throughout the world, who may read the incidents of my life, to take warning in time of the example before them of me, and to realize the force of the saying: 'The way of the transgressor is hard!'—the truth of which is now being verified to me.

"The world must not be allowed to think by anything I have here said that I have intended to reflect upon the instruction and training I received from my own parents. I affirm they did all they could to bring me up in the right way. Circumstances which they could not control threw me among the vicious, and I disobeyed their wise teachings.

"I hereby ask pardon from each and every one whom I have in any way injured; asking that pardon with all the earnestness that only a dying man can; asking also the prayers of all good Christian people that forgiveness may be extended to me, not only by those that I have wronged, but by the Great Father whose laws I have so ruthlessly trampled upon. The forgiveness that I have asked from those whom

I have wronged, I freely and completely give to all who have injured me.

"I thank my counsel, and each one of them, for their devotion to me in my hour of distress. I express my gratitude to Sheriff Adams, Under-Sheriff Winchell, and Deputies Selman and Curtis, for their great kindness to me during the period I have been in their custody. I thank my brothers for their brotherly love extended to me during all the time of my troubles, and to my darling and devoted sisters I render inexpressible thanks.

"Oh, sister of mine, thy love to me will buoy me up in my last moments!

"I commit my soul and the hereafter that is before me to the keeping of the Maker, without whose help I can never expect complete pardon.

"Farewell, brothers! Farewell, sisters dear! The end has come!
                                        TIBURCIO VASQUEZ.

"In jail at San Jose, Cal., Thursday, March 18th, 1875."

WITNESSES: W. H. Collins, Theo. C. Winchell, J. H. Adams, George Beers, H. S. Foote, John A. Ethell, John McGonigle, A. Selman.

After the dictation of the above, Captain Adams suggested that perhaps some advice from the bandit to his former associates would have a salutary effect, coming from so solemn a source.

He then dictated the following:

"To MY FORMER ASSOCIATES: I wish you, who will doubtless expect to hear some last word of farewell from me, whose fortunes and adventures you have shared, to ponder well the few words I now deem it proper to say to you. You must well know that I, who could, had I been so disposed, have disclosed to the authorities and to the world, the perpetrators of many atrocious crimes, might thus have saved my own life. So you can see, if the world cannot, that to a certain extent this expiation is on my part voluntary. I wish you especially to understand that while I deny having committed the immediate crime of which I have been convicted, and for which I am to suffer death, or of having at any time shed human blood, or taken the life of my fellow man, common sense compels me to realize the justness of the law which holds me responsible for the innocent lives lost in the prosecution of my unlawful calling of robbery. The threats of revenge, which I hear have been made by some of you—threats to retaliate by outrages on the community at large, and by the assassination of my captors, the jury who convicted me, or the officers who have held me a prisoner, are foolish and wrong—for all these people have merely represented the law, and have only acted in the interests of society. By the course threatened you could do me no earthly good, but only bring yourselves in the end to my own fate. Take warning, then, by my fate, and change your course of life while you may.

"I, Tiburcio Vasquez, now about to pay the penalty of a misdirected life, say this to you, my former companions, with the solemn earnestness of a dying man.

"TIBURCIO VASQUEZ.

"In jail at San Jose, March 18th, 1875."

WITNESSES: John McGonigle, Theo. C. Winchell, J. H. Adams, Geo. A. Beers, H. S. Foote, W. H. Collins, John Ethell, and A. Selman.

After completing the dictation of the above documents, Vasquez expressed a desire to retire, and bidding a pleasant good-night to his visitors, was left alone with his guard. It had been a scene never to be forgotten. The cold moon shone dimly down through the dusty skylight, rendering the gloomy apartment only more ghastly. It was the bandit's last night but one on earth; and yet—save in lulls in the conversation, when he would gaze abstractedly into the expiring embers of the little box-stove—typical of his own fleeting spark of life— he seemed the most cheerful one of the little party.

Early on the following morning G. D. Hoppes and L. Whittier, of Sacramento, builders of the scaffold on which Mortimer, Estrada, and Cotta were hanged, began the erection of the gallows in the southwestern corner of the jail yard. The structure was visited by over a thousand visitors during the day, and merits a description. It consisted of a platform about ten feet square, supported ten feet above the ground by a stout frame of timbers; eight feet above the platform, and supported on the north and south ends by strong posts reaching eighteen feet from the ground, extended the beam from which depended the fatal noose over the trap. The latter consisted of two doors opening downward and apart—a convenient arrangement for a man who is compelled to "step down and out." Underneath the eastern door were bolted two stout wooden bars of sufficient length to reach across underneath the opposite door when both were lifted to a level with the floor of the platform. Back of this second door, and running parallel with it underneath the platform, was a stout piece of timber with mortises, well oiled, through which worked the two ears of a strong flat bar of iron, and when the doors were in position these ears, when shoved forward, caught under the ends of the wooden bars, and held the trapdoors firmly in place on a level with the platform. To the centre of the iron bar was attached a rope which ran over a pulley and down a narrow box affixed to a post in the rear of the scaffold, and was there fastened to a heavy iron weight. A smaller cord was also attached to this weight, and, when the trap was set, it supported the weight, and was exposed at the height of the railing in the rear of the scaffold. The cutting of this cord, at the proper signal, of course instantly drops the weight upon the other cord or rope, jerks back the iron bar and ears which support the wooden bars, and the doors open, ushering the unfortunate wretch into eternity. The whole action is instantaneous. Cords are also fastened to the underside of the doors, and, running over pulleys, support weights, and the moment the trap is sprung, the doors are drawn back against the posts, which are so padded that there is scarcely a particle of noise, and the witnesses are spared the disagreeable spectacle of loose doors banging against the writhing body of a dying man. It is the most perfect machine of the kind probably ever invented; a fall of seven feet is given, and death is almost invariably instantaneous. When Mortimer fell through the trap he hung motionless. There was absolutely not a particle of swaying of the body, no heaving of the chest, no twisting of the rope. He hung as motionless as though he had been hanging there for a thousand years.

About ten o'clock, A.M., the prisoner was visited by his counsel, Mr. Collins, and the dying statements prepared from Vasquez's dictation of the previous evening, were carefully translated to him by Deputy Selman, and, listening intently, he approved sentence after sentence by an affirmative nod of the head or an occasional word expressive of approval. Some additions were made at the suggestion of his counsel, and with the prisoner's hearty concurrence. His heartbroken sister, Mrs. Laria, was present, and when Mr. Collins came to the concluding paragraph of the "Address to Parents," where he says: "farewell, sisters dear," the bandit for the first time showed emotion. A sudden change swept across his countenance. His eyes were moistened, and he drew forth his handkerchief, and removed the evidence of emotion as quickly as possible. All present were much affected, and for some moments Mr. Collins was unable to proceed.

At the conclusion of the reading, Vasquez declined to sign the statements, saying that he should never again take a pen in his hand; but authorized his name to be attached, repeating his declaration that the sentiments were those he wished to go forth as his dying expressions. His signature was attached, and witnessed by most of those present. Vasquez insisted, however, that before publication, they should be submitted to Father Serda. His request was complied with, and the Rev. gentleman gave his approval without suggesting any changes.

During the day, a large number of representatives of the press, officers from adjoining counties, and other invited guests arrived, and were admitted to the jail to see the prisoner and to inspect the arrangements for his execution.

Following is the form of invitation cards issued:

SHERIFF'S OFFICE,
COUNTY OF SANTA CLARA,
San Jose, March 16th, 1875.

To ——:

SIR—Pursuant to the statute in such cases, you are hereby invited to be present at the execution of Tiburcio Vasquez, at the jail of said county, in San Jose, on the 19th day of March, A. D., 1875, at 1:30 P.M.   J. H. ADAMS, Sheriff.

Present at jail entrance.   *Not transferable.*

The bandit's relatives were with him nearly all the forenoon.

Claudio Vasquez, of Los Angeles county; Mrs. Augustina Bee, a cousin to Tiburcio, with her two daughters, and Amada Maria Vasquez and sister, daughters of Tiburcio's brother, Antonia Maria Vasquez, of Monterey; Manuel Laria, of Panoche Valley; his wife, the prisoner's favorite sister, Maria Antonia Laria; and Francisco Vasquez, of Elizabeth Lake, Los Angeles county. The women exhibited the most intense grief at the parting, but the prisoner bore himself with composure throughout.

Rumors prevailed throughout the day that a number of parties of mounted Mexicans had been seen for the past two days moving from below towards the city, and some affected to believe that a rescue would be attempted. Nothing of the kind, however, was contemplated. An unusual number of Mexicans appeared in town, their object being merely to view the corpse after it had been delivered to its friends and assist at the last sad rites.

Throughout the afternoon there was a constant rush of visitors, and although all were respectful and gazed on the condemned man with no indication in their demeanor of a feeling of vindictiveness, I realized, as I looked upon the coming and going throng, as I never realized before, the horrible ordeal of the death penalty. I had looked upon many a scene of blood and carnage; had moved away the dead and dying upon the battle-field; and had learned that the majority of men, when they know they *must die,* arouse manhood enough to face the mysterious and terrible ordeal with wonderful fortitude. Even the unfortunate victims of the battle-field, mutilated and suffering untold agony, as a rule suffer and die in silence. The "shrieks and groans" of the wounded, as thrillingly and with horrible eloquence depicted in works of romance and even in histories, are things of the imagination. The thousands who survived Antietam, Chancellorsville, Gettysburg, Nashville—all the great battles and skirmishes of our late war, will testify to the truth of this statement. But the condemned man—the man in full health, who knows that tomorrow he must die! At a moment when he would wish to be with his relatives and immediate friends only, or alone with his own thoughts, or communing with his God; or if possible to compose himself, to sleep, to rest, preparing himself for the dread ordeal. It is terrible, in those supreme last hours, to be the constant centre of searching, piercing eyes—to be scanned hour after hour by curious and experienced eyes—to feel that he is being searched to the heart, and to hear whispered comments, hour after hour, on his "nerve" and bearing! I can imagine nothing but the tortures of the inquisition more terrible, more trying! But this man was in the fullest sense of the expression, "equal to the occasion." For each and every visitor he had a manly, affable and self-possessed reception, replying pleasantly and without bravado to all remarks and inquiries.

Having expressed a strong desire to examine the coffin his friends had prepared for him, Sheriff Adams directed Messrs. Truman and Woodson, the undertakers, to gratify his wish; and accordingly about 8 o'clock of the evening of the 18th Mr. Woodson brought the *fine casket* to the jail, and Vasquez viewed it with great curiosity. The lid having been opened at his request, he examined the satin lining, pressed the cushions and remarked, "I can sleep here forever very well!"

After trying on his pantaloons and finding them a little tight, he found fault, but immediately apologized, and remarked that they would answer, as he "should not have to use them much."

During the evening a telegram from the sensation revivalist, Rev. Mr. Hammond, who was then "starring it" in San Francisco, was handed him, reading as follows:

Dear Vasquez: God bless you. Trust in Jesus. He will be with you and love you. I shall continue to pray for you

Yours,   E. P. Hammond.

P. S.—The Governor cannot pardon you, but God can, for Jesus' sake.

Vasquez listened to the reading of the telegram, and smilingly remarked: "Yes, I know if I have any more hope"—pointing upward—"it is in Jesus!"

He retired shortly before midnight, but afterwards remarked to young Adams, the sheriff's son, who remained as guard, that he did not feel very sleepy, lighted a cigar, and conversed as he smoked for half or three-quarters of an hour, and then fell into a sound slumber.

CHAPTER XXVI.

Last act in a life-long tragedy—The soul of the bandit chief Tiburcio Vasquez is swung from Time to Eternity—Details of the execution—One of the most astonishing exhibitions of nerve and coolness, without 'bravado" on record—The march to the gallows—An instantaneous and painless death—Last sad rites by the relatives—The sister's midnight vigils at the bandit's tomb—Resurrection of the body by the relatives, who feared the grave had been robbed.

Vasquez's last morning on earth found him as imperturbable and cheerful as ever. He arose early, dressed himself tidily for the solemn event so near at hand, and ate a substantial breakfast. At eight o'clock his relatives and friends came to pay their last visit, most of them remaining until nearly noon.

Soon the usual throng of visitors began to pour in, and during the whole morning, up to the moment of the execution, a dense crowd of people occupied the space in front of the high fence which shuts out the jail yard from view. In the saloons about town the principal topic of discussion was Vasquez's "courage," and—to the discredit of "human nature"—bets were offered and taken as to whether the bandit would die "game." Vasquez's counsel, Mr. Collins, spent some time with his unfortunate client, and about an hour and a half before the execution, Father Serda called for the last time, and was occupied in religious services with the prisoner until the time arrived to read the death warrant.

Sheriff Adams, deeming it an unnecessary cruelty to compel the unfortunate man to stand upon the scaffold during the tedious reading of the document, which had to be translated as the reading proceeded, decided to go through the ceremony within the prison. The newspaper representatives, sheriffs, physicians and a few others only were admitted.

As the solemn document was read by Under-Sheriff Winchell, and translated sentence by sentence, all present narrowly watched the expression of the prisoner's countenance, and could not detect the slightest indication of weakness.

At the conclusion of the reading, Sheriff Adams said, "Vasquez, the time has come to march to the scaffold."

"All right!" was the quick reply, and shaking hands calmly with those present, and saying, with an affable bow, to each one, "Good-bye!" signified his readiness for the ordeal. Under-Sheriff Winchell, and Deputy Selman led the way, followed by the condemned, supported on either side by Sheriff Adams and Father Serda. Various sheriffs and reporters brought up the rear. So densely was the jail-yard crammed with spectators, that the solemn procession had to crowd the way to the gallows.

Vasquez bore a small crucifix before him as he moved forward and ascended the scaffold. Taking his place on the drop, some moments of respite were granted to allow him the last rites of the Catholic church, a white robe or shroud being first thrown over his shoulders. The prisoner gave his responses in a calm, distinct tone, and did not exhibit the slightest agitation. The dense throng of spectators gazing upon the solemn scene preserved the most perfect silence. On the scaffold besides the sheriff and his deputies, Father Serda, and one or two reporters, were Sheriff B. F. Ross, of Hollister, Sheriff H. N. Morse, of Alameda; ex-Sheriff Harris, of Santa Clara; Sheriff Orton, of Santa Cruz; ex-Sheriff Wasson, of Monterey, and one or two others.

The religious ceremony ended, Vasquez quickly pulled off his coat, and handing it to Winchell, proceeded calmly to remove his collar, and bared his neck for the rope. He was then pinioned with straps, at the elbows, wrists (buckled to a strap securely fastened around the hips), at the knee, and again at the ankles. Under-Sheriff Winchell then placed the fatal noose over the bandit's neck.

Even at this supreme and appalling moment, Vasquez maintained the most absolute command of nerve—the most perfect composure, turning his neck to assist the officer in working the knot closely under the left ear. Winchell made no mistake or blunder, as often does happen in such cases; but the hangman's knot does not always slip easily; and in this case the rope was somewhat stiff, and in using the necessary force it suddenly slipped so tight to the neck as to impede the circulation. Within a few seconds suffocation would have ensued.

The doomed bandit simply turned his head, and giving Winchell a meaning look, exclaimed in Spanish:

"*Pronto!*" (quick!)

It was his last word!

The next moment the black cap was drawn over his head.

Winchell stepped back, the sheriff gave the signal, and the next instant the soul of Tiburcio Vasquez passed from time to eternity!

The time was 1:35 P.M.

The same phenomenon that occurred in Mortimer's case was repeated here. The body fell perpendicularly seven feet, dislocating the cervical vertibra and snapping the spinal cord, and the body remained as still and immovable as though it had been hanging for a month.

Death was instantaneous!

And yet the heart did not cease altogether to pulsate until the lapse of six minutes and a half. At the end of twelve minutes the physicians, Drs. David Todd, of San Francisco, and A. J. Coney, J. N. Brown and W. S. Thorne, of San Jose *pronounced* life extinct.

The body was allowed to hang for twenty five-minutes, when it was taken down and delivered to the sorrowing relatives for interment. The remains were enveloped in a fine suit of broadcloth, and placed in a magnificent casket, and borne to the residence of Gaudaloupe Bee, of Santa Clara (a beautiful town three miles distance from San Jose), whose wife was a cousin of the bandit, and there laid out in state.

There was a general expression of surprise among officers and citizens generally at the courage and manhood exhibited by Vasquez in his dying moments. His cunning avoidance of capture for so long a time had impressed them with a belief that he was a cowardly dog, and would have to be dragged to the scaffold like the wretched cur Mortimer.

At 9 o'clock on the evening of the execution the writer accepted an invitation to accompany Under-Sheriff Winchell to the residence of Mrs. Bee, where the body of the dead criminal was lying in state, as though he had died a martyr in some glorious cause.

The house was a modest little cottage in a pleasant portion of the town, neatly kept, and the grounds made pleasant and inviting by shrubbery and flowers, which grow so prolifically in that climate.

The body was neatly laid out on a raised platform covered with black cloth, near the centre of the room. The body was neatly dressed. The arms peacefully folded across the breast and holding a crucifix. The countenance looked perfectly natural, exhibiting none of the hideous distortions characteristic of cases of hanging or strangulation. It presented the appearance of one peacefully sleeping. Roman candles were burned in silver candlesticks placed at intervals around the body.

The female relatives of the dead bandit were seated about the room gazing mournfully and silently at the remains, while the male relatives and friends were gliding spectre-like through the various apartments, occasionally stopping a few moments to gaze at the dead, and then passing out to converse in solemn groups, or wandering about dejectedly alone.

On the following day the body was followed to the grave and interred with all the ceremony that affection could devise.

The dread that the body would be stolen either by doctors or by ghouls who would take the head and preserve it for exhibition, as was done in the case of his famous prototype, Joaquin Murieta, caused great anxiety among the relatives, and especially of his grief-stricken sister, Maria, and night after night she jealously guarded the grave, until utterly prostrated by the ghostly vigils, and other friends for a time guarded the (to them) sacred spot.

On Thursday, the 29th of March, in the presence of officers and friends, the grave was opened to relieve the fears and anxiety of the latter, and the coffin raised to the surface. On removing the lid, it was found that the body had not been disturbed. The face exhibited an advanced stage of decomposition, considering the brief period that had elapsed since the execution, and the clothing was covered with mould.

It was again returned to the earth, where it will probably be allowed to "rest forever well," as the bandit had prophesied when he examined the untarnished receptacle prepared for its "repose."

The successor of the redoubtable Vasquez, his former lieutenant, is now carrying on an organized system of robbery in the southern portion of the State, and determined efforts are being made to effect his capture and the destruction of his infamous band.

H. M. Hayes, county clerk of San Benito county (formerly a portion of Monterey) received from the county clerk of Santa Clara county, Cornelius Finley, a certified bill of the expenses attending the keeping, trial, and execution of Vasquez. Following are the items:

John H. Adams $1,214.13
W. R. Rowland 43.25
B. F. Ross 57.50
M. C. Briggs 165.55
C. Finley 82.00
P. J. Malone 900.00
Cash paid witnesses 260.00
Total $2,722.43

The bandit cost the State of California from the time of the Tres Pinos massacre over $40,000.

THE END.

The Mexican American

An Arno Press Collection